This book was compiled on the initiative of TANGRA TanNakRa ALL BULGARIAN FOUNDATION and the CENTER FOR RESEARCH ON THE BULGARIANS

THIS BOOK IS PUBLISHED IN 2001.
THAT IS 1836 YEARS AFTER THE BEGINNING OF BULGARIAN STATEHOOD IN EUROPE (165 AD) AND 1320 YEARS AFTER THE CREATION OF DANUBE BULGARIA (681 AD) BY KHAN ASPARUKH.

BULGARIA – THE OLDEST EUROPEAN STATE,
EXISTING UNDER THE SAME NAME FOR OVER EIGHTEEN CENTURIES,
AND SAFE-KEPT UNTIL TODAY BY THE BULGARIAN NATION.

Prof. Dimitar Shishkov, editor
Ass. Prof. Plamen Pavlov, introduction

ISBN 954-9942-24-4

JOHN ATANASOFF

THE FATHER OF THE COMPUTER
THE BRILLIANT AMERICAN SCIENTIST, WHO WAS PROUD OF HIS BULGARIAN ROOTS

Portrait by Simmie Knox, 1995, Iowa State University

Greenland Sea
White Sea
Norwegian Sea
Atlantic Ocean
Gulf of Bothnia
Gulf of Finland
Skagerrak
North Sea
Baltic Sea
Irish Sea
English Channel
Bay of Biscay
Black Sea
Bulgaria
Sofia
Adriatic Sea
Aegean Sea
Tyrrhenian Sea
Ionian Sea
Mediterranean Sea
of Gibraltar

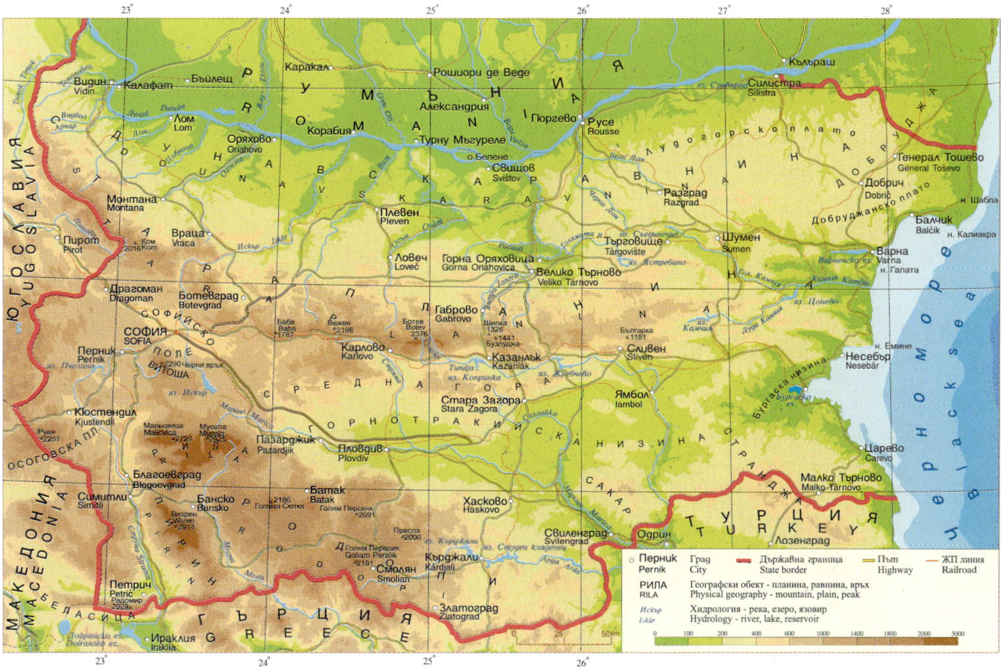

Bulgaria, my father's people, I salute you.

John Vincent Atanasoff

Bulgaria. In the Valley of Roses.

Rila Monastery – spiritual center of Bulgarians

THIS BOOK IS DEDICATED
TO THE 100TH ANNIVERSARY
OF THE BIRTH OF JOHN ATANASOFF –
THE INVENTOR
OF THE FIRST ELECTRONIC DIGITAL COMPUTER.
A LEGACY THAT HAS CHANGED THE WORLD!

PRIDE IN BULGARIA

Modern Bulgarians need, among many other things, a well-grounded national confidence. The source of self-confidence is our history and the talent of people with Bulgarian blood in their veins. In the past century, one of the highest peaks in that respect was John Atanasoff, the inventor of the first electronic computer in the world. The significance of each and every action is determined by its consequences. Atanasoff's invention started the information revolution, which has changed the world. What did John Atanasoff do in fact? The idea of a computer with program operation had been known a hundred years before he began constructing his computer. That idea belonged to the English mathematician Charles Babbage but was not realized because of the technical difficulties of building it with mechanical components. Before John Atanasoff, a great number of mechanical calculating machines were built. However the big breakthrough was made by John Atanasoff who abandoned mechanics and designed electronic circuits for calculating by use of a binary system of numbers. Nowadays, we see that quite natural and simple but the genius prevailed over tradition. The wheel is also simple and natural but many civilizations developed to perfection without inventing it.

The principles of John Atanasoff's computer, though seemingly outdated today, are the basis of the thousands of millions of computers, without which modern society cannot exist. Every Bulgarian knows and prides in the holy brothers, St. Cyril and St. Methodius, who created the alphabet of all Slavonic peoples. Similarly, John Atanasoff, a man of Bulgarian extraction, opened the road to the world information society.

Blagovest Sendov
20 April 2001

JOHN ATANASOFF

MY FATHER'S LAND

As I dedicate to the people of my father's country this Bulgarian version of a paper which I have written, my emotions run full. I have so much to say to you, but words come slowly, and you will have to listen as I say what I must.

My father was born 1876 January 6 as our people prepared for a revolt from Turkey. When the revolt became imminent, the ruling Turks told the people of Boyadzik to leave their homes to be burned. But as my grandfather with my father in his arms fled, with my grandmother behind him, a small group of Turkish soldiers shot him through the chest. The bullet which killed my grandfather left a mark on my father's head which he carried throughout his life.

After two step-fathers, my father came to the US at the age of 13 and was left alone at the age of 15. After such an incredible beginniing, he graduated from Colgate University and married my mother, an American whose grandfather fought in our Revolutionary war. Father always wanted to bring his wife and children to Bulgaria but it did not happen.

I have always felt the heredity I received, the blood of two different peoples, served to buoy my spirits.

And now as I grow old, I feel most fortunate. I have received a warm welcome from my father's people, an important award, The Order of Cyril and Methodius, First Class, was made a Foreign Member of the Bulgarian Academy of Sciences, and I maintain highly esteemed contacts with many friends in Bulgaria.

Bulgaria, my father's people, I salute you.

John Vincent Atanasoff

ON THE BULGARIANS – THE NATION THAT GAVE BIRTH TO JOHN ATANASOFF'S FATHER

IN THE STEAD OF A PREFACE

Bulgaria lies in the center of the Balkan Peninsula, on a busy crossroads of differing cultures. According to statistics, the country holds one of the first places in the world in the number of archaeological monuments, being second only to Greece and Italy in Europe. The present-day land of the Bulgarians constitutes one of the ancient hearths of European civilization on the continent. The earliest data of human activity on Bulgarian soil have been estimated at over 100 thousand years ago – the Paleolithic period or the Old Stone Age. Since then human activity and culture have left their mark. Some particularly interesting finds have been discovered in the **Karanovo** burial hill near the town of Nova Zagora, in which cultural layers of almost 40 thousand years can be traced, dating from the late Paleolithic to the Neolithic periods. Many caves keep traces from the Ice Age, the most impressive ones being in the **Magura Cave**, famous for its cave art. The ancient people painted and engraved expressive hunting scenes, dances, as well as, animal, totem and pantheistic cult figures. The prehistoric inhabitants of the Bulgarian lands became highly developed during the Eneolithic or the Chalkolithic periods. Thirty years ago, a civilization, older than the Mesopotamian and the Egyptian one was found in the Bulgarian lands – the **Varna Chalkolithic** burial mount from the fifth millennium B.C. The oldest gold objects, including objects symbolizing power, were found there.

During the Bronze Age (3100–1200 B.C.), the life of the local population changed. These were the **ancient Thracians**, who formed a nation in the first half of the first millennium B.C. The Thracians were not only shown to be the oldest historic inhabitants of these lands, but Ancient Thrace served as a consolidation center of the **ancient Indo-**

Europeans. The most ancient Thracian monuments were contemporaries of the Old Egyptian Kingdom. Thracians influenced world culture by their contacts with the ancient Greek civilization. Herodotus indicated that the Thracians were the second largest people in the Old World. Homer described them as allies of Troy in the 8th century B.C. **Esceles, Euripides, Aristophanes** and other leading authors of the antiquity wrote about the Thracians.

The powerful Hellenic influence in its mature forms shaped the culture of the Thracians as a synthetic one. The cult of the Thracian **Dionysus** played a major role in the creation of Greek comedy and tragedy. The myths and the cult of the famous Thracian singer **Orpheus** penetrated deeply into the spiritual life of the ancient civilization. Orpheus was most probably a Thracian king-priest from the Mikene epoch, who was personified in mythology into a **Heros** (an immortal human who has turned into a god), symbolizing art, wisdom, music, healing, clairvoyance and rule. Similar to Orpheus is **Zelmoxis** (Gothic priest who lived as a hermit) was a famous prophet and healer. Some Orpheic elements can be found in Christianity today.

We know of Thracian art from their elaborate burial tombs. They are highly concentrated in some regions, especially in Thrace, where John Atanasoff's forefathers were born. The peak of their art took place between the 4th century and the beginning of the 3rd century B.C., when the famous **Kazanlak Tomb** was built. The golden **Panagjurishte treasure** is a classic example of the artistic achievements of the Thracians. Ancient Thracian finds are being discovered today. For example, the temple near the **village of Starosel**, located in the Plovdiv region, was uncovered during the summer of the year 2000. Recent exhibitions of Thracian art organized in Western Europe and America have made people aware of their interesting culture.

The Thracians' belief system – their religion has been found on numerous monuments, like the cult stone slates of the **Thracian Horseman** (Heros), as well as the gold and silver vessels, found in other treasures. The ancient Greeks accepted, and through them – the Romans, some Thracian gods: **Ares** – identified with the Roman **Mars**; **Artemis** – originally **Bendida**, the Thracian god-mother; **Dionysus** – identified with the Roman **Bacchus**; **Asclepius** – identified with the Roman **Aesculapius**, etc. Mankind knows these ancient Thracian gods today. Their names are synonymous with war, medicine, etc. However only a few people know that those were not Hellenic mythological personages but Thracian religious figures. The same is true of ancient Thracians like **Orpheus**, who was born in the Bulgarian mountain called Rhodope mountain and **Spartacus** (the leader of a slave revolt in Rome) who came from the region of the present-day town of Sandanski at the foot of Mount Pirin.

In 346 B.C., the Macedonian Kingdom occupied Thrace for a period of about 50 years. The ancient **Macedonians** were a people related to the Thracians. According to some scholars, they were part of the Thracian tribal structure like the **Odrysians, Bes** and **Dacians**. During the 5th century B.C., Macedonia played an important role in the Peloponnesian Wars and, in the following century, it obtained hegemony in the Balkans. The Hellenic influence upon the ancient Macedonians was more pronounced than that over the other Thracian tribes, although they all remained "barbarians" to the ancient Greeks. **Philip of Macedonia** reformed the Thracian town of Pulpudeva and gave it his name – Philipopolis (present-day Plovdiv). World hegemony, reached by **Alexander III the Great** (336–323 B.C.), however favored neither the ancient Macedonians, nor the Thracian "world" as a whole, but promoted the Hellenic military-administrative oligarchy.

By 46 A.D., after continuous wars and resistance, the lands of the Thracians became part of the **Roman Empire**. During the 2nd–3rd centuries, our lands constituted one of the most flourishing Roman provinces with highly developed towns – **Philipopolis** (Plovdiv), **Augusta Trayana** (Stara Zagora), **Serdica** (Sofia), **Naisus** (Nis), **Pautalia** (Kjustendil), **Durostorum** (Silistra), **Marcianopolis** (Devnja), **Nicopolis ad Istrum** (a town near present Veliko Turnovo), etc. Thracian lands attracted settlers from the Near East and veterans from Rome. Special roads were built and a streamlined system of communications was created (unsurpassed by the modern period of the 19th–20th century). The establishment of the Roman statehood, and the demographic and ethnic contacts led to the domination of the Latin language, especially to the north of the Balkan Mountains, although the Hellenic cultural characteristics were preserved in Thrace and on the Black Sea coast.

In 330 A.D., Constantine I the Great moved the capital of the Roman Empire from "old" Rome to Byzantium (Constantinople/Istanbul), named **Tsarigrad ("Kings' City")** by the Bulgarians. This however took place only after Constantine briefly considered setting up his capital in ancient **Serdica**, now known as Sofia, the present-day capital of Bulgaria. Following the separation of the Empire (395), our lands entered the Holy Eastern Empire (Byzantium). Many of the significant personalities in Byzantium had Thracian origin, including several emperors. One of them was the **"most Orthodox"** emperor, **Marcius** (450–457), who came from present Plovdiv. Also, **Emperor Justinian I**, called the Great (527–565), who was the most remarkable Byzantine ruler of that thousand-year long empire, was Thracian. The early Byzantine culture developed in the Bulgarian lands. The people were some of the earliest followers of Christianity in Europe. Important church events, like the **Council of Serdica** held in 343 A.D. which left long lasting traces in the religious life of the whole Christian world, took place in present-day Sofia.

Yet another ethnic-cultural component of the present-day Bulgarians, is made up of the **Ancient Bulgarians** who have given their name to the present Bulgarian state. They are the fundamental ethnic component of the medieval Bulgarian state. Since antiquity, they had been a highly developed nation with statehood, ethnically Indo-European. It is believed that their ancient heartland was in Middle Asia in the region of the mountains of the Pamirs and Hindukush. Two famous states were founded there in antiquity, called by some authors "Balgar" and **"Balhara"**. With their highly developed social structure, ancient Bulgarians were culturally dominant in Central Asia for long periods. They created rich culture in the area of the philosophical understanding of the world, state government, social structure, military arts, script, language, building and astronomy. The **Ancient Bulgarian Calendar** is an impressive achievement with its perfect astronomical and mathematical accuracy. It is based on an original calendar of the year and a 12-year-cycle calendar. The constellations in that masterpiece of ancient Bulgarian thought bear the names of animals. UNESCO has recognized the calendar of the ancient Bulgarians as the most accurate of all the ones known until modernity.

The European presence of the Bulgarian state may be traced back to the 2nd century A.D., as is indicated in the *Name List of Bulgarian Khans*. The calculations refer to the reign of the legendary leader, **Avitohol**, the originator of the **Dulo Dynasty**, circa 165 A.D. Those centuries, little known in Bulgarian history, are related to the "Great Migrations". As a result some Bulgarian communities were forced to move to Armenia (the so-called "Bulgarians of **Vund**") and Panonia (present Hungary where they were later known as the Panonian Bulgarians). The main part of the nation fought powerful opponents like the Avars and Turks together with Byzantium. In the 7th century, Bulgarians led by the great **Khan Kubrat** created a powerful state union, known as the **Old Great Bulgaria**. It was an ally of Byzantium in its grandiose wars against the Avars and the Persians. Emperor Hyraclius bestowed the highest Roman-Byzantine title of Patrician on Khan Kubrat and gave him rich presents as a sign of respect. One of the sensations of modern East-European archaeology is the treasure from the village of **Malaya Peréshchepina**, near the town of Poltava (Ukraine) where that great ruler of Bulgaria was buried. The marvelous objects, gold jewelry, a scepter, a beautiful sword, etc. are kept

at the famous Hermitage Museum in St. Petersburg. They are evidence of the political power of Old Great Bulgaria and the authority of its ruler.

After the Chazar aggression during the middle of the 7th century A.D., a part of the Bulgarians remained in the structure of the new Chazar Khaganate (the tribes of Bat-Bayan, which formed the state of the so-called **"Black Bulgarians"** near the sea of Azov in the 10th century). The larger part of the Bulgarians migrated and founded new states – **Volga Bulgaria** and **Danube Bulgaria**. Some of them tried to establish their statehood in Macedonia (the people of **Kuber**) and Italy (**the Bulgarians of Altsek**). **The Panonian Bulgarians** had autonomy in the structure of the Avar Khaganate. Of all those **"many states"**, the most potent one has been the present-day Bulgaria in the Balkans, founded by Khan Asparuh, and also of the Volga Bulgaria (present Autonomous Republic of Tatarstan in the structure of the Russian Federation), founded by **Khan Kotrag**. The two large medieval Bulgarian states were situated far from each other at a distance of more than a thousand kilometers. The Danube State accepted Christianity during the 9th century A.D. and thus became the third cultural power in early medieval Europe.

The Volga state adopted Islam in the 10th century A.D. The Volga Bulgarians built a splendid Islamic civilization fighting against the steppe peoples and the Russian principalities. During the 8th century A.D., they were forced in becoming vassals of the Tatar (Mongolian) "Golden Horde". Finally, Tsar Ivan the Terrible of Russia destroyed their state in the middle of the 16th century. Even today, the ruins of their capital **Bolgar Veliki** are an impressive sight. Subsequently the Russian Empire subjected the Volga Bulgarians to strong assimilation pressures. The Soviet regime was particularly severe, enforcing the incorrect ethnic name of "Tatars" on them. Presently, there is a movement of intellectuals for resuming of the name of "Bulgarians" and the restoration of the original name of **"Bulgaristan"** of the Republic of Tatarstan.

In the Balkans, the powerful Bulgarian state, headed by **Khan Asparukh** (680–700), united the ancient Bulgarians with the descendants of the ancient Thracians and the Slavonic tribes of the so-called Bulgarian group who settled in these parts in the 6th–7th centuries. The latter comprised many tribes, inhabiting Moesia, Thrace, Macedonia and partly the lands of present Greece, Albania, Serbia (including Kosovo) and Romania. Byzantine ambitions to conquer those tribes met a strong barrier – the state created by Khan Asparukh. Danube Bulgaria (the present state of Bulgaria) was created after a decisive victory over the Byzantine army near the delta of the River Danube (681). Its first capital was the town of Pliska. The territory of the state included Moesia with present

Dobrudja and vast lands to the north of the Danube. Thanks to its ethnic tolerance, Danube Bulgaria became a magnet for the surrounding Slavs who gradually were "Bulgarianized". Asparukh perished somewhere in the northeast during a war against the Chazars around the year 700. Tradition required the Khan be made into an epic hero who built **"great towns"** and fortifications **"between the Danube and the Sea"** to protect his people. His brother, **Khan Kuber**, created a "second Bulgaria" in the Balkans (also around 680) by rising against the Avars and retreating into the region of the town of Bitola in present-day Macedonia. Kuber's forces were smaller so he submitted to Byzantine supremacy and established close contacts with the surrounding Slavs.

Khan Tervel (700–721) headed the powerful Danube Bulgaria when the Arabs attacked the Balkan Peninsula. In 718 A.D., he stopped the aggression and saved Byzantium and the whole of Europe from the advance of the Arab Caliphate in its strive to conquer the "world capital" of Christianity, Constantinople. Emperor Justinian II gave Khan Tervel the Byzantine highest-ranking title of **"Caesar"** for the Bulgarians' support in the war (the title comes from the name of Guy Julius Caesar, the great emperor of Rome). That is a unique case in the history of Byzantium and medieval Europe. **Khan Krum** (802–814 A.D.) introduced a new type of legislation and created an organized Bulgarian state. In 811 A.D., Byzantium attacked the Bulgarians and set the Capital Pliska, on fire. The Bulgarians struck back immediately – Krum's armies defeated the Byzantines at one of the Balkan passes. The emperor himself, Nickiphorus II was killed in battle. Since Emperor Flavius Valens (378 A.D.), no emperor had perished in battle. Byzantium was in shock and sought the help of King Charlesmagne of the Franks, recognizing his title of "Emperor". Bulgarian culture of the pre-Christian period reached its apogee during the reign of **Khan Omurtag** (814–831 A.D.). The state expanded up to the Middle Danube region, the Tisa river (present-day Hungary) and the Dnepar river (present-day Ukraine). The administrative reforms, started by Krum, were further developed. Bulgarian lands spread out to the south almost up to the Aegean Sea and present-day Albania under **Khan Presian** (836–852 A.D.). Bulgaria became the third "great power" in medieval Europe, together with the Byzantine Empire and the Frankish Empire.

Almost two centuries after the foundation of the state, **Khan Boris I** (852–889 A.D.) christened the Bulgarians. He adopted the Christian name of Michael and built the first Bulgarian churches and monasteries. Subsequently, the Bulgarian Church canonized him; he remains in the traditional historiography as **"Saint Tsar Boris-Michael"**. The creation

The Ancient Bulgarian Diaspora (I millenium BC - VIIth Century) - The movement of a horse civilization and its answer to challenges of time and history.

The solar twelve-year-cycle calendar of ancient Bulgarians.

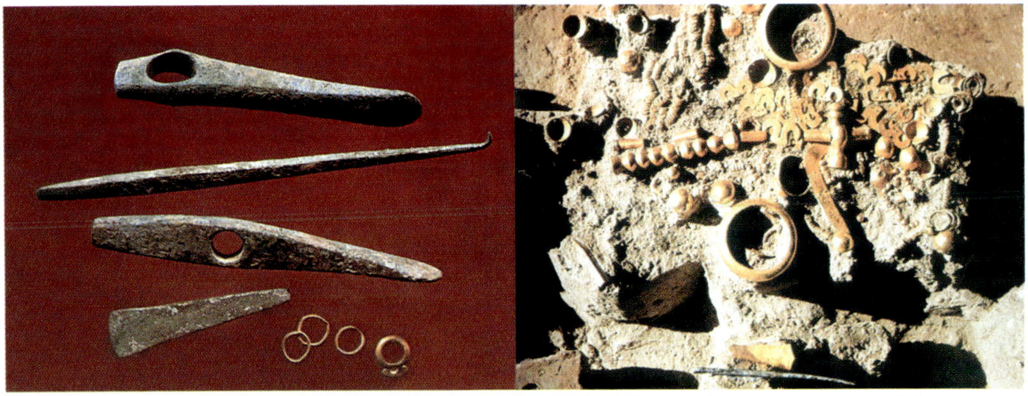

Artefacts from the Late Chalkolithic necropolis, Varna, Bulgaria - the most ancient gold, discovered in Europe, 6 millennium BC.

The central mural-painting in the Kazanluk Thracian Tomb - a masterpiece of Hellenic painting from the end of 4th c. and the beginning of 3rd c. BC. UNESCO monument.

Simeon the Great (893-927) – Tsar (Emperor) of Danubian Bulgaria, painter Dimitar Giudjenov.

Volga Bulgaria - the Earliest State in Northeastern Europe

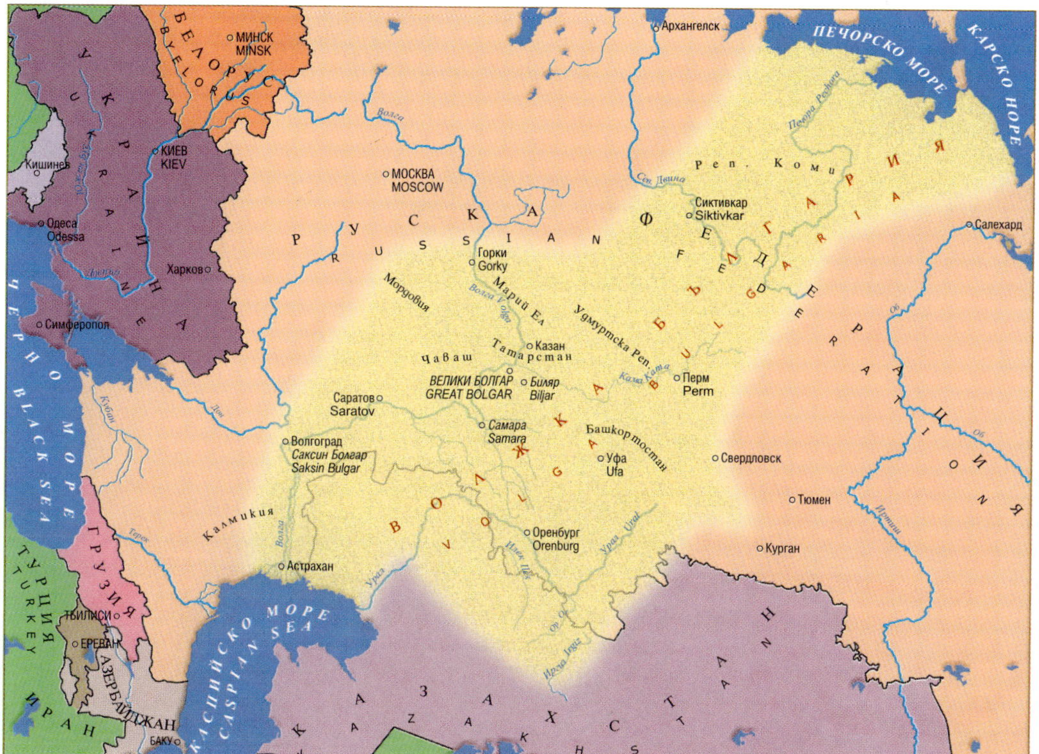

The Holy Brothers, St. Cyril and St. Methodius – the spiritual patrons of Europe. A 19th century icon from the Crypt of St. Alexander Nevski Cathedral in Sofia.

Bulgarian States: A Shield for Europe

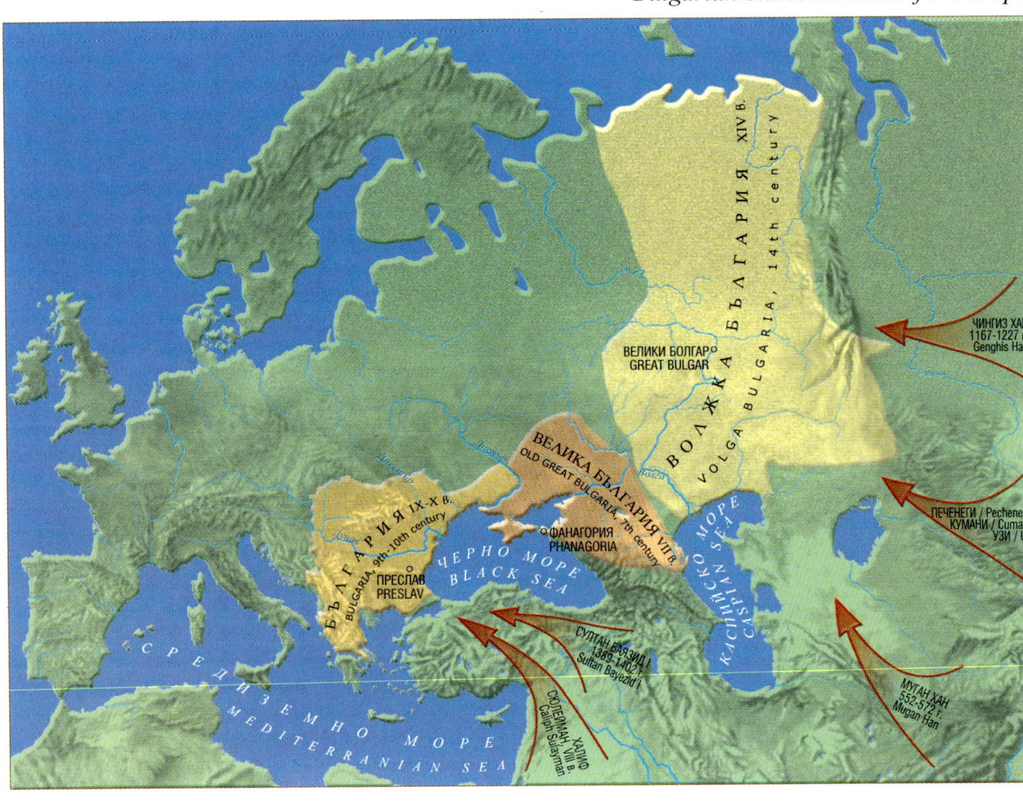

The monument to Patriarch Euthymius in Sofia – the scholar, clergyman and defender of Veliko Tarnovo besieged by Turks.

The Hill of Tsarevetz with its fortifications, the heart of Veliko Tarnovo

The triumph of Bulgarian will for spiritual freedom and church independance in the time of Ottoman domination. A litograph by artist N. Pavlovich (1872).

The April uprising of 1876. The military leader of the uprising, Georgi Benkovski at the head of his „Flying Brigade“. A painting by P. Morozov (1909).

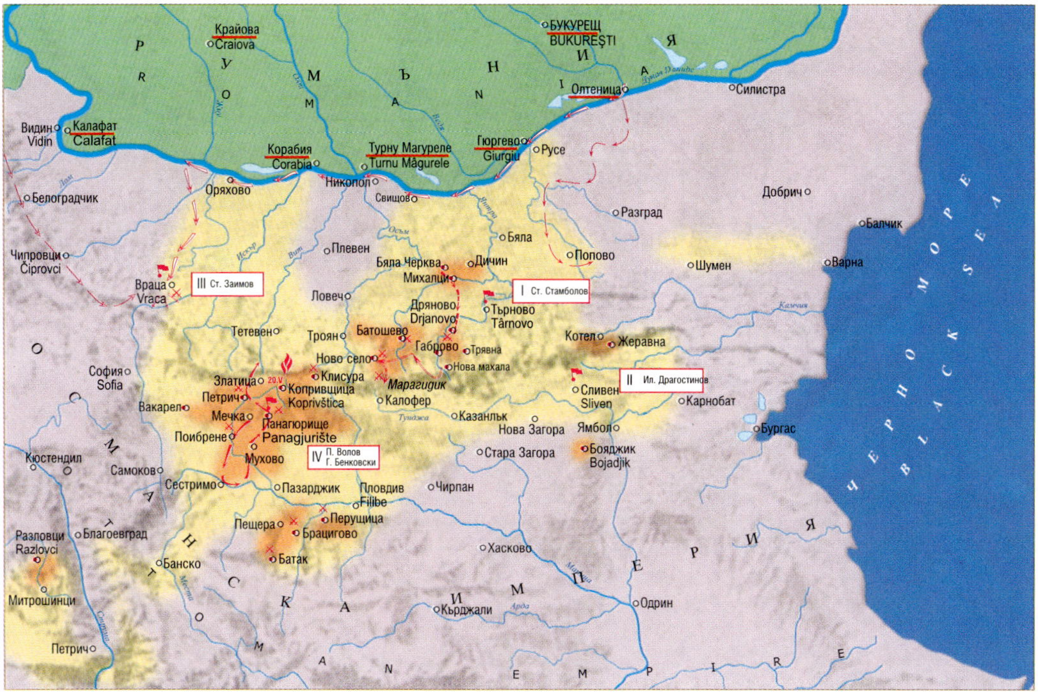

The April Uprising against Ottoman Empire (1876).

Bulgaria according to the San Stefano Peace Treaty (1878).

Bulgarian Academy of Sciences - central building. A painting by A. Aleksiev (1999)

The National Theatre „Ivan Vazov“ in Sofia.

The central building of Sofia University „St. Kliment Ohridski“.

and implementation of the Bulgarian-Slavonic script by the holy brothers, **Saints Cyril and Methodius**, was of extreme importance from a historical and cultural perspective. The Vatican has declared St. Cyril and St. Methodius patrons of Christian Europe. Through Orthodoxy, the alphabet which they created, was accepted by other nations. Today, it is used in Macedonia, Russia, Ukraine, Belarus, Yugoslavia and Mongolia. That writing system was dominant in the Romanian principalities of Wallachia and Moldova and in Lithuania in the past.

The politics of Boris-Michael were continued by his son, **Tsar Simeon the Great** (893–927) who was highly educated in Constantinople and possessed the capacity of a great statesman. He had literary talent and organized the translation of many Christian Orthodox books from the Greek into the Bulgarian language. He is considered the creator of the Old Bulgarian Literary language. Simeon moved the capital to Veliki Preslav and almost doubled the territory of the country, which now lay on three seas – Black Sea, Aegean Sea and Adriatic Sea. He knew the ancient Greek and Byzantine culture and managed to turn Bulgaria into a powerful state with an enormous influence in the world of its time. His reign is rightly called a **"Golden Age"**. Sir Steven Runciman refers to Bulgaria at that time as to the "First Bulgarian Empire".

The majority of Bulgarians have been faithful to the Orthodoxy. Albeit its diverse community, the Bulgarians have hardly been "sterile" and have always been open to different spiritual processes and phenomena. A **"Bulgarian heresy", the Bogomilism**, was born during the reign of Tsar Peter. Its emergence was caused by the influence of the old dualistic doctrines and by the people's opportunity to read and interpret the Bible in their mother tongue. The priest **Bogomil**, probably a poor monk, was the founder of that heresy. The Bogomil heresy possesses a range of original traits; it was moderately dualistic and pronouncedly ascetic. The Bogomil ideas, portending that Satin created the existing world, which was full of inequity, spread beyond the borders of Bulgaria. They had a strong impact on Christianity – the French **Chatares** and **Albigensians**, the Italian **Patarens**, the **Bosnian heretics** (the present Bosnian Muslims are their successors), the Russian **Strigolniks**. The dissidents in Serbia, Croatia, Hungary and even in distant England considered the Bogomils their spiritual mentors. French religious rebels were proud to call themselves **"Bougres"** (Bulgarians in faith), highlighting their connection with their senior Bulgarian brothers. Those ideas were persecuted severely by the Catholic establishment but they had their reflection in the Reformation and the Protestant ideologies in the West.

Despite the difficulties, the Bulgarian Kingdom continued to be a significant political power under **St. Tsar Peter** (927–969 A.D.). Byzantine intrigues however caused the aggression of the ruler of Kiev Russia, Svjatoslav. The Norman-Russian occupation brought about the false "help" of Byzantium, resulting in a heavy blow to the Bulgarian Kingdom by driving Svjatoslav out, Emperor John Tzimiskes occupied Eastern Bulgarian lands with the capital of Veliki Preslav in 971. The Western lands whose center was present-day Macedonia preserved their freedom. The able **Tsar Samuel** (997–1014) moved the state center of Bulgaria to Ochrid. The "Bulgarian Epopee" in the struggle against Byzantium was marked by brilliant victories, including the liberation of the old capital of Preslav, and by heavy defeats. In 1014, after the defeat of Samuel's army, Emperor Basil II (called Bulgarokiller) captured 15 000 Bulgarian soldiers. He blinded them all, leaving one man in a hundred with one eye so that he could lead them back. That barbarism and that catastrophe ended the first period of the history of Danube Bulgaria (1018). Bulgaria was occupied by Byzantium for a period of about 170 years.

In 1186–1188, after many uprisings, Bulgarians from Moesia liberated their lands from Byzantine rule. The brothers, **Peter and Asen**, led them. Capital of the Bulgarian Kingdom became Veliko Turnovo. The reign of **Tsar Kaloyan** (1197–1207) and **Tsar Ivan Asen II** (1218–1241) was exceptionally fruitful. Being great commanders and diplomats, they expanded the borders with brilliant negotiations, decisive wars and wise treaties, bringing lasting peace and prosperity. In 1204, Kaloyan became the first eastern ruler who defeated the invincible knight horsemen. Ivan Asen realized a territorial expansion comparable to that of Simeon the Great. During the following decades, however, the Bulgarian Kingdom suffered from the attacks of the Tatars (Mongols) and was shaken by political crises, including the big uprising of the peasant king **Ivailo**. The state withstood the hardships. The "golden sunset" of medieval Bulgaria took place during the reign of **Tsar Ivan Alexander** (1331–1371). Arts and culture developed in accord with the pre-Renaissance in Western Europe. The days of the free Bulgarian Kingdome were nearing their end, due to the movement from the southeast, the "wave", of Turkish Muslims. The "king's city" of Turnovo was captured by the Ottoman invaders in 1393. By 1396, the last free Bulgarian lands had been occupied.

The Turnovo Literary School exerted a strong cultural influence on the Orthodox world, particularly during the time of the great writer and spiritual leader, **St. Patriarch Euthymius** (1371–1394). The impact was especially felt in Moscow, Russia. At the end of the 14th and the beginning of the 15th century, the spiritual leaders, heads of Churches of Russia, Lithuania, Moldavia, Wallachia and Serbia were Bulgarian. St. Kiprian of Moscow (in Russia), Ephrem of Serbia, Nikodim Tismanski (in Wallachia), were revered as national saints by their peoples. Grigori Tsamblak, the famous Bulgarian clergyman and writer, ran away from the Ottoman invaders, acquired the unique characteristic of being a representative of several national literatures of that epoch – Bulgarian, Serbian, Moldavian, Russian and Byzantine.

The darkest period of Bulgarian history continued five centuries. During those difficult centuries, the Ottoman Empire had a policy of discrimination of the Christian population, especially the Bulgarians, and of ethnic assimilation. As a result of the Islamic nature of the Ottoman occupation, mosques were built. Arabic script was introduced for official and religious documents, and many Christian shrines were demolished or turned into Muslim temples. Many Turks, predominantly soldiers, settled within the borders of present-day Bulgaria. The so-called **"blood tax"** was especially heavy. It required the "donation" of a boy from each family, sent to Asia Minor, where he adopted Islam and trained as a "janissary" – a soldier and administrator without parents and without consciousness of home and homeland. The janissary and the volunteer army of Turkey, called "bashibozuk", were the most merciless agents representing the Sultan in Bulgaria.

Many uprisings and rebellions marked the period of Ottoman rule. They were most numerous at the end of the 17th century. Three large uprisings marked that period: the **Second Turnovo Uprising** (the first one was in 1598), the **Chiprovo Uprising**, organized by the Roman Catholics in Bulgaria, and the **Uprising of Karposh** in Northern Macedonia. The "Haiduks" rebel movement continued throughout the centuries of foreign domination. Armed companies of Bulgarians crossed the space between the Danube and the Aegean Sea and the mountains of present Albania avenging the injustices and crimes of the authorities. That military and political experience served as a basis for the organized national liberation movement in Bulgaria.

The new Bulgarian Revival began in the middle of the 18th century. The struggle for Church independence and religious openness, the publication of books and periodicals in Bulgarian, the foundation of secular Bulgarian schools and the granting of the official status of the language and culture of the Bulgarians were some of the initial steps in the process of reviving the nation. A very important moment was the writing of "A Slavo-Bulgarian History" by the monk, **Paisiy of Hilendar** (1762), and its dissemination in the form of handwritten copies at the beginning. The traditional **"chitalishta"**, reading clubs, were preserved, elevating the national spirit. There, thousands of young Bulgarians came into contact with the values of European culture. The national consciousness and desire for political freedom increased immensely. The church-national struggle, which developed into a massive civil movement in the middle of the 19th century, had secular and not clerical characteristics. It turned into a struggle for the national emanation, forcing Constantinople to recognize the Bulgarians as a separate nation and to distinguish them from the amorphous mass of the so-called "rome-millet" (the Christian population in the empire). The Bulgarians gained democratically their recognition from the Universal Patriarchy in Istanbul, which was in the forefront of the assimilation aspirations of the Greek "Megali Idea". The apogee of this unprecedented, by its scale, upsurge of civil activity was the so-called **"Bulgarian Easter"** in 1860 when the Bulgarians voiced their will to defend their national, religious and human rights.

The influence of the Russo-Turkish wars of the 18th–19th centuries was enormous. It generated the myth of **"Grandfather Ivan"** – the Russian giant from the North who would liberate his brothers, the Christians in the Balkans. The actual Russian interests for influence in the Balkans supported the fable. Unfortunately the wars did not bring freedom but only encouraged thousands of Bulgarians to emigrate to the North – to the Danube principalities and Besarabia, which was part of the Russian Empire. Even today, thousands of ethnic Bulgarians inhabit the southern parts of Moldavia and Ukraine, keeping their origins, language and customs.

The participation of Bulgarian volunteers in these wars, especially in the Crimean War (1853–1856), prompted Russia to plan and organize the liberation of Bulgaria from Ottoman rule (although with a certain delay in comparison with the policy towards Serbia and Greece). The conditions in the Balkans did not favor the Bulgarian cause because of the closeness to the main imperial centers and the fact that the Bulgarian lands were the basic supplier of raw materials for the Ottoman war machine and bureaucracy. The neighboring Wallachia and Moldavia (united in Romania in 1859), Serbia and Greece succeeded in overthrowing the Ottomans relatively easily thanks to the geopolitical circumstances. The Bulgarians however had to overcome not only the degenerating Ottoman state, but also the plundering appetites of its neighbors. In 1862, **Georgi Rakovski**, the philosopher of the Bulgarian National Revolution, created the **First Bulgarian Legion** in Belgrade. He trained the young men with the aim of organizing an uprising in the future. Many Bulgarian emigrants had obtained good military education abroad; others occupied important posts in the Ottoman Empire and sought diplomatic ways to achieve the independence of their country. In 1869, the **Bulgarian Revo-**

lutionary Central Committee was established in Bucharest. Its chairman was the writer, **Ljuben Karavelov**, who organized the preparation of an uprising from the territory of Romania.

Vasil Levski was a key figure. He was called simply **"Dean" ("monk")** or **"Apostle"**. That former monk succeeded in organizing a solid network of local revolutionary committees and to train many assistants and followers. The Ottoman police persecuted him for several years and eventually caught, tried and hung him, in Sofia. People consider him a holy person and the most revered martyr in the whole thousand-year-old history of Bulgaria. The **April Uprising** of 1876 was the turning point in the national liberation resistance of the Bulgarians. It was particularly rigorous in the region of Thrace where **Georgi Rakovski** was in charge. Thousands of innocent victims perished in it. Thousands of revolutionaries sacrificed their lives for Bulgaria. The great poet, **Hristo Botev**, was one of them.

In the stormy 1876, **John Atanasoff's** father was born in the **village of Boyadjik, the Yambol region**. The Turkish soldiers burned down the village during the dramatic days of the uprising. John Atanasoff's grandfather holding his baby son in his arms was killed by a bullet, which grazed the baby and left a scar on his forehead. Later, John Atanasoff's father immigrated to the United States.

The cruel suppression of the April Uprising raised the **"Bulgarian Question"** before the democratic societies of the world. A wave of protests, rallies and actions for the collection of relief supplies for the suffering Bulgarians swept across Europe – from Slavonic Russia to distant England and Ireland. **"Bulgarian horrors"**, the reports of the American journalist **McGahan** covered the front pages of the European and world press. The great French writer, **Victor Hugo**, wrote, "There should be put an end to the empires which kill!" The leading European intellectuals spoke out in support of the Bulgarians: **Darwin, Gladstone, Mendeleev, Dostoevski, Tolstoy, Turgeniev, Garibaldi** and many others.

The Great Powers could not ignore the Bulgarian cause, which they had been disregarding for decades. After several unsuccessful diplomatic attempts to give autonomy to Bulgaria, divided into two regions (eastern with the capital of Veliko Turnovo and western with the capital of Sofia), Emperor Alexander II of Russia declared war on Turkey in 1877. Together with the Russian soldiers, Fins, Poles, Romanians and many Bulgarian volunteers participated in this war. After a year of many epic battles, like in the Shipka Pass and near Pleven, Turkey was forced to sign a peace treaty. Thus, Bulgaria regained its independence on 3 March 1878. Its territory had to include almost all time-honored Bulgarian lands

(Moesia, Thrace and Macedonia) whose ethno-cultural characteristic was defined by the dominating Bulgarian element.

In July 1878, the Great Powers revised the **San Stephano Peace Treaty at the so-called Berlin Congress and separated the Bulgarians. To the North of the Balkan Mountains (Moesia), an autonomous principality was created as vassal to the Sultan.** It included the Sofia region and was called the **Principality of Bulgaria**. Southern Bulgaria (Thrace) became Eastern Romalia with the center of Plovdiv. It had administrative autonomy but politically and militarily it was under Ottoman rule. Macedonia and Odrin Thrace remained under full Ottoman domination. Romania obtained Northern Dobrudja and Serbia – the region of the big town of Nis. The epic struggle for independence continued in the territories under foreign occupation, especially in Macedonia. The tradition of the Apostle Levski was followed and it culminated in the **Ilinden-Preobrazhenie Uprising** of 1903.

Despite the disappointment of the unjust Berlin Treaty, the Bulgarians took to restoring their state. The Constitutional (Great) National Assembly sat in the historical capital of Veliko Turnovo. It created the **Turnovo Constitution** – one of the most democratic constitutions of that period. Bulgaria became a constitutional monarchy with a powerful parliament and modern legislation. The first Prince of free Bulgaria, **Alexander I Batenberg** (1879–1886) ruled the people who realized the Unification of the two autonomous territories in 1885. The Unification was conducted despite the opposition of the Great Powers. Bulgaria gained international authority as a modern European state during the mandate of **Stefan Stambolov** as a Prime Minister (1887–1894). He was a remarkable politician and statesman and was called the Bulgarian Bismark. The role of the monarch increased under Prince (later Tsar) **Ferdinand Sax-Koburg-Gotha** (1887–1918). The multi-party political system functioned exceptionally well. In 1908, Bulgaria denounced the remaining traces of dependence on the Ottoman Empire and declared its sovereignty. In 1912–1913, Bulgaria was the backbone of the allied Balkan states against the Empire in the war to liberate the **"enslaved brothers"** in Macedonia. Bulgarian soldiers demonstrated extreme courage. Airplanes were used, for the very first for military use; they introduced new methods in the artillery warfare; etc. The people's exalted upsurge was however cut short by the politics of Serbia and Greece and by the undertaken attack in the back by Romania. In the First World War Bulgaria had no other choice but to side with Germany because of the unfulfilled national unification. It suffered a severe catastrophy together with Germany and their allies. The heroism of the Bulgarian army was futile because the attempts to liberate and unify Macedonia failed. The national catastrophe became a fact with the signing of the peace treaty in the Paris suburb of Neuilly in 1919.

At the time of **Tsar Boris III** (1918–1943), the country was with a reduced territory and hostile surrounding, shaken by social cataclysms and fierce internal political struggles. In spite of that, all domains of the economy continued to modernize; scientific research was supported; education and arts developed. **Alexander Stambolijski** (1919–1923) was one of the eminent Bulgarian Prime Ministers of that period. He was ideologist and leader of the Bulgarian Agrarian Union, a party, which made decisive reforms but also made some grave political and diplomatic mistakes. The political conditions were grimmer because of the interference of the Communist International with its serious terrorist acts, especially the one that took place in September 1923 and the assault on The Church of St. Nedelja in Sofia two years later. That was followed by cruel repressions on the part of the right-wing forces. However, despite the hardships and the extremes, Bulgarians continued to trust the Turnovo Constitution and to cherish their democracy.

The name of Boris III is related to the unprecedented saving of the **Bulgarian Jews** from the German Concentration Camps during the Second World War. Some 50 000 Jews were saved from deportation to the concentration camps, protected by the democratic forces, the Bulgarian Orthodox Church and many leading intellectuals. Although linked to the "Axis" countries, Bulgaria managed to refrain from sending troops to the Eastern Front thanks to the flexible politics of its governments and of the Tsar Boris III. Unfortunately, at the Paris Peace Conference of 1947, the victors did not consider the historical and ethnic rights of the Bulgarians and gave Macedonia to Tito's Yugoslavia. In that part of the nation, the brutal experiment of creating the so-called Macedonian nation and language on an anti-Bulgarian basis began. Despite that, as a state with a longstanding historical experience marked by set backs and great sufferings, Bulgaria was the first to recognize present-day Macedonia (1991) and has supported it ever since then in the complex reality of the Balkan politics.

After the coup actuated on the 9 of September 1944, and supported by the Army of the Soviet Union, the post-war democratic system was formally restored in Bulgaria. Soviet interference, however, placed the Communist Party in the forefront and repressions and social experiments began. **Georgi Dimitrov** returned from Moscow in 1945. He was known as the "winner at the trial of the 20th century" in Leiptzig, which was staged by the Hitler political machine against three Bulgarians, accused of setting fire to the Reichstag. Dimitrov was "elected" Prime Minister in 1946. He was also the General Secretary of the Bulgarian Communist Party. Under the keen eye of Stalin, the Bulgarian democratic system was substituted with a totalitarian system. During **Vulko Chervenkov's** term as a Prime Minister (1950–1956), the so-called personality cult, yet another name for dictatorship, was imposed. State and party finally merged during the long period of totalitarian government under **Todor Zhivkov** (1956–1989). In the 1970s, Bulgaria achieved economic stabilization and a certain modernization of industry and culture. The decline of the communist "real socialism" was, however, inevitable.

Modern Bulgarian democracy was restored in November 1989. Bulgaria elected its new leaders, President **Zhelev** and President **Stoyanov**, and the Prime Ministers, **Lukanov, Popov, Dimitrov, Berov, Videnov**, under the circumstances of its functioning parliamentary democracy. Since 1997, **Ivan Kostov** became the Prime Minister of the Republic of Bulgaria. The country is quickly integrating into the large European family with its model of ethnic tolerance, based on the traditional Bulgarian democratic values and historical experience. It is not by chance that Bulgarians are a factor of stability in the Balkans, despite the difficult and complex social and economic transition. The leaders of Bulgarian democracy have the historical and civilization support of the nation and they are able to face the challenges of the future with dignity and wisdom.

This is, in short, the history of the ancient nation from which **John Vincent Atanasoff's** father came and that gave rise to the brilliant inventor from America who was proud of his Bulgarian origin. We dare say that in retrospect, his invention was epochal, and that it is one of the most significant events of modern history. Today, mankind lives differently; it is another mankind! And we hope for the best...

Associate Professor Dr. Plamen Pavlov,
President of the Agency for Bulgarians Abroad

CHRONOLOGICAL TABLE

YEAR	BULGARIANS	EUROPE	THE WORLD
AD 165	The first entry into the *List of the Bulgarian Khans*, the earliest written testimony of the existence of a Bulgarian empire in Eurasia	The Roman empire. Emperor Marcus Aurelius (161–180)	The Han dynasty in China, AD 25–221. The Parthians in Persia: Vologesus (148–190)
681	Danubian Bulgaria founded by Khan Asaparukh. Possible emergence of Volga Bulgaria: the late 7th century.	In the West: the Frankish Merovingian dynasty, 511–751. In Byzantium: Emperor Constantine IV (668–685)	The Tang dynasty in China, 618–906. Ummayad caliphate, 690–750.
718	The Bulgarian Khan Tervel defeats an Arab army before the walls of Constantinople, thus saving Europe from Muslim invasion	Byzantine emperor Leo III (717–741): beginning of Iconoclasm. In the West, the Frankish ruler Charles Martel defeats the Arabs at Poitiers (732)	Khazar invasion of Azerbaijan Arabs and Tibetans invade Kashgar (717). The Caliph Maslama marches against the Khazars (727)
864	Conversion of Bulgaria to Christianity: Khan Boris later known as Prince Michael-Boris (852–889)	Novgorod founded by the Varangian Riurik (862). In Byzantium, the emperors Theophilos and Michael III, 843–867. The Saxon dynasty in England, 827–1016. The Carolingian dynasty in France, 843–987	Early Japanese dynasties, 710–1160. Arab invasion of the Mediterranean.

YEAR	BULGARIANS	EUROPE	THE WORLD
1205	The Bulgarian Tsar Kalojan (1197–1207) defeats the Crusaders at Adrianople	The crusaders of the Fourth Crusade capture Constantinople (1204). The Latin empire is founded.	The Khural of the Mongols proclaims Temuchin Great Khan under the name of Genghis Khan (1206)
1230	The battle at Klokotnica: Tsar John Asen II (1218–1241) defeats the *despotes* of Epirus, Theodore Komnenos	Fifth Crusade, 1217/21. King of France: St.Louis IX (1226–1270)	The Mongols capture Kwaresm, 1219/21. Genghis Khan dies (1227). His huge empire begins to disintegrate.
1396	The Vidin Kingdom of John Sracimir falls to the Ottomans. The whole of Danubian Bulgaria is turned into an Ottoman province.	In Muscovy: the Great Prince Basil III (1389–1425). In Bohemia, John Hus burned at the stake as a heretic	Tamerlain defeats Sultan Bajazid I at Angora (1402). The sultan is taken prisoner.
1400s	The Ottoman military and administrative organization is introduced into the Bulgarian lands	Movement for an ecclesiastical union. Hussite wars. End of the Hundred-year war between France and England	Christopher Columbus discovers America (1499)
1550s	Tsar Ivan the Terrible captures Kazan: Volga Bulgaria conquered by the Russians	The Reformation. Outbreak of the revolution in England: early 1640s	Portuguese sailors reach China, 1516/20. The Portuguesse reach Japan (1542)
1660s	Anti-Ottoman uprisings in the Bulgarian lands, 1686/89	The Christian league wages a war against the Ottoman empire, 1683/89	The earliest French colonies founded in Canada: Quebec, the city of Montreal

YEAR	BULGARIANS	EUROPE	THE WORLD
1700s	Beginning of the Bulgarian National Revival st. Paisy of Hilandar completes his *Slav-Bulgarian History*	The Enlightenment: Ch. Montesqieu, F. Voltaire, J.-J.Russeau. Outbreak of the French revolution (1789). Napoleon Bonaparte rises to power (1799)	French colonists found the city of New Orleans, in Louisiana (1718). Discovery of New Zealand and Australia, 1768/69. Declaration of Independence of the USA (1774)
Early 1800s	Dr. Peter Beron publishes his textbook (called the *Fishbook*, 1824). G.S. Rakovsky was born in Kotel	The Congress of Vienna (1815). The Concert of Europe comes into being. The first railroad is opened in England (1825)	The Democratic Party is founded in the USA (1824)
1830s–1840s	D. Zeljazkov opens the first textile factory in Bulgaria (Sliven, 1835). V. Levsky was born in Karlovo (1837)	In England, the beginning of Chartism (1838/48); Parliament passes a bill of a ten-hour working day for women and teen-age workers.	France conquers Algeria. American-Mexican war, 1846/48
1850s	Emergence of the organized liberation movement of the Bulgarians, 1856/78. G.S. Rakovsky publicizes the first plans of Bulgaria's liberation	The Crimean war, 1853/56. Revolution in Spain, 1854/56	The Republican Party is founded in the USA (1854)
1860s	Movement for an autonomous Bulgarian church (Exarchate), 1860/72. V.Levsky builds the Internal Revolutionary Organization in Bulgaria, 1869/73	Unification of Italy, 1860/70. Austria becomes a dual monarchy, Austria-Hungary (1867)	Civil war in the USA, 1861/65. The US buys Alaska from Russia (1867). The Suez canal is openend (1869)

YEAR	BULGARIANS	EUROPE	THE WORLD
1870s	April uprising, 1876. Russo-Turkish war and Liberation of Bulgaria, 1877/78	Franco-Prussian war, 1870. Unification of Germany. Commune of Paris, 1871. The Eastern crisis, 1875/78	Egypt declares bankruptcy (1876). The British establish their control over the Suez canal.
1878	The Kingdom of Bulgaria is restored as a Principality	The Congress of Berlin.	The Triple Alliance begins to disintegrate.
1885	Unification of the Principality of Bulgaria and Eastern Rumelia	The Eastern question is transformed into a Bulgarian crisis.	The British fight the French over the Sudan
1908	Bulgaria declares its full independence and is internationally recognised as a sovereign state	The earthquake in Sicily	The revolution of the Young Turks in the Ottoman empire
1914	The investigation of the Carnegie commission supports the Bulgarian national claims	The biggest Trans-Atlantic Liner, Bismarck, is launched.	Outbreak of World War one
1919	Bulgaria signs the Treaty of Neuilly	Civil War in Russia	The Versailles system is established world-wide.
1939	Program of a "peaceful revision" of the existing borders	Outbreak of World War Two	John Atanassof, an American of Bulgarian descent, creates the first prototype of the modern computer
1945	The Bulgarian army fights its way into the Alps in the war against Germany	The post-war division of Europe according to the agreements of Yalta and Potsdam	The end of World War Two

PREFACE FROM THE EDITOR

John Atanasoff, a half English and a half Bulgarian name, peaked the interest of the Bulgarians in 1970. As it turned out, “the father of the computer” had not only a Bulgarian sounding surname but his roots were Bulgarian as well. This book is an attempt to respond to the enormous interest in the fascinating personality and the everlasting endeavor of this great man.

This work centers on the lawsuit, unprecedented in its scale and importance, for the patent rights of the Honeywell Computer Corporation against the Sperry Rand Corporation and its subsidiary, Illinois Scientific Development (ISD), 1967–1973. The decision of the Federal Court of Minneapolis (U.S. District Judge Earl R. Larson) of 19.10.1973 finally and categorically determined John Atanasoff's priority in the invention of the century. The book is an extended biography of the American inventor John Vincent Atanasoff, son of the Bulgarian, Ivan Atanasoff, who was orphaned during the April Uprising against Turkey of 1876. The book narrates the long life and work of the man and the creator of the first electronic computer in the world. It also tells of the Bulgarian roots of the inventor, his two visits to this country, his gratefulness, and the place of Bulgaria in his huge heart.

The aim of the book is to overcome the 50-year-long distortion of the history of the computer revolution. Even today, in certain reference literature, Bulgarian publications included, authors continue to refer to Mauchly and Eckert as the actual inventors of the computer. The Bulgarian scientific community has undertaken the task of restoring the historic event of John Atanasoff's fundamental contribution to computer technology.

Judge Larson's decision states that the universal digital electronic computer ENIAC, designed in 1943–1945 by John Mauchly and John Eckert, is based largely on the unpatented ideas of the inventor John Atanasoff and his associate Clifford Berry, whose ABC computer was made in 1939–1942. The Court's decision was confirmed and substantiated by the scientific documentation of the event.

The authoritative American scientists Arthur and Alice Burks undertook the investigation of determining who was, or were, the inventors in the early 1980s and financed by official US institutions. Burks participated in the work on ENIAC and was the second person that received the most prestigious Computer Pioneer Medal (1982) from the IEEE – Computer Society. John Atanasoff was the fourth scientist to receive that award in 1984 – awards are often unfair. The spouses analyzed tens of thousands of pages – lawsuit protocols and exhibits, including the most inaccessible documents; they studied the scientific work of Atanasoff and Berry in the early 1940s and finalized their conclusion with the help of Atanasoff's rich archive.

Here, the two main books on John Atanasoff – the first monographs of the journalists Clark R. Mollenhoff in English (1988) and Nicolay Bonchev in Bulgarian (1990) form the basis of this book.

It is based also on extensive materials available in English and to a lesser extent in Bulgarian, consisting of monographs, collections and scientific periodicals. The major sources used are provided by John Atanasoff and his associate Clifford Berry, Alice Atanasoff, John Atanasoff's wife, A. Apokin and L. Maystrov, Arthur and Alice Burks, John Eckert, H. Goldstein who have co-authored along with John Von Neumann and Burks, the famous report on the electronic computing machines in 1945, A. Mackintosh, John Mauchly, B. Randall. Authentic letters and documents have been studied. Interviews given by John Atanasoff and some of his Bulgarian acquaintances are included. His father's memoirs (Ivan Atanasoff) and conversations with his mother, Iva Atanasoff, have been used. N. Bonchev's investigations in the village of Boyadjik, the birthplace of Ivan Atanasoff, also have been drawn upon.

As an eyewitness, I would like to explain how Bulgaria 'discovered' John Atanasoff. In the autumn of 1970, Georgi Alipiev, Dipl. Eng., noticed his name in the foreword of the Russian translation of a book by R. S. Richards, Electronic Digital Systems: "It seems that the origin of all electronic digital systems starts with the computer of Atanasoff and Berry." He mentioned this to Cyril Boyanov, Dipl. Eng., who in his turn informed Professor Blagovest Sendov. The latter had just returned from a research trip to London where he had used the letters of recommendation of three British professors to gain access to manuscripts in the British Museum. There, he had studied the files of Charles Babbage describing his two machines, his other inventions, his mathematical heritage and even the letters of Babbage to Lady Augusta Ada Lovelace, Byron's daughter. Sendov sent a letter to John Atanasoff which found him in the State of Iowa, U.S.A. That was the beginning of the correspondence between the two scholars, that was followed by Atanasoff and his family's first visit at the invitation of the Bulgarian Academy of Sciences to Bulgaria.

About the peculiarities of this book. All superfluous quotation marks have been deleted. Almost everywhere, the capital letter stands for the left quotation mark. Journal names are written in italic.

I thank most sincerely the TANGRA Foundation and its co-chairmen Mr. Petko Kolev and Mr. Dimitar Dimitrov who asked me to compose the book and made it altogether possible.

Sofia, 20 February 2001 **Dimitar Shishkov**

THE LONG AND ENLIGHTENED LIFE OF A MAN WHO FOUND OUT LATE THAT HE WAS A SCIENTIFIC GIANT

But who was the man who achieved so much and, still, was deprived of the attention of the public and of his peers in science? During his whole life, Atanasoff remained inventive and strange, out of the ordinary, even after having been left dejected for some time. Sometimes he seemed to be an irreparable outsider because of his disparity with other people doing his job or for his persistence not to do things the way other people did them.

He was a very bright child. At 13 (starting high school), he decided to become a theoretical physicist, choosing a basic science whose broad scope and structure matched his interest in the separate components of the material world. Now emphasizing proudly his Bulgarian origin, then he was simply a typical American – an amazing Huck Finn in science.

[...] His style of work shaped at an early age and remained unchanged through the years:

"I worked on calculating machines in the way I approached any other problem. I amassed everything on the issue whilst I exhausted it all. After that it strained me until it wore me out. Sooner or later, the new idea would occur to me. And I would start realizing it straight away."

William Gardner, The Independent Inventor.
Datamation Journal, September 1981

The genius, the inventor of the modern electronic computer, John Vincent Atanasoff, of Bulgarian origin, died at the age of 91. His long life resembles a film script – the story of a great man. His inspiration has changed fundamentally the course of human life; it has caused the last great revolution – the computer one; and also, it has laid the foundations of the information society at the end of our century and the beginning of the new one. But it is a story of great dissatisfactions, delayed recognition and enormous personal financial losses. For six years on end, one of the largest and complex lawsuits for patent rights between two well-known American corporations, related to the work of John Atanasoff, continued.

[...] The scholar did not consider the computer his major invention. In his life, he patented more than 30 inventions including the first device for detonating hydrodynamic sea mines, equipment for detecting and recording strong seismic and sound waves, mail sorting systems, electrical quartz watch and a range of designs for military purposes.

Dimitar Shishkov

THE ROUTE TO THE INVENTION

Nikolay Bonchev

ALGORITHM TO SELFDISCOVERY

Like the claims of the Seven Ancient Greek city–states to be the birthplace of Homer, Seven North American states can claim association with the fame of John Atanasoff – New York, Florida, Iowa, Wisconsin, Illinois, Maryland and Minnesota, not counting the Federal District of Columbia. Unlike John Von Neumann who was initially educated in Chemistry, John Atanasoff 's education was an "ecclectic mixture" of Electrical Engineering, Mathematics and Theoretical Physics. In the 20th century, that particular "mixture" created the computer. Like the philosopher's stone, this invention has empowered man; it developed and enriched man's knowledge and skills in all spheres of life.

John Vincent Atanasoff was born on 4 October 1903 at the farm of his maternal grandfather near Hamilton, New York. At that time, his father was a correspondence school student of Electrical Engineering, working at a number of electrical jobs in the area of Hamilton, including the northern part of the State of New Jersey. There, in the town of Lindhurst, 6-year-old John learned how to read, having been taught by his mother. A year later, he entered a public school, a foundation school for predominantly well-to-do parents. He attended similar schools at the towns of Osteen and later Brewster and Old Chicora, Florida, where the family moved in 1912. John Atanasoff said, "My father worked at a series of electrical engineering positions (people were poor then and kept looking for better jobs) before he settled in Florida… We were four children, all ailing… But we got stronger in Florida." Iva Lucena, his mother and mathematic teacher, had ten children, of whom eight survived: John, Ethelyn, Margaret, Theodore, Avis, Raymond, Melva and Irving. She was a demanding mother but never disciplined her children. She encouraged them all and was particularly glad of her first-born son's talent and fascination with science.

The father had a restless disposition, often making unexpected decisions. After a year at Osteen, the family moved to Brewster where Ivan Atanasoff obtained a job at a pharmaceutical company. His job was to build an electrical power plant at Brewster. He maintained the plant and the other electrical equipment of the phosphate mine for 10 years. In 1913, the Atanasoff family lived in a two-bedroom frame house with electric lights. The family bought their first automobile. Together with his father, young John made his first steps in electrical technology. He preferred his toys with batteries, wires and lamps. The son was especially proud when, as a nine-year-old boy, he found and corrected faulty electric wiring in a back-porch light of the house.

Young John read many of the books in his father's library; he believed that he could learn everything through reading. But nothing impressed him as much as the instructions to the Dietzgen slide rule and the logarithmic table, which "miraculously" simplified calculations. They made even his favorite books, "The Faerie Queen" by Spencer and Ruskin's essays, drift into the background. The father had ordered the slide rule but he was absorbed by his work repairing the electrical equipment of the mine damaged by Florida's frequent electrical storms. He hardly noticed that John had got hold of the brand new slide rule. "The slide rule became the food of my thoughts," Atanasoff recalled in his memoirs. Not only did the child learn how to find correct mathematical answers with it, but also became interested in the mathematical principles behind its operation. Something extraordinary happened with the nine-year-old boy – the favorite baseball was abandoned and its place was occupied by the persevering, and passionate study of logarithms (initially from the short slide rule manual and later from other sources). In a conversation with Bulgarian journalists (Otechestvo, 1979, 9), Atanasoff said that as a student he could use freely logarithms with base 2 and 10 taken from tables. In addition, he studied trigonometric functions with pleasure. He found a book from his father's library, which included introduction to differential calculus and also a chapter on infinite series and how to calculate logarithms. He started reading that book without any knowledge of elementary algebra. At the beginning, his mother gave him the help he needed. Later, the child progressed individually – step by step. He encountered the unfamiliar "n" sign. Only several weeks later in another book on series, he was able to find what that symbol meant (given as n!).

John studied radio technology from books published in Great Britain. In his memoirs, he wrote that the book on radiotelephony described the electrical discharge as the only means of generating electromagnetic waves. The triode, the first electronic tube, which could amplify such vibrations and work in a circuit for their generating, had been invented only a few years before. The book contained information, which Atanasoff would remember when designing the first computer – information about the magnetic conductor developed by Valdemar Poulsen. Initially, the magnetic conductor could be used for imprinting memory of sound vibrations but its later modifications would serve as a slow memory for the computing machine. That year, John started studying Physics, Chemistry and Astronomy. He explored these new waters with more confidence, reaching farther and farther. And then, something happened.

It was from his mother's eighth grade arithmetic textbook that he first read a chapter on numbers base system other than 10. He studied it carefully and later he was convinced that this early understanding of mathematical base system other than base 10, together with the mastering of logarithmic calculations, played an important role in his later work on computer technology.

In 1918, the family moved to Old Chicora, Florida. They owned a large farm with wide uncultivated areas and an orange grove. John finished the Mulberry High School deciding that he wanted to become a theoretic physicist. Why did he choose that area? Why did the son have a preference for Physics when the father knew Mathematics and was engulfed in electrical engineering? We can hardly find a categorical answer. Yet, we should note that in that period, the first decades of the 20th century, Physics was a leading science with "unlimited" opportunities. The relativity theory was launched; the structure of the atom and its nucleus was being investigated; the laws of movement of elementary particles were found. That is to say that Quantum Mechanics was created.

In 1921, the Atanasoff family settled finally at the town of Bradley Junction. The children enjoyed the picturesque surroundings where they could go swimming, fishing or hunting. The big family stayed at the new house until 1975 when its members scattered in different states.

After completing high school maintaining "A" grades in 1920, John did not have money to go to university. For a whole year, he worked as a phosphate surveyor. Then he entered the University of Florida at

Gainesville. He studied Electrical Engineering because that course included disciplines closest to theoretical physics. Electronics was not taught but he became interested in it. He studied practical mechanical construction of forging, hammering, pressing and shaping machines as well. The knowledge and skills acquired would be applied in the construction of the first computer some 15 years later. According to the English biologist, John Holdaine, "the road in science is made not only by those who can think well but also by those who have skillful hands". John worked as a waiter and also gave private lessons while he studied at the university.

In September 1925, holding a Bachelor of Science Degree in Electrical Engineering with a straight "A" academic average, he accepted a teaching fellowship at Iowa State College at Ames and became a postgraduate student of Mathematics. As a graduate student, he was awarded a teaching assistant. He taught two mathematics classes to undergraduates and worked seriously on his master's thesis in mathematics.

However he was still only 22 years old and liked immensely the socials given by the Dixie Club for students from the South. It was there that, the handsome young Floridian met the attractive twenty-six-year-old Lura Meeks, a home economics major. She came from an Oklahoma farming family who had moved from state to state in search of better farmland.

Soon after receiving his master's degree in mathematics in June 1926, John Atanasoff married Lura. That did not stop John from becoming a doctoral candidate at the University of Wisconsin. In March 1929, the family moved to Madison, Wisconsin, with their one-year old daughter, Elsie. The winter semester had already started and Professor J. Van Vleck (in the 1960s, he became Nobel Laureate for his work on magnetism, in which Atanasoff took part) objected to Atanasoff entering his class on Quantum Mechanics in the middle of the semester. Nevertheless, and over his objections, Atanasoff attended the class just the same. He enrolled in the courses in Electrodynamics and Mathematical Theory of Elasticity in the same way and, when the semester was over, he succeeded in completing all three courses. Of the 25 graduate students in Prof. Vleck's class, only five passed the final examination. The professor indicated that Atanasoff's test was the best one. Atanasoff worked on his doctoral dissertation during the 1929/1930 academic year and also taught mathematics at the University of Wisconsin. Prof. Vleck was Atanasoff's supervisor on his doctoral studies but he took leave for a year and was substituted by Prof. Gregory Wentzel from Zurich, Switzerland. He became a close friend with Prof. Warren Weaver who taught Electricity and Magnetism. Their paths crossed many times in subsequent years.

Atanasoff completed his doctoral dissertation on the topic of "The Dialectic Constant of Helium" and received his Ph.D. as a theoretical physicist in July 1930. In his thesis, Atanasoff extended the Rayley-Ritz method and succeeded in calculating the dielectric constant. After that, he examined the results experimentally. In fact, the work on the thesis was his first experience in serious computing. Later he recalled, "Such calculations required many weeks of hard work on a desk calculator, the Monroe, which was the only one available at the time. I was also amazed by the enormous quantity of calculations required by the process of approximating the solution of partial differential equations – the fact that eventually motivated my work in the area of automatic calculating."

Atanasoff returned to Iowa State College where he was given the rank of assistant professor of Mathematics and Physics (1930–1936), and later – associate professor (1936–1942) and professor in absentia (1942–1945).

As of the beginning of the 19th century, the mass device for calculation was the mechanical calculator – the simple desk machine. The arithmometer with a turning shaft, introduced by Leibnitz at the end of the 17th century, was perfected and mass-produced in the 1820s thanks to one Thomas from Alsace. The arithmometer with a cogwheel was even more widely used. It was designed at the beginning of 18th century by Poleny from Italy but was generally accepted after having been improved on by Odner from Russia in 1873. Independently, the adding machines, based on the development of Pascal took on. A keyboard adding machine was patented by Pamley in the United States in 1850. Russian mathematician, Chibishev, introduced some important principles. In 1888 Burrows patented a keyboard calculating machine with a printing device in the United States. Despite the advancement of mechanical calculators during the 19th century – speed, reducing friction, eliminating blocking, substituting levers with keys – they had reached the limit of their development at the end of the century. The inertness of the moving parts did not allow the rotating speed to be increased over 400–500 rotations per minute; the human factor contributed to errors at the input of data and in the operations with the intermediate results of calculations. The latter shortcoming was overcome in the so-called complex calculating machines with machine input of intermediate results. The optimal solution to the problem would have been the programmable calculating automatic machine, which Charles Babbage (in Great Britain during the mid 19th century) first proposed their construction based on the mechanical principle. His brilliant ideas were a century ahead of their time but were not forgotten – they inspired several generations of inventors who applied them. Their realization came to pass when the first automatic electromechanical digital computer, an extremely heavy and massive machine (MARK 1) was constructed by Howard Iken, who together with the IBM Corp. created it for Harvard University in 1944.

The new machine used perforated paper tape and the electromagnetic elements of the communications technology. The perforated tape for the program memory, the binary key (the commutation element), and the electromagnetic switch were borrowed from telegraphic technology. The ten-step switches and the switchboard for manual commutation of electrical circuits were borrowed from telephone technology. These new elements had many advantages in comparison with the existing mechanical computing devices. The electrical principle of calculating with the help of the small electromagnetic switch, created an easier amplification of the signal, greater speed of calculation and better data input and output. Despite the fact that MARK 1 presented digits by mechanical means (cogwheels were used), the electromechanical principle of computing allowed a speed of 0.3 seconds in addition and subtraction, 6.5 seconds in multiplication, and 15 seconds in division. MARK 1 substituted 20 operators working with manual calculators, yet its memory was small and its programming was very time consuming.

In the last quarter of the 19th century, two mathematicians, Charles Pierce in the U.S.A. and Frege in Germany, created independently of one another, the so-called Logic of Relations or Predicate Logic. In the early 1880s Pierce brought forth the idea of a calculating machine based on the Truthfulness tables. He found that the logical operations of NOT-AND and of NOT-OR were enough to express all other operations, i.e. all logical relations. About half a century later, Atanasoff used similar logical operations in his ABC computer, realizing them technically in logical schemes. A student of Pierce, Markand, worked on the construction of electromechanical logical machines with switches and binary memory. There was an interesting parallel between the principles of commutation elements used by Markand and by Atanasoff. The former used several levels of intensity of the magnetic field to realize switching, while the latter realized switching by using vacuum electronic tubes controlled by different voltage levels. However, binary switch memory of Markand corresponded to binary condenser memory of Atanasoff. Pierce predicted the creation of an electrical mathematical-logic-based machine for computing "a la Babbage".

ON PERFORATED CARDS AND ELECTROMECHANICAL MACHINES

Until the third quarter of the 19th century, the mechanical desk calculator and the slide rule entirely satisfied the needs of the scientific and technical calculations. The need for an instrument capable of fast calculation was not yet felt by the scientific and technical circles. So the ideas of Babbage and Pierce had to wait for their realization until the following century. It was not until 1880, when the United States experienced an acute need for fast processing of the data resulting from the national census. It became clear that the keyboard machines, that were then manufactured and the new ones built by NCR and Burrows could not cope with the task. The processing of the 1880 census data was completed in 1887 when the new census of 1890 was forthcoming. The estimation was that the new data would be processed in 10 years' time, which was unacceptable because the constitution demanded that the redistribution of the seats of the members of Congress be made in a timely manner. Herman Holerith, a mine engineer of German origin, undertook the task of designing a device for fast processing of the census data. After some unsuccessful attempts to use perforated tape, he decided to apply perforated cards of the size of a dollar note in his electromechanical calculating machine. From 1884 until 1889, Holerith patented his basic perforated card machines – a device for reading perforated cards, a tabulator, and a sorting machine. To that he also added a simple and a complex perforator and some 28 other patents. This started the new electromechanical age of the development of world calculating technology. The perforated card calculating machines are known as "calculating analytical machines". According to the classification of D. Okan, they are called "statistical machines". But their most widely used name is "tabulating machines".

Initially, Holerith used his machines for statistical processing of data on the contagious diseases in the population and the death rate they caused. In 1880, the first machine processing of census data was carried out in the United States and Austria simultaneously. It turned out that with the help of the tabulating machines the time of processing was reduced four times and the data could be combined and analyzed. In 1896, Holerith founded a firm for the serial production of tabulating machines – Computing Tabulating Recording Company. His machines were used all over the world by state governments for census data processing. Machines for accountancy were also designed, but their major application was in statistical processing. During the first quarter of the 20th century, other firms, competing with the Holerith's company, were established in the United States and elsewhere. Holerith sold out his company in 1911 and, after several mergers with other companies, it started the international corporation of IBM in 1924.

Tabulating devices were mass-produced in the industrially developed countries in the early 1930s. Their calculating power was constantly increasing at the cost of raised complexity. IBM became a major factor, in the scientific development of this area. It stimulated the application of computing technology at the universities by creating computational laboratories and by training specialists. Professor Vannevar Bush built a differential analyzer at the Massachusetts Institute of Technology in 1929 and 1930. It was an analog device measuring the turns of a shaft by means of a 10-base number system. Some of the Babbage's principles were applied in the Bush Differential Analyzer.

During the 1930s, IBM developed and produced a wide range of perforated card machines, some of which could record data of other scientific equipment on perforated cards. It is interesting to note that in a letter addressed to John Atanasoff dating from the late 1930s, IBM stressed that they would never make electronic calculating machines! Only a decade later, in 1946, the electronic calculating analytical machine IBM 601 appeared. The president of IBM was dismissed in the mid 50s for having caused losses to the company because he did not foresee the development of the electronic computer industry.

FROM THE INITIAL ATTEMPTS OF CALCULATING TECHNOLOGY TO THE DEVELOPMENT OF THE ABC

The research tasks in quantum mechanics and other fields of physics on which Atanasoff and his students at Ames worked required the calculating of large systems of linear algebraic equations. But the solution of systems of 10 and more equations with 10 unknown quantities with an electromechanical calculator was practically impossible because of the time it took. The way out was the mechanical solution of the equations. And Atanasoff began to explore the possibilities of that mechanization in 1933. Later he recalled that the only large machines of the tabulating type were the ones made by IBM and Remington Rand. But they could only add figures recorded on perforated cards. A similar machine was installed at the Statistics Department of Iowa State College. So after his return from Wisconsin, Atanasoff began examining that equipment. He believed that it was the biggest computing device at that time although it did not possess the calculating capabilities of the Monroe calculator. With the assistance of A.E. Brandt from the statistics department, he started looking for a problem in theoretical physics that could be solved by the IBM tabulator. Atanasoff wrote later in his memoirs, "First, we thought of applying it to the analysis of complex spectra but on close analysis we determined that the IBM equipment would not perform the job. Then we thought that by using some additional devices we might enable the IBM equipment to solve the problems we had devised. In this we succeeded." The Journal of the Optical Society of America published their paper on this experiment in February 1936.

There are at least two reasons for looking at this successful attempt by Atanasoff in the field of calculating technology. Firstly, because it is the first proof of his inventiveness in this field, documented in a scientific publication. Secondly, because calculating analytical technology of that period was not disunited from the invention of the ABC computer.

The period when Atanasoff started working on calculating machines was characterized by the fact that, after the design Holerith's machine of 1913, printing and adding tabulators began to be built. The notion of the tabulogram was created – the printed out tables with the results of the calculations. In 1921, the tabulator was improved by attaching to it a commutation board. In 1931 calculating multiplying perforators were introduced and in 1936 – perforated card machines with letters and digits were made.

Towards the mid-1930s, scientific research needed fast computing devices. However even the most sophisticated makes of electromechanical machines (desktop calculators and tabulating machines) could not meet this requirement. IBM produced tabulators for automatic processing of stacks of perforated cards. The most advanced device of that type was IBM 601 – a multiplier with cross addition of the data. That multiplier could read the numerals "memorized" on perforated cards and make calculations on a given formula, entered by commuting a switch. The formula could contain one multiplication and three additions or subtractions so that it added to the increasing total sum (always positive).

The early predecessors of the electromechanical “calculating giants” were ahead of their time in terms of their actual necessity with about four decades because the theoretical and technical preconditions for their creation already existed. Only at the end of the 1930s, half a century after the work of Pierce and Markand, science and technology experienced the need for fast computing machines with large memory. Large automatic digital calculating machines, using the principles of Boolean algebra and the electromechanical element base (electromechanical relays) were designed by researchers in the developed countries. In Germany, Konrad Zuse built a calculator whose digits are presented with a floating comma. The term is floating point. In the U.S.A., George Stibits created a relay machine for calculating complex numbers, and also the series of makes (from II to V) for Bell Telephone Laboratories. At Harvard University, Howard Iken built the notorious Mark I – the electromechanical realization of the Babbage project together with the IBM engineers, Lake, Hamilton and Durfy. Although they were not still born, those electrical giants were “morally outdated” because the computers were being designed at that same time. In particular, the ABC computer provided the basic principles for the creation of the ENIAC and the computers with memorizing programs.

In this exceptionally fruitful period for the calculating machines, IBM built an electronic version of its relay multiplication machine, IBM 681. In it, vacuum electronic tubes were used to produce partial results, and electromagnetic switches moved those results. Brian Phelps’ patent was based on that design. At the ENIAC court trial (1971–1973), it was found that Eckert and Mauchly borrowed from the Phelps patent claims 83, 86 and 87 for the patent of ENIAC. Judge Larson deemed that Phelps experimented successfully his device in 1942 – long before he filed his application on 27.04. 1945. Therefore, Eckert and Mauchly did not have the right to claim before the United States Patent Office their priority in patenting the ENIAC on the ground that their application was filed earlier than Phepls’. The heart of the machine patented by Phelps – the electronic multiplying device – was connected electronically with the mechanical part of the machine (the reading, perforating and power blocks). It calculated with a speed of 8 000 impulses per second, whereas the perforated card block had only 23 impulses/sec, i.e. the latter was 350 times slower.

Despite the apogee of the calculating-analytical technology, the compilation of tables, i.e. the large part of scientific research was done by hand until nearly the mid-1930s. Professional mathematicians doing calculations possessed a real psychological barrier; they would not give up their "sacred work in the temple of science" away to the machine. In England, the astronomer Lesley Comrie was the first to introduce calculating-analytical machines in the scientific calculation of the tables on the movement of the Moon in 1933.

The task, which Atanasoff and Brandt wanted to solve with their perforated card machine, was related to the spectral analysis. That was one of the most effective methods of qualitative and quantitative exploration of substances. They studied the so-called linear spectrum. It should be pointed out that spectroscopy is the field of Physics, which deals with the study of the emission and retraction spectrums of substances. Its objective is to measure the wavelength, intensity, position, width and structure of the spectral lines. Thus, important information about the structure and energy states of the electron shell of atoms, the properties on atomic nuclei and isotopes is obtained. Molecular spectroscopy is a source of data on the relationships of different parts of the complex molecules, their oscillations and energy. By 1928, it had been practically impossible to determine the chemical composition of complex organic substances with a large number of atoms in their molecules – their specters were too difficult to analyze. Spectroscopy began coping with this task only after the Indian scholar, C. Raman, found the effect of combinational diffraction of light subsequently named after him and won the Nobel Award for Physics. At this diffraction, along with the primary specter, spectral lines of longer and shorter waves are also observed. So Atanasoff and Brandt dealt with the analysis of complex specters – one of the difficult problems facing chemistry and physics, as well as astronomy. For that purpose, they used a tabulator, working with eight-digit numbers. The electrical perforator was capable of copying a random part of the perforated card onto another card. Of course the calculating-analytical set contained a sorting machine, which classified the cards and ranked them in the order of the digits perforated in a given column (for which it was tuned to sort). The speed was 100 times slower than the speed of the first electromechanical computers of the late 1940s (e.g. Mark I) and 900 times slower than the speed of the ABC computer.

The method used by the two scholars was quite effective – standard equipment was applied. The results were obtained directly in numbers, so it was not necessary to check them with an arithmometer. That made it possible to assign assistants to operate the equipment.

The above mentioned paper, Use of a Perforated Card Device for Analyzing Complex Spectra by Atanasoff and Brandt was accepted by the journal of the American Optical Society on 20.11.1935. It came out only two months later – in the February 1936 issue, of the journal. The paper shows the exceptional correctness of the authors. After detailed descriptions of their work and the advantages of their method, the authors made an important announcement. They informed those interested in their new method that the British Tabulating Machines Company, London, has produced a rolling total machine, which makes the use of any additional equipment unnecessary and completely eliminates the use of B-cards. Using that imported piece of equipment could solve any problem in spectral analysis, the authors admit.

The authors extended their gratitude to the tabulator department of the IBM for the kind cooperation in the supply of machines and devices. However three decades later in connection with the processes in Minneapolis and Baltimore, IBM was ordered to submit to the court all documents from the archives, in which the name of Atanasoff was mentioned. In one of those letters, the company said, "Atanasoff should not be allowed near the tabulator". Atanasoff wrote in his memoirs, "We had not made any alterations or damage to the IBM tabulator but it seemed that someone in the IBM Company was nervous when we published the paper with a photograph."

Although successful, the analysis of complex spectra with the help of calculating-analytical technology was only a test of the penultimate occasion for Atanasoff – the solution of systems with a large number of algebraic equations by means of the available calculating technology. This is what Atanasoff in his memoirs stated, "The prospects of solving my problem by means of digital language were favorable. At that moment, I would not have persisted perhaps any more if I hadn't got two more thoughts in my thinning bag of ideas. One was that the big tabulator could be adapted for the solution of the problem if additional devices had supported it. In the end, the limited capacity of the tabulator and the difficulty of the support made me give up the idea." Atanasoff added to the insufficient calculating capacity the limited amount of operating memory and the large dimensions of the machine. He said that at that time the IBM tabulator was the biggest digital device. The Iowa State College possessed a machine, which could tabulate and add 40 of the 80 columns of the perforated cards, but there were machines, which could tabulate and sum all 80 columns divided into 10 fields of 8 columns each. Atanasoff argued that even then he had ideas about the importance of the "fast", i.e. the operating memory, and the "slow", i.e. the permanent memory of a calculating machine. He explained the classification of the fast and slow memory with the time necessary for the access to the memorized data and indicated that the fastness of the calculating machine depended on the speed of the "fast memory". As far as the IBM tabulator with 80 columns was concerned, its operating memory was kept in its internal digital discs with a capacity of 80 log210 ~ 266 bytes. That is the "top standard" of the current calculating technology. Atanasoff thought that the slow memory of the perforated card device had in fact a much larger capacity if that was understood as the memorizing of data on cards and its return to the machine for secondary processing. "I understood that the new machine, which I wanted to build, had to have a fast memory with a capacity much larger than 266 bytes. The advantages of such a memory were obvious and corresponded to Babbage's concepts, despite that I did not realize that at that time."

Atanasoff studied many mathematical devices and found that they could be classified into two categories – analog and digital. Nobody at that time used the term "digital", so Atanasoff distinguished the analog machines from the "real computing machines". In 1936, we made one last attempt to build a small analog calculator. He worked with Glen Murphy, an atomic physicist from Iowa State College, creating the Laplaciometer. They used it for geometric surface analyses. According to Atanasoff, that machine had the shortcomings of all analog devices – its accuracy depended on the separate parts of the machine.

Atanasoff's preliminary calculations in 1937 indicated that a computer with a binary principle of calculation could be built for the purpose of solving systems of linear algebraic equations. The input and output device for the IBM machine was made during his attempts to solve such systems. But the calculating capacity of the tabulators was insufficient and the use of many machines was expensive. Atanasoff surveyed the prospects of building a specialized tabulating-type machine. The result was negative – such a machine would have extremely large dimensions and unsteady marketing.

The invention of the first automatic electronic numerical computer (1937–1942) was in response to the needs of increasing the speed of scientific calculations of the 1930s.

The Second World War opened a vast field for the application of powerful digital computing machines in the military domain. At the end of the 1930s and the beginning of the 1940s, the electromechanical computing giants appeared. Their place was taken in two or three years' time by the electronic digital computers, which inherited some of the features of the electromechanical machines: permanent programming, control of numbers and calculations in which digits are represented by a floating point.

THE DAWN

Many Iowa State students remember with affection their "attractive and devoted" tutor. He had not had a peace of mind for many months – he wanted to find a machine, which would compute automatically the enormous calculations for his students. The analog and electromechanical machines did not meet his requirements. Atanasoff remembered those years, "I was unhappy at that moment in my professional career. I was forced to reach to the conclusion that if I wanted to have a machine for the solution of linear algebraic equations, I had to build it myself. I was leading a full life and I had to do many things. I did not want to research this area but I made as reluctant turn in this direction."

His research interests shifted to the applied science. Atanasoff described the process of his creative reorientation, "Ideas did not come quickly. The failures stifled my imagination. Then I remembered what my English teacher, James Far had told me, "If you have to do something unpleasant, don't abandon it, don't stop doing it and in the end it might give you pleasure". I didn't think that that rule would turn me into a pianist but I continued applying it because I had to do many things, which I didn't find attractive." Atanasoff was seized by the passion of the inventor, which dissuaded him from his adolescent dream of becoming a theoretical physicist. He was pleased that he had become a university lecturer – no matter how much he was occupied with his students, he would "maneuver" and find time for his idea. At first, the very idea seemed utopian. Later, he would remark not without irony that he thought it "quite clever" to shift to another medium the structure of the Monroe type calculating machine, which was too familiar to him. But that attempt was of course unsuccessful. Seven years later, Mauchly and Eckert would also start with that idea. Atanasoff considered the possibilities of automation of computations. Gradually he reached, the conclusion that the new machine should have a separate memory, detached from the computing functions, and also that the method of calculation should be digital rather than analogue. Also Atanasoff thought of a number system with a base different from 10. However the ideas could not easily have taken shape and that upset him.

He concluded that in order to meet the requirements of scientific research, the new machine had to have a capacity for much larger memory. He investigated the biggest existing machines. The concept of "memory" did not exist then – Atanasoff had to introduce it. He wrote in his memoirs, "Turning to the science and technology of 1936, I was convinced that a new computing machine had to be capable of memorizing a large volume of data. I called that "memory" almost from the beginning. The word seemed natural to me, as I suppose to other people. I did not know well the work of Babbage at that time and I was not aware that he termed the same notion "store". I like the word and perhaps I would have adopted it. I also like "memory" because it is analogous with the brain. Even at this early stage of my work on computers, I had a notion of the importance of fast and slow memory. The speed of access to fast memory was similar to the speed of the computer itself. We also have access to slow memory but for longer periods. In the 80-column tabulator of IBM, the only fast memory, the biggest existing at the time, was in its internal counters of 266 bytes." So Atanasoff called the memorizing device which is known today as operating (internal) memory "fast memory" and distinguished it from the external (periphery) memory. He also affirmed the existence of a "very slow memory" in the perforated card, on which the calculations of the tabulator are recorded. It is taken out by hand and is put into the machine for further processing.

He was a specialist in electrical engineering and selected the methods and materials very carefully. The present task was not standard though and he swayed from one extreme – the good old mechanics, which "hypnotized" him with its presumed reliability – to another – electronics. Of course in the 1930s, when Atanasoff was laying the foundations of the design of the computer, electronics was just making its first steps. On the one hand, he was attracted by the stability of the mechanical motion of the familiar axes and the simple elements for displaying numbers – the dials of the mechanical counters. On the other hand, his qualification and experience in electrical engineering and physics urged him to use the electrical state of some electrical circuit board for the purposes of calculating. But he was uneasy about the then existing preconception that electronic tubes were unreliable and unstable.

Atanasoff's testimony at the ENIAC trial of 15.06.1971 is recorded in Volume II of the trial protocols of the Federal Court of Minneapolis.

Atanasoff had to choose a memory element after having decided to use the binary system. The prospective list was:

1. A completely mechanical system with two equilibrium positions, effected by a mechanical force.

2. A moving piece, similar to the anchor of a polarized switch, moved by an electromagnet.

3. A small piece of ferromagnetic material, whose two stable states are the directions of the magnetizing of the material; the state would be changed by a magnetic field.

4. Some circuit boards with vacuum electronic tubes with two stable states (a similar board is used in the binary counter used for counting impulses created by cosmic rays).

5. A small condenser, whose two stable states are the two charges resulting from electrostatic charging.

All these prospective "candidates" were accepted in some way in the computing technology. Atanasoff included a semiconductor element in his Manuscript of 1940 because he had the intuitive idea that such elements could have an amplifying effect. But he did not pursue the idea. He sought a simple, cheap, reliable element with two stable states – one for the logical 1 and another for the logical 0. He reached to the conclusion that a small magnetic element with two magnetized states could be used. But the calculations proved that such an element did not have a chance – it would have needed additional amplification with electronic tubes, which were expensive. In the end, Atanasoff decided on condensers. Their signals are sent directly to the electronic tubes by a logical arithmetic device without mediating amplifiers. The "Achilles' heel" of these attractive elements was the gradual leakage out of their electrical charge. They could be used for only about five minutes. But the problem found an elegant solution – Atanasoff used an electronic circuit board, which recognized the initial state of the condenser and automatically restored it. It is worth mentioning that he reached to this decision in a peculiar bionic way, related to his memories of childhood. When he was sent to the shops, he was afraid of forgeting what he was ordered to buy. So he helped his memory by repeating, "A dozen eggs, a pound of butter, a dozen eggs, etc." So Atanasoff thought at first that the additional charging was necessary when the condensers participated in the calculation process. Later, he was convinced that during the initial conversion of the

Ivan Atanasoff, John V. Atanasoff's father during the first years following his arrival to the US

John Atanasoff's mother, Iva Purdy Atanasoff, 1900

John V. Atanasoff
as a baby
with his mother
circa 1905-1906

Ivan and Iva Atanasoff, Florida, 1955

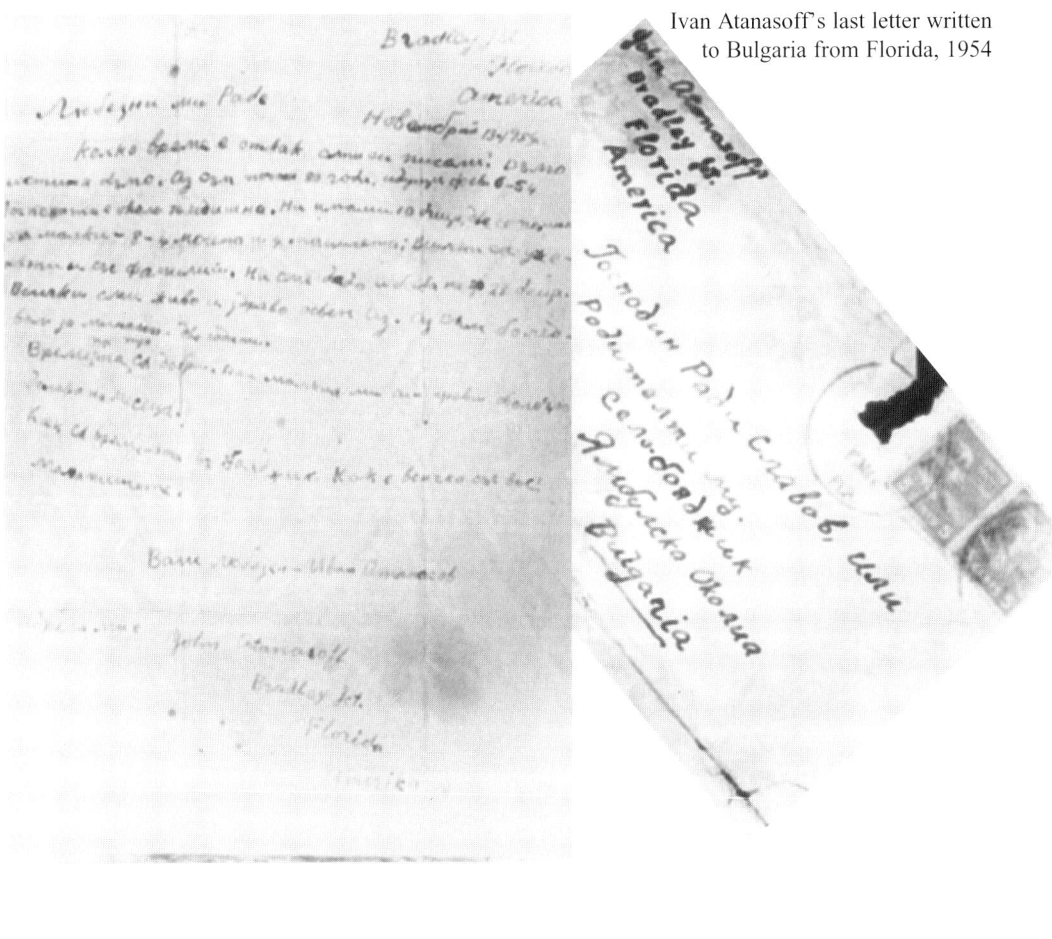

Ivan Atanasoff's last letter written to Bulgaria from Florida, 1954

The village of Boyadjik, birthplace of Ivan Atanasoff, John V. Atanasoff's father, 1936

The headstone of John and Iva Atanasoff

John Atanasoff – Professor
at Iowa State College, 1926

Lura Meeks Atanasoff shortly after her marriage
in June 1926.

John V. Atanasoff, in the middle of the second row, with the Graduate Students – Doctoral Candidates, at the University of Wisconsin, 1930

Clifford Berry holding vacuum tubes that were part of the ABC's memory bank, 1941

Clifford Berry and the original ABC, circa 1942

State University of Iowa building

Perforated (keypunch) card showing the AB Computer as the fore-runner of all modern computers.

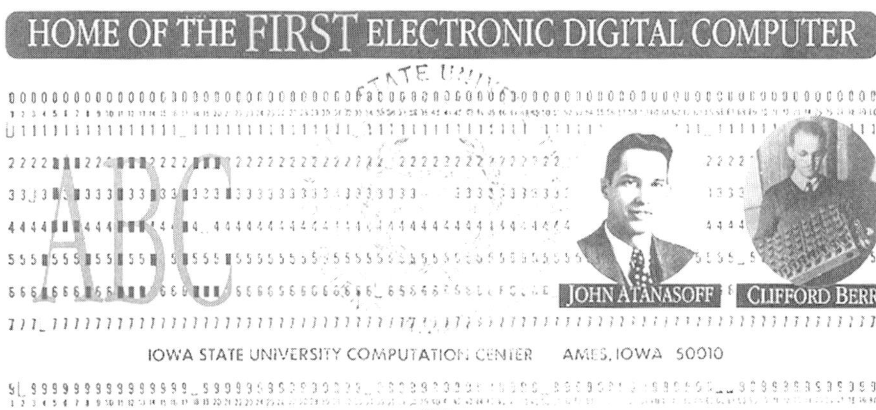

Judge Earl R. Larson

John W. Mauchly holding a section of the BINAC circuitry

John V. Atanasoff and his children Elsie, Joanne, and John

John V. Atanasoff started his own company, the Ordnance Engineering Company (TOEC) in 1952

10-base to 2-base system, the idle condensers should be in standby condition, i.e. should be charged. The same was necessary at the output stage, when binary numbers were changed into decimal numbers. This standby state was also needed in other cases, e.g. when the operator had to restore some of the processes or when he had to leave it idle for some time. In the end, it turned out that the machine would not become much more expensive because of the additional charging of the condensers.

According to Atanasoff's original idea, the computer had to "possess logic" created by the use of electronic tubes. The approach of the inventor was generally bionic. He explains in his Manuscript of 1940, "Finally, the author [of these lines] found another type of circuit diagram, which was stable and completely satisfactory in any respect. That circuit diagram worked on new calculating technology principles, which resemble the functioning of the human brain when calculating silently. The circuit diagram considers what is contained in a given [memorizing] element, what should be added to it or subtracted from it, and a [third] memorizing device receives a signal, which redirects the transfer from the previous discharge. I imagined it [the circuit diagram] "as a man with a soldering iron – it chooses the right answer and substitutes it for what is contained [in the condenser]... Thus, the overall complexity and the expenses [for the production] of the computer have been considerably reduced."

Atanasoff applied the economy of human silent calculation – it does not use counting numeral by numeral but skillfully employs memorized addition and subtraction tables. The "man with the soldering iron" or the constructor "teaches" the electronic arithmetical device. So it can produce the right sum, or difference, independently, on the basis of any pair of binary digits which have been entered. Incredible – even today, half a century later, multiplication and division is done on the basis of tables by modern super-fast processors.

So, Atanasoff designed the major structural units of the future computer in the course of a year – from the beginning of 1938 until 1939. The creation of the logical arithmetic device took longest. He did not test the designed diagrams but he "was convinced that the project would be successful". The inventor realized that, for the further development of the computer, he would need the help of a specialist in electronics. Also, he needed to use the mechanical engineering workshop of the College. As using it free of charge was impossible, he applied for a grant of $ 650 to the Dean of the Graduate Studies Department. It was accepted in March 1939. Part of the money was paid to "a very special student" of electrical engineering. Professor H. Anderson had recommended Clifford Berry without any hesitation. According to Anderson, Berry was a very gifted student experienced in electronics, who combined his skill in making mechanical constructions with his patience in bringing his work to perfection. In fact, the project was also attractive for Berry because he had to choose a topic for his Master's Thesis. Atanasoff liked the short 21-year-old young man for his frank eyes and firm handshake. At the short interview, Berry grasped the project quickly and his clever questions convinced Atanasoff that he had found a valuable assistant. In his memoirs he wrote, "I think that the selection of Clifford E. Berry was one of the best things that could have happened to the project."

CLIFFORD EDWARD BERRY

Instead of the summer, the two of them started work in September, at the beginning of the semester. However Berry did not wait until September and used the summer months to study the theoretical project of Atanasoff. So when the constructing work started, during the first weeks, the assistant offered his own ideas. The newly formed research team set up its office in the overpopulated building of the Department of Physics. They put a wall across a 12-meter long hallway in the students' workshop in the basement, which was cool in the summer and heated and dry in winter. The two of them felt particularly happy because of the closeness of the mechanical shop. Three long years – until the completion of the ABC – their private corner would be a magnet for them.

The first task on the project was to experiment with the new electronic methods of calculation, which Atanasoff had developed theoretically. They wanted "to breathe life" into them. But since nobody before them had tried anything similar, Atanasoff had moments of anxious premonition and of enthusiastic excitement. He was convinced that the logical circuit with electronic tubes would be capable of adding and subtracting in accordance with the voltage given to their lattice. They both tried to prove as quickly as possible that they were making a novel calculating machine. That is why, in this initial phase, Atanasoff decided to abandon the idea of building a specialized computer for solving systems of linear algebraic equations. He wanted the team to focus on making a simple but reliably working laboratory model – an electronic tube device, which adds and subtracts using Atanasoff's method. For the time being, the memory cylinders of the future machine consisted of a Bakelite disk with capacitors mounted along the radiuses of its two sides. Berry worked out quickly the electronic tube logical circuits. For two months – until the demonstration in October – the first electronic computer was assembled and activated. They demonstrated the prototype in November. The audience was amazed that something resembling a school electrostatic machine, connected to about twenty electronic tubes, gives correct sums and differences of given numbers. The device could add and subtract binary equivalents of 8-digit ten-base numbers, using the simple rules of binary arithmetic. A feature of the new machine was that calculation was done by a serial method – binary discharge after binary discharge. But the most revolutionary characteristic was that electronic tubes did the arithmetic operations of addition and subtraction for the first time. That was achieved not by counting but by direct logical operations, analogous to the processes in the human brain when calculating silently. The digital use of electronic vacuum tubes, which until then were used for the processing of analog signals, was started. The model had another novelty in calculating machines – a capacitor regenerative memory, which was separate from the arithmetical device. The inventors organized a special demonstration session for the college elite in December. They were allotted $ 850 to build a computer for solving systems of linear algebraic equations.

Thus, in the span of a year and a half, Atanasoff laid down the basic principles of calculation with electronic means. After their experimental approbation with the prototype model, the Atanasoff – Berry team started the construction of the actual ABC computer. The beginning was in 1940 and the work was finished in 1942.

Atanasoff was disappointed to find during one of his later visits to Ames that the ABC was moved out of the building and taken apart. Neither he, nor Berry were informed. Only parts of the computer are preserved.

THE FIRST ELECTRONIC COMPUTER

Allan Mackintosh!*

During the late 1930 and early 1940 many complementary and competing attempts were made to develop electromechanical and electronic computers in the US (by Atanasoff, Henry Howard Aiken, Van-

* Allan Mackintosh is professor of experimental solid-state physics at the H. C. Orsted institute of the University of Copenhagen and director of NORDITA, the Nordic Institute for Theoretical Physics, in Copenhagen

nevar Bush, Mauchly and George R. Stibitz), in England (by Turing and his colleagues) and in Germany (by Konrad Zuse and Helmut Schreyer). There are many excellent sources on the history of these efforts, among them a collection of the original papers of these computer pioneers*, and Atanasoff himself has chronicled the events surrounding his invention of the electronic computer.

Atanasoff's contribution is becoming increasingly recognised in the computer literature – he is acknowledged as the inventor of the computer in several recent books – but physicists are still surprisingly ignorant of the fact that this supremely important machine was invented not by an engineer, nor indeed by an experimental physicist, but by a theorist. Furthermore, his primary motivation was not to construct a device but rather to solve problems in basic research, and his approach was not to develop existing technology but to formulate a radically new set of principles for attaining his goal. At a time when the value of basic research in physics is being questioned in many parts of the world, it is especially pertinent to promote an appreciation of the reasons why so many modern inventions of major importance, including the computer, have been made by physicists.

The originality and indeed audacity of the approach to computing that Atanasoff conceived in the Illinois roadhouse may be appreciated by comparing it with other devices available at the time. Most computations were performed on electromechanical calculators, able to add, subtract, multiply or divide two numbers at a time; large operations were done on IBM (Hollerith) tabulating machines that used punched cards- the Iowa State statistics department, for example, had such a machine. But these were simple "adding machines"; the most advanced scientific computer at that time was Bush's Differential Analyser, a mechanical analog computer based on a decimal system. Atanasoff's approach was the diametrical opposite of this.

THE PROTOTYPE

Although Atanasoff was convinced that he had found the right principles for electronic computation, translating these principles into practice would obviously require a prodigious effort. In this effort he received vital assistance, as he always emphasises, from the late Clifford E. Berry, who worked with him as a graduate student from 1939 to 1942.

* Randell, B. (ed.). The Origins of Computers: Selected Papers

It is clear that they were both obsessed by electronic computing during this time. Atanasoff recalls how busy they were with other matters, but notes that "I do not remember a single instance in which either of us did not have time for the computer; our hearts were really in this adventure."

The prototype, which worked reliably and accurately from the beginning, was not of course a very impressive computer. It could only add or subtract 8- digit numbers, and using paper and pencil was undoubtedly much quicker for the purpose. Nonetheless the device bears the same relation to electronic computing as, for example, the Wright brother's airplane bears to aeronautics. "Once our prototype had proved successful, we both knew that we could build a machine that could do almost anything in the way of computing", Atanasoff wrote later. Allowing for a certain degree of hyperbole, this was true enough. By demonstrating the viability of the principles, the prototype opened up the path that led directly to the modern computer.

The Atanasoff – Berry Computer (ABC). In 1940 he wrote a detailed description of his computer design in connection with grant applications. The proposal indicated the type of problem he had in mind:

It is the main purpose of this paper to present a description and exposition of a computing machine which has been designed principally for the solution of large systems of linear algebraic equations...

Utility. In the treatment of many mathematical problems one requires the solution of systems of linear simultaneous algebraic equations. The occurrence of such systems is especially frequent in the applied fields of statistics, physics and technology. The following list indicates the range of problems in which the solution of systems of linear algebraic equation constitutes an essential part of the mathematical difficulty:

1. Multiple correlation
2. Curve fitting
3. Method of list squares
4. Vibration problems including the vibrational Raman effect
5. Electrical circuit analysis
6. Analysis of elastic structures
7. Approximate solution of many problems of elasticity
8. Approximate solution of problems of quantum mechanics
9. Perturbation theories of mechanics, astronomy and the quantum theory

It is customary to describe ABC as an uncompleted machine.It is perhaps more accurate to characterise it as a functioning but fallible computer. The electronic computing part, designed essentially to calculate eliminants between pairs of equations up to 29 unknowns, was a brilliant success. Even with the faults in the binary card system, such an eliminant could usually be obtained accurately.

Considering the remarkable speed with which this project was carried out, it is reasonable to assume that the problem with the binary card system would have been solved within a few months, either by eliminating its occasional faults or by replacing it. IBM input – output systems that would have been perfectly satisfactory for the purpose (and that were later used on ENIAC) had existed for decades, and by demonstrating the power of his computer in practice, Atanasoff could surely have obtained financial support to purchase what needed. Thus, if his efforts had not been terminated by the war, ABC would very likely have been fully operational by 1943. The history of electronic computing would then have been very different, but the results would ultimately have been the same, because Atanasoff's ideas were communicated to Mauchly, who with Eckert, exploited and developed them in a further superb accomplishment of electronic computing, the construction of ENIAC.

THE INFLUENCE OF ABC

In their history of ENIAC*, the Burkses summarise Atanasoff's achievement.

So, clearly, Atanasoff had achieved a great deal in his pioneering efforts. He invented a novel form of Serial store suitable for electronic computation. He also conceived, developed and proved the fundamental principles of electronic switching for digital computation, principles encompassing arithmetic operations, control, base conversion, the transfer and restoration of data, and synchronisation. He designed a well balanced electronic computing machine utilising this memory and these principles and having a centralised architecture, arithmetic, any controlled circuits and imput – output devices. His was the first specialized electronic computer ever invented: Indeed, it was the first electronic computer of any degree of generality ever invented. Finally, even though his machine was relatively slow, processing pulses at the rate of 60 per second as compared to the ENIAC's 100 000, and the ENIAC differed in other important respects, Atanasoff's principles for electronic computation played a crucial role in the circuitry of the ENIAC and all its successors.

* Burks, A.W., A.R. Burks. The ENIAC

John V. Atanasoff even contributed the original idea that resulted in the ENIAC, the idea that the machine he had developed could "be converted into an analyser".

In the spring Samuel Caldwell who was working on the design of the new MIT Differential Analyser, visited Atanasoff and told him about the use of electronics in the new analog machine Atanasoff, who 'knew that we could build a machine that could do almost anything in the way of computing, ' immediately realised that his own electronic digital computer could be converted into an integraph to solve differential equations. On 31 May he wrote to Mauchly:

The figures on the electronic differential integraph seem absolutely startling.

During Dr. Caldwell's last visit here, I suddenly obtained an idea as to how the computing machine which we are building can be graph. Its action would be analogous to numerical integration and not like that of the Bush Integraph which is, of course, an analog machine, but it would be very rapid and the steps in the numerical integration could be made arbitrarily small.

Mauchly was very enthusiastic about the computer, and on 28 June, 1941, he wrote to a colleague:

"Immediately after commencement there, I went out to Iowa State University to see the computing device which a friend of mine is constructing there. His machine, now nearing completion, is electronic in operation, and will solve within a very few minutes any system of linear equations involving no more than thirty variables. It can be adapted to do the job of the Bush differential analyser more rapidly than the Bush machine does, and it costs a lot less. My own computing devices use a different principle, more likely to fit small computing jobs."

In fact, due to the confusion of the war and the ineffectiveness of the lawyers and university officials involved, this patent was never applied for, even though Atanasoff's report was later declared to be more than adequate for a patent application.

The war, which brought Atanasoff's efforts in computing to an abrupt halt, created the opportunity that Mauchly and Eckert exploited so brilliantly. They direct a team of engineers (including Arthur Burrs) who created INCA, the world's first general purpose computer. Although they inherited the basic ideas of electronic digital computing from Atanasoff, INCA was much faster and larger than ABC, with thousands rather than hundreds of vacuum tubes, and it could be programmed for different problems by modifying the circuitry through a plug board. It also contained many novel features that were of decisive importance for further progress in electronic computing. Mauchly and Eckert deviated from Atanasoff's fundamental principles by using a decimal rather than a binary calculational base, but this turned out not to be a viable approach. On the other hand, the British Colossus, which was constructed slightly earlier than ENIAC, used binary logic, and though less flexible, it could also be programmed to some extent through plug boards. The development of the stored- program computer also proceeded more or less simultaneously in the US and Britain; the first working program on an electronic stored – program computer was run on 21 June 1948 at Manchester University. Soon thereafter commercial stored – program computers became available – the Ferranti Mark I in Britain, and UNIVAC from Mauchly and Eckert's company- and the computer revolution was truly launched. In recent years, interest in special purpose computers, analogous to ABC, has revived, especially in connection with the solution of scientific problems. (Translator's and Editor's note B.Penkov – J.Gustavson. Checkpoint, 3 (1986)5, Floating Point Systems, Portland, Ore)

The astonishing similarity between ABC and a modern vector processor for solving linear equations has been analysed in detail in a recent article; the basic principles are the same, but the speed differs by roughly a factor of 10!

THE LONG PATH TO RECOGNITION

In 1947 Mauchly and Eckert applied for a patent, based on their work on ENIAC, that covered essentially all aspects of electronic computing. The patent was issued in 1964 and Sperry Rand, who in the meantime had acquired it, began to collect royalties. Honeywell declined to pay, and Sperry therefore sued. Honeywell's lawyers learned of Atanasoff's work – indirectly, through a book by R. K. Richards* – and consulted Atanasoff in 1967. He observed that some parts of the ENIAC patent were derived from his own work on ABC, and was consequently called as a witness in the court case in 1971–1972. The trial was a gargantuan affair, lasting 135 working days, involving 77 witnesses and filling over 20 000 pages of transcript. In his decision, Judge Larson declared the ENIAC patent invalid because, among other reasons, the subject matter was derived from Atanasoff. Despite the enormous economic interests involved, Sperry did not appeal the decision. In his judgement, Larson sum-

* Richards, R. K. Electronic Digital Systems

marised Atanasoff's achievement: In December 1939, Atanasoff completed and reduced to practice his basic conception in the form of an operating breadboard model of a computing machine.

This breadboard model machine, constructed with the assistance of a graduate student, Clifford Berry, permitted the various components of the machine to be tested under actual operating conditions. The breadboard model established the soundness of the basic principles of design, and Atanasoff and Berry began the construction of a prototype or pilot model, capable of solving with a high degree of accuracy a system of as many as 29 simultaneous equations having 29 unknowns. By August 1940, in connection with efforts at further funding, Atanasoff prepared a comprehensive manuscript, which fully described the principles of his machine, including detailed design features. By the time the manuscript was prepared in August 1940, construction of the machine, destined to be termed in this litigation the Atanasoff – Berry computer or "ABC", was already far advanced. The description contained in the manuscript was adequate to enable one of ordinary skill in electronics at that time to make and use an ABC computer.

The fascinating story of Atanasoff's achievement provokes a number of reflections about research and innovation. The sagacity of those who should have been concerned with promoting these activities frequently left much to be desired. Atanasoff found it difficult to obtain recognition of the importance of his work, or backing for it from funding agencies – with the honourable exception of the Research Corporation. Iowa State deserves credit for supporting him at its inception, but the officials concerned clearly had no concept of its significance, and their obtuseness cost the university dearly when they failed to apply for a patent. Atanasoff also attempted to interest IBM in his ideas, but could not convince them of the potentialities of electronic computation. After the war, he worked on computing again for a while at the Naval Ordnance Laboratory, where he and John Von Neumann had mutually enlightening discussions, but the project was cancelled and he was moved to what his superiors considered more important tasks.

THE MYSTERY OF CREATION

The way in which Atanasoff conceived the basic principles for his computer is a classic example of the creative process, which is familiar to most research scientists. He started with the long and frequently frustrating process of immersing himself in all aspects of the problem, without making much obvious.

But when he had absorbed all this information, and his mind had time to work on it, largely unconsciously, the perfect solution became apparent to him while he was engaged in a completely different activity. To the uninitiated, his 200 mile drive through the dry state of Iowa might seem just a particularly inefficient way of obtaining a drink, but Atanasoff knew perfectly well what he was doing. He had appreciated that the mind needs variety and relaxation to perform its creative mysteries.

Atanasoff devised a design for an electronic digital computer that was so perfect that it is difficult, even with the benefit of hindsight, to see how it could be improved upon with the resources that were available to him.Not only did he describe this design (in an article that is a major milestone in the history of computing), but he and Berry converted it into a practical and operating machine with their own hands. Some might regard this as eccentric behaviour for a theoretical physicist, but when asked about the origins of his inventive skills, Atanasoff replied: "I couldn't have had a better training. Theoretical physics is a uniquely effective discipline." Indeed any problem in basic research that strains a student's personal resources of imagination and ingenuity to the utmost is an effective preparation for a career as an innovator. It is not a coincidence that so many major advances in technology have been made by research scientists. The ultimate springs of innovation have always been located in the scientific enterprise, and the frontiers of science and technology are inextricably intertwined.

From **Burks, A.R., A.W. Burks. The First Electronic Computer**

STRONG ROOTS

Nicolay Bonchev

"The special, Slavonic blood in my veins that I have inherited from that land has helped me much in my life... As a Bulgarian, I have an eager, creative nature too..."

John Atanasoff

In May 1876 by the village of Boyadjik near the town of Yambol, Bulgaria, one of the last Ottoman bullets fired during the crushing of the April Uprising against Turkish rule, scared the forehead of a baby boy. That was Ivan Atanasoff – the future father of the man who was destined to invent the computer. Miraculously, the baby survived in the hands of his own dead father, Atanas. That is how the hard life of the orphaned boy began. At the age of 13, his uncle took him to America and left him there to become a self-made man. During his variegated life, Atanasoff met and married a teacher of Mathematics, called Iva, with Irish and French blood in her veins. His wife bore eight children, one of whom was christened by his mother John-Vincent. The future would show that the second name was prophetic because "Vincent" meant "victorious", and Atanasoff did really win.

THE HERITAGE: THE ATANASOFF ROOTS

Young John would often hear his father tell about his birthplace, Boyadjik, which he left at the age of 13 in 1889. The images of the Russian soldiers did not fade away in Ivan Atanasoff's mind. One recurring scene was particularly vivid in his memory – many black bulls grazing in the fields near the Azmak River (present Kadnitsa), the right tributary of the Tundja.

The people of Boyadjik fought for their independence several times in the 19th century. Volunteers from the village participated together with the army of the Russian commander Dibich in the Russian-Turkish War of 1828–1829. McGahan, an American journalist as a member of the International Enquiry Commission, investigated the brutalities in the suppression of the April Uprising (about 80 villages and towns were burnt down and tens of thousands of Bulgarians were slain). He visited Boyadjik and found that the percentage of literacy of the Bulgarians after the five-centuries-long Ottoman rule was the same as that of the independent nations like England and France. One of the reasons for this incredible fact, was the circumstance that education was free even in the poorest of villages. The funds collected as donations by the communities were used to recruit the best teachers. That was the case of Boyadjik too and it created a typical desire for enlightenment in its inhabitants.

THE BLOOD-STAINED SPRING IN BOYADJIK

On 10 May 1876 (24 May according to the present Gregorian calendar), the inhabitants of Boyadjik celebrated the day of the saints, the brothers, St. Cyril and St. Methodius.

On 28 March 1983, The International Planetary Center at the Smithsonian Astrophysical Observatory in Cambridge, MA U.S.A., approved the naming of asteroid No. 2609, discovered in Crimea, after the names of the Cyril and Methodius brothers. In the official document issued in English, it is highlighted that they are honored as the "apostles of the Slavs, great Slavonic enlighteners, designers of the Slavonic script". The work of the two remarkable medieval scholars and saints is inseparable from the historical fortune of the Bulgarians because it was Bulgaria who saved their heritage and passed it on to other neighboring nations. Had it not been for Bulgaria, their names would have been but footnotes or details in the major encyclopedias today. In the 1990s, Pope John Paul II made them patron "Saints of Europe".

Bulgarians have honored Sts. Cyril and Methodius since the 10th century. During the 19th century, a holiday of Slavonic script and culture was established throughout the Bulgarian territories. It was observed not only by the Orthodox Church but also by schools, reading clubs (cultural centers throughout the Bulgarian lands), peoples' assemblies, pagan rituals, name days and private family days on 10 May according to the old calendar.

In the autumn of 1875, young intellectual Bulgarians, who had studied or lived abroad, felt the terrible controversy between their national self-consciousness and the medieval circumstances of their lives in the shadow of the decaying Ottoman Empire. They decided to focus the nation's energy in their "Freedom or Death" slogan. At a secret meeting in the Danube town of Giurgiu, they decided upon organizing an uprising. Thus, it was only natural for them to select May 11th for the date of the uprising. That day was both symbolic and convenient because of the fairs and ensuing festivities. Actually, the uprising started earlier in many parts of the country. In the Sliven Revolutionary Region, Apostle Ilarion Dragostinov (officer at the English railway company, which maintained the lines to Constantinople, Vienna, Bucharest, Galac, Odessa) kept the initially appointed date. In the village of Boyadjik, between the towns of Nova Zagora and Yambol, the people met at the "horo" – the communal dance.

And the uprising began.

And a few days later the Boyadjik slaughter (known as "genocide" now) started. More than 150 people were massacred. A folk song was composed commemorating that event.]

The service in the church finished and the annual school examination began with songs and recitations at the school decorated with peonies and greenery. Then with the music, the merry communal dance the horo, began. Suddenly gunfire interrupted the flute and horsemen attacked the people. Those were Circassian plunderers. The holiday was covered in blood... The Turks pillaged the village and finally rode away as quickly as they had come.

The church bell tolled gravely – because of those massacred. People got together and decided to take measures against such attacks in the future. The people of Boyadjik armed themselves using the Circassian attack as an argument before the Turkish authorities. The village built fortifications and dug trenches. Observation points and permanent security guards were set up. Villagers from neighboring settlements sought refuge in Boyadjik.

Some Circassians were sent to capture two of the village leaders and to take 120 horses away. However one of them was killed and they all fled. Later one sultan would be accused that he endangered the Empire with his actions in Boyadjik. He excused himself in the presence of the British Ambassador to Turkey, Sir Elliot, that he had telegrams from the supreme commander with orders to destroy eight enlisted villages.

In his report of 22 August 1876, the English Consul in Burgas, Charles Brofy, reveals the predetermined character of the repressions, "I know from a good source that seven other rich villages were marked for destruction under the pretext of being rebellious."

Yana, Ivan Atanasoff's mother, later told her son that one morning when the crops were ripening they got up and saw the whole hilltop red with the caps of the Turkish soldiers. The bells tolled and everybody assembled in the churchyard.

On 12 August 1876, Skyler wrote, "I saw human sculls and bones in the fields."

The victims and the sufferings of the people of Boyadjik received broad reaction from the diplomatic circles and the press of many countries in Europe and America. The April Uprising, covered in blood, contributed for the declaration of the Russian-Turkish War of liberation. Lord Strangford from England who spoke Bulgarian wrote many articles unveiling Ottoman brutality. His wife, Lady Strangford, sent massive relief support to the people from Boyadjik. Some of the objects donated by her are still kept in the village.

THE ORPHAN FROM THE APRIL UPRISING

Ivan Atanasoff, the orphan from Boyadjik, died in Lakeland, U.S.A., at the age of 80 in 1956. Since then, his wife has been living with her eight children. They encouraged her to write her memoirs. The sight of 75-year-old Iva Lucena was weak but, to please her children, she learnt to type. The information about her husband's early years is most interesting. It spans the time from his birth in 1876 until his graduation from Colegate University, U.S.A. in 1901 and his marriage to Iva.

Here, we describe the significant events in the life and the shaping of the personality of young Ivan, which Iva Atanasoff has recorded on the basis of her husband's stories. Data from the Atanasoff family in Bulgaria have been added.

The Atanasoff family earned their living by farming, cattle breeding and trade in the 19th century. The taxes of the Sultan, however were high. Sometimes the same tax was collected several times. Often, the villagers had to sell their property in order to pay their taxes.

At that time of hardship, in 1875, John's grandfather, Atanas Ivanov, married Yana Zhelyazkova from the neighboring village of Omarchevo. He spoke Turkish and was on good terms with the Ottoman authorities. But he could not bear the Ottoman rulers, for which they despised him.

Ivan Atanasoff learned about his father's peril in the Boyadjik massacre from his mother. This is how Iva Atanasoff tells about the event in her memoirs.

"The clashes between the Bulgarians and their plunderers were numerous. Although plotting an uprising, the people of Boyadjik and the other villages had not bought and stored weapons. They were defenseless. They had heard about the slaughtering in other parts but they were not ready.

One morning in 1876, Boyadjik awoke besieged by troops and threatened by a cannon on the opposite hill. Atanas dug hurriedly holes in the roots of the mulberry trees and hid the family gold coins in them. He covered them with clay and earth. Then he went to meet his fellow villagers in the square. They discussed the situation and sent truce envoys to the Ottoman general. [...]

The villagers were taken out of the village to the village grazing fields. Only the children and old people were left behind. In the meadow, the men could run to save their lives but the foot soldiers and the horsemen followed them. The only hiding places were the deep ravines.

Atanas ran very fast because of his wife and his child. The sultan and two other horsemen reached him. He begged for mercy but they shot him and the bullet scratched the head of the baby. Yana was pushed on the ground probably by one of the horses and lost consciousness for some time. When she regained consciousness, she saw her husband lying on the ground dead. She could not see the baby because he was partly hidden in his hands. She saw a child and took him up but it was not her baby. She returned to her husband and there laid her son. When she pulled Atanas' arm to pick up the child, he breathed out for the last time.

Yana hid in the ravine with another woman and then decided to go to another village where they had relatives. On the way, the two women met an acquaintance that sent farewell to his kin. A little later, he was caught and a Turkish sword cut off his head before their eyes. His body rolled down the hill. The two women hid in the cornfields and finally reached the nearby village.

A little after they reached their relatives, the village was suddenly attacked and everybody fled. The only hideout Yana could find was an empty wine cask. It was deep but there was a ladder next to it. Yana went down to its bottom. From there she could not go out without help. She remained four days in the cask without food and water. Nobody could hear her cries for help. Her breasts were in blood because of her attempts to breastfeed the baby. She began to knock on the walls of the cask when she got exhausted from shouting. An old lady who was looking for eggs heard the strange knocks. Yana and the child were found."

[...] The young widow suffered from lack of means and went back to Boyadjik to look for the buried gold. But she did not find anything there – the mulberry trees were uprooted. Only Atanas' wedding present for her – a string of gold coins, which she carried sewn in the hem of her skirt – was left...

A year after the horror of the massacre a widower with an eight-year-old child asked for Yana's hand. Gospodin was not as wealthy as Atanas, but nevertheless, he had a large stable with a roof covered not with straw but with tiles. Yana accepted the proposal and soon found that she had not made a mistake. Gospodin was a good and kind husband, and looked after Ivan as his own son.

Ottoman repressions continued and Yana's family was exiled again. She hid in the forest and lived with other fugitives in an abandoned school building in Sliven for two years...

Times changed for the better when Russian troops defeated the Ottoman. As before, the people of Boyadjik lived from the wheat that they sow. Many of them continued to breed sheep and bulls.

Constantine, young Ivan Atanasoff's uncle [his mother's brother], adopted the Protestant faith after having been influenced by a Methodist missionary. He departed for the U.S.A. and registered as a law student. He returned to Bulgaria for a short time and told interesting things. In America, he had seen reaping machines and had understood what a relief they will be for the peasants in his rural country. He managed to convince the representative of a German firm in Bulgaria to sell the Zhelyazkov family in Omarchevo a harvester at a low price. Its appearance was a great event for all villages in the region. The owners harvested the fields of all neighbors.

IVA ATANASOFF'S MEMORIES OF HER HUSBAND, IVAN ATANASOFF

"[...] They [the relatives] had greater ambitions for Ivan. He cherished a desire for more knowledge and higher education than he could have obtained in Bulgaria."

Below, we give a summary of Iva Atanasoff's memoirs.

Uncle Constantine offered to take Ivan on his trip to the United States. Naturally, the invitation pleased the boy who wanted to go there. To pay for the trip, his mother sold some of the land, which his father had left as his inheritance. They took a train to Germany and there they boarded a steam ship...

New York was of course the most spectacular sight the boy had ever seen. To the end of his life, Ivan would not forget his first impression of the Statue of Liberty. Until then, he had not been to a big city and so he thought that New York filled the horizon in all directions. The cheap hotel, in which his uncle booked them, seemed a palace to the boy. On this trip, Constantine had taken his family with him – his wife and his two little children. His wife was Greek with keen black eyes...

The family moved to an apartment in New Jersey soon. The uncle traveled daily to the college where he studied law. Ivan found a job with an owner of a seedbed garden. The boy had to cover a large distance every day carrying his lunch, which consisted of half a loaf of bread. After his seasonal job at the garden, he took another job in a dairy. Time passed. He spent more than two years in America. Ivan worked at various places and already spoke some English. His uncle decided that it was time for him to attend school.

The local vicar recommended a good preparatory school. Ivan could work to pay his fees. The boarding school had some three hundred boys and girls. The students met Ivan warmly and he enjoyed their company. The school turned into a real home for the boy.

The record book of the school registered the boy as John Atanasoff (K. Mollenhoff maintains that the change of the name was made by the immigration authorities on Ivan's arrival in the United States). John is naturally the English variant of Ivan. So he washed dishes, peeled potatoes, and did all sorts of jobs to pay his fees and his board. He studied arithmetic and English. He had always been good at arithmetic but he found it difficult to understand the problems in English; the system of measuring weight and length was also new for him. But he coped successfully with the difficulties.

Uncle Constantine returned to Bulgaria after having finished his studies. He did not take his farewells with John. That hurt the boy but he thought that they had decided not to cause nostalgia in him and not to make him return with them.

His first summer job was in the town of Ocean Grove on the Atlantic coast. The restaurant was called "Lillygor Pavilion". John waited at tables, washed dishes and cleaned the swimming pool.

The following school year, he registered at the same school. His prospects seemed brighter because he had saved during the summer and had kept his job at the boarding school kitchen. But he fell ill. He tried to finish the regular program of studies but he had to use a dictionary all the time. Studying after work in the kitchen continued long into the nights. That caused a mental confusion, which continued for two months. Probably it was a nervous breakdown caused by fatigue. Mrs. Reece took good care of him.

John spent the second summer vacation as a waiter at Widimer's Restaurant in Atlantic City. He returned to the boarding school and was ready to begin his studies when his cousin, Zhelyazko Petrov, arrived from Bulgaria. John realized that he could find a job more easily than his cousin, so he offered his place to Zhelyazko. According to information from the Atanasoff's family, Zhelyazko studied Physics. He died of tuberculosis. John was not aware of the fact that it was too hard to find any job at that time.

John went to Philadelphia and luckily found a job with a man who rented rooms. He could have stayed there but he saw an advertisement for job training in electrical engineering at the General Electric Company. That attracted him. So he went to Skenektody and found that it was a false rumor. In fact, he could not find any job there. His savings were waning quickly, so he started on foot for Amsterdam, some 40 kilometers away. He stopped in all small towns on his way hoping to find a job. Sometimes he earned his lunch cutting trees and cleaning farmyards.

An old woman stopped to talk to him near a church one evening. She said she had a job for him. So in the morning after breakfast, he went to her house. He had to cut firewood for her from a small house, which had been pulled down. He was hungry at lunchtime but he was not invited at the table. He continued working until darkness. The woman opened her purse and took out a 25-cent coin. John was so dismayed that he neither protested, nor refused to accept it.

In Amsterdam, he was allowed to sleep at the gas factory. Somebody told him to look for Pastor Cook of the Baptist Church. He was known for helping those in need. Pastor Cook promised John to help him find a job. He invited him to stay for lunch. So John could wash and mend his appearance.

The priest found him a job to look after a sick horse. John thought, "Now I'm right where I was three years ago in Bulgaria – looking after a sick horse." Then he was a liftboy in a clothes shop and a wrapper of underwear at a factory.

Some time passed and Father Cook talked him into writing his life story. A friend of the pastor's corrected the text and made it interesting. So John started going around churches, dressed in his national costume, to talk to the congregations about his life. The people were eager to help him to continue his education.

In September 1895, twenty-year-old John registered at the Colegate College with his savings of $ 200. That sum covered the fee for the first year. He finished the second year with a loan, which he paid back during the following summer. John lived at the residence of West Hall. The annual rent for the unfurnished room was $ 18. His roommate and he installed an oil heater, a folding bed, a table and a chair, which they bought from a departing student. The expenses were brought to the minimum by cooking in the room. A large loaf of bread cost 6 cents, milk was 5 cents for a quarter, stewed beef was 8 cents a pound. They could buy apples and potatoes cheaply from the farms around.

The finances of the student were scarce in spite of the seemingly low prices. There were not many job opportunities in that town. During the vacations, John worked in the retail trade. Books did not sell well though. One summer, he could earn some money by selling stereoscopic postcards published by Underwood and Underwood. During the following summer they did not sell at all. Obviously, the market had been overexploited the previous year.

During his last year, he started selling Belmer hangers for trousers. That consisted of two wood pieces held together by a wire spring, which pressed trouser edges or skirt belts. Those hangers were a novelty and sold at $ 3 a piece.

John did not find his studies at the college difficult. He spoke Good English and his studies of Latin and Greek helped him guess the meaning of unfamiliar words. Mathematics was easy and he even earned money by giving private lessons in Algebra and Geometry. He was also interested in Physics and Chemistry and studied them successfully.

His college years however were not occupied with studies only. He played baseball well enough to have his nose broken. Also, he played football – the family has kept a photograph showing him his team. A band of honor shows that he won a running contest. It is quite clear that he had to keep in good physical condition.

Although John was a member of the Baptist Church, he attended the services of the other sects, which were trying to attract more students. He met many girls from Hamilton at various public initiatives. They invited him to visit their homes, so he visited the families of Miss Smith, Miss Nelson and Miss Page. The Tue family had no grown up children, but Mr. Tue liked John's singing in their family quartet.

In the second semester of his senior year, John noticed a young lady at the Methodist Church and drew her portrait on the cover of the Sunday School Quarterly magazine. She wore a hat of dark red velvet and a fur collar in black and beige. He was introduced to her but the two of them did not exchange any words. That is why the young lady was strongly surprised to receive a note, in which John was asking for permission to call on her. The name was Iva Purdy. She lived with her parents on a hill some 2.5 km from Hamilton.

After the ceremony of the conferment of his Bachelor's Degrees, John hired a cab, to visit, with Iva, her sister in another town. He was still dressed in the traditional graduation gown and wore the four-cornered mortarboard. He was rightly proud of them. He's photographed with his diploma before going with Iva to the graduation ball in the evening. It was raining so the two of them had to walk in the rain. They must have looked like two wet mice when they entered late for the dinner. There was some lamb and peas left for them and they enjoyed it and the desert while speeches in praise of the college and the professors and the graduates were made.

That evening the young couple decided to marry in the near future. Iva intended to teach the following year to pay for the piano, which she had bought. Christmas was set for their wedding day. The wedding took place at her home in the presence of about thirty guests. The bride wore a cream dress with applications, decorated with pink roses, and the groom was in a new blue cheviot suit. Pastor Smith pronounced the words, which joined them into a family, and his wife played the Wedding March. The best men and witnesses were Ethelyn Cook and Floyd Purdy. The menu for the wedding feast was consulted with the caterers and the doctors. So the result was steaks with oysters, chicken salad and bread sticks, biscotti, "angels' food" biscuits, fruitcake, ice cream and coffee. The young family received many gifts of linen and silver. The newlyweds had a one-week honeymoon, after which John went to sell hangers in Baltimore and Iva returned to her classroom. Every fortnight he would pedal on his bicycle for fifty kilometers to spend Sunday with his wife.

From the book **Джон Атанасов. Изобретателят на компютъра**

THE BEGINNING

JOHN ATANASOFF

THE BIRTH OF DIGITAL ELECTRONIC COMPUTATION

I am writing a historical account of what has been an important episode of my life. During the last half of the 1930s, I began and later, with Clifford E. Berry, pursued the subject of digital electronic computing. Included were my conceptions of computing, and the construction both of a prototype and of what I later called the Atanasoff-Berry Computer (ABC), to honour the memory of Berry's extraordinary competence. My contacts with computing began much earlier, though, and I will mention something of those events.

The year 1913 made an impression on my mind because so much seemed to happen then. My family lived in a house in Florida on the premises of a phosphate mine where my father was an electrical engineer. Early that year, my father decided that his position required him to have a better slide rule than the one he had. Now, my father did not really need that new slide rule so the new slide rule was left for me, with its book of instructions. That slide rule was my meat. In two weeks or thereabouts, I could solve most simple problems with it.

Can you imagine how a boy of nine-plus, with baseball on his mind, could be transformed by this knowledge?

Early in high school, I decided to study theoretical physics as my life's work. At the University of Florida, however, I studied electrical engineering because it was the most theoretical course given.

In September 1925, I started my graduate work in mathematics at Iowa State College (now University).

In the period between 1925 and 1928, I taught mathematics at Iowa State College and continued graduate work in mathematics and physics.I received a master's degree in mathematics in 1926 at ISC. In March of 1929, I went to the University of Wisconsin to continue my work for the doctorate. I received my Ph.D. in physics in July 1930. My thesis was titled "The Dielectric Constant of Helium." My major professor was John Hasbrouck Van Vleck. This work demanded long calculations with a table computing machine /tabulator/ to solve the equation of Shreudinger.

This was my first experience in serious computing. Such calculations required many weeks of hard work on a desk calculator such as the Monroe, which was all that was available at the time. I was also impressed that the process of approximating the solution of partial differential equations required a great many calculations, a fact that ultimately motivated my work in automatic computing.

After receiving my doctorate, I returned to Iowa State College. I paid increased attention to the equipment of the International Business Machines Corporation housed in the Statistics Department. While this tabulator did not permit the mathematical dexterity of the Monroe, it nevertheless represented the largest "computer" of the day.

As the only man in theoretical physics at ISC, I did not have much competition. I was soon made assistant professor of both mathematics and physics. About that time (1934) I commenced to give attention to the formal process of approximating the solutions.

STATE OF THE COMPUTING ART (1934–1937)

As I came to feel the basic need for more powerful means of computing, I commenced to examine, in more detail, the types of apparatus that were available and I soon saw that computers fall into two classes, analog and digital.

In analog computers, a number is represented by a physical quantity in the machine as measured by some system of units.

A digital computer also requires some entity to represent numbers. Here, however, the representation is not a simple one-to-one relationship, but is determined by a kind of algorithm called the Hindu-Arabic number system. While historically this system used numbers to the base 10, we intend no such restriction, for in theory any greater than unity can be used as the base. My own device, to be described later, and most modern computers use the base 2.

It seemed clear to me that the advantages of the analog approach had been largely explored and found wanting, except in some special cases requiring relatively low accuracy. For most of the purposes of technology and science, we were left with a digital approach. To make this fully effective would require a new and original art.

I thought I knew how a computer should work. First it would have to add and subtract, and later one could compound these operations into multiplication and division. At the time, I wondered if anyone had devised a definition of multiplication that was not based on addition, but the four elementary operations of arithmetic are interrelated, and all computing theoreticians have had to go along with that fact. From the start, I was interested in carry-over; it is the crux of the digital method.

What is the stuff with which the digital numbers are to be represented? In those days I had little precedent as to the architecture of a new digital computer of a larger size-that is, capacity. The only attempt at a machine of sufficient capacity for my purposes was the differential analyser, an analog device that did not seem promising. In simple computers and even in the tabulators, the medium of representation was always mechanical, often the rotation of a shaft, and I must admit that I was inclined to follow this precept.

Even at this early day, the principal other medium that occurred to me was an electric state of a circuit. I had studied electrical engineering and physics, and I had also studied and experimented with electronics, then in its infancy. So it was perhaps natural that my mind turned to this medium in which I had my greatest expertise.

At an early point in my thinking about digital computers, I looked at the effects of a change in the base of the number system. How would the structure of a computing machine depend on this choice?At that time, I had only a vague idea of a computing machine. I hoped that the nature of the arithmetic for the various bases would indicate which one would be most advantageous for a computer. However, these thoughts led me to a conclusion that has stood the test of time.

In looking over the 1936 art in computing, I had become convinced that a new computer should provide for a much larger retention of data. Almost at the start, I called this "memory." The word seemed natural to me, as I suppose it did to others since it is still in use in a wide field including computers.

I now quote from the transcript of the testimony I gave in federal court on June 15, 1971:

"Well, I remember that the winter of 1937 was a desperate one for me because I had this problem and I had outlined my objectives but nothing was happening, and as the winter deepened my despair grew and I have told you about the kind of items that were rattling around in my mind and we come to a day in the middle of winter when I went out to the office intending to spend the evening trying to resolve some of these questions and I was in such a mental state that no resolution was possible. I was just unhappy to an extreme degree, and that time I did something that I had done on such occasions – I don't do it anymore – I went out to my automobile, got in and started driving over the good highways of Iowa at a high rate of speed.

I remember the pavement was clean and dry, and I was forced to give attention to my driving, and as a consequence of that, I was less nervous, and I drove that way for several hours. Then I sort of became aware of my surroundings. I had, of course, been aware of the road before, but then I became aware of where I was and I had reached the Mississippi River, starting from Ames and was crossing the Mississippi River into Illinois at a place where there are three cities, one of them is Rock Island.

I drove into Illinois and turned off the good highway into a little road, and went into a roadhouse there which had bright lights. It was extremely cold and I took off my overcoat. I had a very heavy coat, and hung it up, and sat down and ordered a drink after which, I realised that was no longer so nervous and my thoughts turned again to computing machines. Now, I don't know why my mind worked then when it had not worked previously, but things seemed to be good and cool and quiet. There were not many people in the tavern, and the waitress didn't bother me particularly with repetitious offers of drinks. I would suspect that I drank two drinks perhaps, and then I realised that thoughts were coming good and I had some positive results.

During this evening in the tavern, I generated within my mind the possibility of the regenerative memory. I called it "jogging" at that time. I'm thinking about the condensers for memory units, and the fact that the condensers would regenerate their own state, so their state would not change with time. If they were in the plus state, for instance, they would stay in the plus state; or, if they were in the negative state, they would stay in the negative state. They would not blink off to zero. Or if you used two positive changes, would retain their individual identity and would not leak across for each other"*.

During that same evening, I gained an initial concept of what is called today the"logic circuits." That is a nonratcheting approach to the interaction between two memory units, or, as I called them in those days, "abaci." I visualised a black box which would have the following action:

* Mackintosh, A.R. The First Electronic Computer.

suppose the state of abacus 1 and the state of abacus 2 would pass into the box; then the black box would yield the correct results on output terminals.

During that evening in the Illinois roadhouse, I made four decisions for my computer project:

- I would use electricity and electronics as the media for the computer.
- Inspite of custom, I would use base- 2 numbers (binary) for my computer.
- I would use condensers for memory, but "regenerate" to avoid lapse.
- I would compute by direct logical action, not by enumeration.

Atanasoff's approach was the diametrical opposite of this, involving instead;

- A method of computation that was digital (for the sake of precision) and based upon the logical manipulation of binary numbers.
- A means of computing by electronics (for the sake of speed for control, logic and arithmetic operations.
- The preliminary concept of a computing machine, with an architecture in which the computational function and regenerative binary memory are separated.

These three are among the fundamental principles on which modern electronic computing is based.

I am now amazed and pleased to find that all of my four decisions relate to structures that are in use in modern computers. It is true that I did not invent the modern dynamic memory, but this memory uses capacitors for memory and the refresh cycle directly derived from my jogging or regenerative ideas.

Since the trip to Illinois, I had used more than a year working mostly on jogging and logic circuits for adding and subtracting. I now felt much more confident that the project would be a success, and I know that I could not go on alone. So, early in the spring of 1939, I made an application for a grant from the dean of the graduate school. I planned to hire an assistant and to have a small budget for materials and shop work.

In selecting an assistant, I felt that I should choose an electrical engineer, since students entering graduate work in physics did not have the mechanical or electronic skill. Soon after having these thoughts, I met Harold Anderson, a professor of electrical engineering, on the sidewalk in the centre of the campus and told him of my need. He already knew of my interest in computers, and he answered in a moment, "I have your man – Clifford Berry."

I would have chosen to go to work on the computer during the summer of 1939, but that was not possible. We started actual work at the beginning of the fall quarter of 1939.

THE COMPUTER PROTOTYPE

Even before the fall quarter had begun, Berry had studied my plans, and we were soon involved in a discussion of how we should proceed. We both agreed that the theoretical aspect of these plans, however necessary it had been, would have to be reduced to practice. Each portion of my design would have to be built, examined, and fully tested. In the end, we would compose these parts to form a prototype of a computer to see if the portions would coact as I had planned. Parts of the whole were not fully designed, and we would have to devise them and bring them to fruition.

As I have said, I chose condensers (or capacitors) as the element for memory, because a condenser can give a good voltage to actuate a vacuum tube, and because the vacuum tube will give enough voltage to charge the condenser.

We next had to study how condensers would operate as memory elements, and soon learned that almost any condenser would work. I suppose that the reader will have gathered that I was delighted with the concept of jogging. Jogging is reminiscent of the little boy going to the grocery store and reciting, "a dozen eggs, a pound of butter, etc.," Over and over, hoping to arrive at the store before his memory has failed.

Vacuum tubes gave electronic digital computing a start, but transistors and integrated circuits brought it to its present state.

At that time, vacuum tubes were the only active element available for electronics. In those days, it was hard to get a low-voltage, direct-current source, and so we wished to use alternating current for our tubes. This limited us to heater type tubes. The only objection was that the heater types used much more power for the heat source.

Almost as soon as the prototype was completed, it began to work very well. Our visitors who understood what was going on were surprised to find so much structure giving additions and subtractions that were correct. Of course, our explanation to them had to cover base-2 number theory. Several of those who witnessed these first trails are still alive.

There is little doubt that the prototype was completed near the end of 1939. My memory said November 1939. Much later, during cross-examination in court, counsel for defense (Sperry Rand) showed me material purporting that this was not until early in 1940. In recross, material was adduced by counsel for the plaintiff (Honeywell) showing that the first demonstration was in October 1939.

The prototype was, of course, a crude device. It could just add and subtract the binary equivalents of decimal numbers having up to eight places. Nevertheless, CEB and I regarded this machine as a great success. It settled many doubts about how an electronic computer should be built.

1. The device was digital, not analog like the differential analyser.
2. While the clock system was mechanical, all computing was electronic.
3. For the first time, vacuum tubes were used in computing.
4. The advantageous base – 2 number system was first used.
5. Logic systems were first employed in computing.
6. All computation was done in a serial manner.
7. Capacitors (or condensers) were used as memory elements.
8. A rotating – drum memory contained the capacitors.
9. What I called jogging (others call it regeneration or refreshing) was first used in computation.
10. While the prototype did not shift or detect sign, the changes needed for these processes were obvious and could be immediately applied, thus providing the essentials for multiplication and division.

Clifford E. Berry and I were pleased to have access to method of computing with the just described. Once our prototype had proved successful, we both knew that we could build a machine that could do almost anything in the way computation.

During the early years, our computer had a title relating to the solution of large systems of linear algebraic equations.About 1968, I became aware that it would be discussed at length – and because I wanted a title that would honour CEB for his extraordinary ability and effort in developing this computer – I renamed it the Atanasoff – Berry Computer.

In order to get started fast, I decided to take a chance and estimate the size of the machine. I knew a few dimensions of the various parts that were to go into it. I was repeatedly trying to estimate the number of vacuum tubes I would need for this digital electronic computer. Arbitrarily, we had decided that it would operate in 30 fields, and so would require 30 add-subtract mechanisms. Without much figuring, I made an estimate of the size of the total machine and arrived at roughly the size of an office desk.

I ordered a lot of angle iron for the frame. People saw these irons at the back entrance of the physics building and wondered about them.

I heard someone replying to a question, "Oh, Atanasoff thinks he is going to make a computer out of those angle irons."

At that time, the largest digital device was the IBM tabulator. The one we had at Iowa State College could tabulate and sum 40 columns of the 80 provided by the punched cards. We knew machines existed that could tabulate and add the full 80 columns each. We planned for 3000 bits of memory, which would in fact calculate at a speed of about 30 times that of the largest IBM tabulator.

When one starts a new and strange project, one must expect that it will be in financial trouble from the start. I had received some aid from ISC, and expected and did receive more from time to time. I knew, however, that I should seek other source for the funds necessary to complete the computer project.

In my requests to ISC, I had used a two-page write up, but in asking others for help, I needed something better. During the spring and summer of 1940, I used my spare time to write not only what we had done, but also what we proposed to do during the remainder of the project. This paper, finished on August 14, 1940, was reprinted by Brian Randell in The Origins of Digital Computers (1973).

I had been corresponding extensively with different organisations that supported research in the sciences, and also with several corporations. My records of the period show an exchange of about 30 letters before support for my project was gained. They also reveal that I submitted my manuscript to three foundations with which I had corresponded. One of these, Research Corporation, after a review of our efforts to that time, made a grant of $5330 for the completion of my computer.

I felt that the work we were doing on computers should be patented, and so, at an early stage, I had investigated the subject of patents at ISC. It seemed clear to me that there was no firm policy on the subject. I learned that the Iowa State College Research Foundation (ISCRF), which I consulted concerning a patent application, did not regard its own patent counsel as adequate for this task. I then spent some time investigating the source and quality of counsel; after several contacts, I was referred to Richard R. Trexler, a Chicago patent attorney. When ISCRF and I ultimately entered into a contact for the proceeds of a patent on my invention ISCRF agreed, in principle at least, to Trexler as our patent attorney.

No official pronouncement was made on the terms of a contract, or even on the necessity for a contract, until Charles E. Friley, president of ISC, received the letter of March 24, 1941, from Howard Poillon of

Research Corporation granting the $5330, a considerable amount of money in those days. Then, from a seeming absence of any policy, the situation changed drastically, and ISC policy was suddenly firm. I am still not exactly sure how it all came about, but I have since seen a letter from Friley to ISCRF saying that ISC should hold onto rights to the patent on my invention. I soon heard from ISCRF. The first words came to me verbally; in substance, I would not be allowed to use the grant until I signed a patent contract with ISCRF in July, 1941.

At the time I first contacted Trexler (August 6, 1940), I was finishing my manuscript on "Computing Machines for the Solution of Large Systems of Linear Algebraic Equations", and I supplied him with a copy. This did not satisfy Trexler, so CEB, with some help from me, drew up an extensive specification covering the details of the patent; together we directed a drafts man in making the patent drawings.

* * *

At this stage in my scientific career, I usually attended the winter meeting of the American Association for the Advancement of Science (AAAS), which in those days was scheduled between Christmas and New Year's. So, late in 1940, with my family, I turned my car eastward, and after other activities, on December 26 I attended the meeting in Philadelphia for three days. My interests were wide, and I frequently moved between the sessions of the various societies. There were, of course, no papers on computing in the modern sense, but I was interested in calculation in general. As a consequence of this, I visited what I clearly remember was a more than ordinarily dusty, chalk filled classroom assigned to John W. Mauchly for giving a paper on an application of a harmonic analyser, which he had constructed, to some weather phenomena. After the paper was presented, I advanced to the podium.

He was very enthusiastic about his analog electrical system for doing Fourier transforms, which had been the subject of his paper. In Mauchly I had met another person who was interested in computation; at that time not many such people were around, and we talked for most of an hour in this first meeting. In the end, we shook hands and promised to write.

About the Atanasoff-Mauchly meeting Mollenhoff* wrote: The discussions dealt with Atanasoff's "pulse" principle (electronic digital computing) as opposed to the "analog" or mechanical principles of the

* Mollenhoff, C.R. Atanasoff: Forgotten Father of the Computer.

Bush differential analyser that had been built by Vannevar Bush at MIT. Atanasoff had refused to discuss more details of the computer but promised to explain his theories in detail if Mauchly would visit Iowa State.

Mauchly was "excited" about the prospect of the visit to Iowa State and the possibility of seeing what he believed was an electronic computer that would perform faster than the Bush differential analyser and could be constructed for "$2 per digit unit".

Mauchly (JWM) made good on his promise to write. My files do not have his first letter, but they do have a letter from me on January 23, 1941, answering him and inviting him to come and see me. JWM was pleased with my invitation, and we wrote a succession of letters. My memory is that he arrived about dark on Saturday, June 14, accompanied by his young son, Jim.

My memory is very clear that he first saw the computer with his son and my family.There was no one else around, this being Sunday, and this checks with his letter saying he might spend Friday at Iowa City. The computer was covered with a sheet to prevent dust from settling on it. The machine was still in construction at this point.

I believe that JWM and his son left Ames early on Friday June 20. Meanwhile,two-thirds of our waking time was spend talking about computers. He read my manuscript and would have liked to take a copy home with him, but I did not allow him to do that. He read all parts of this description of our machine and discussed it with me. Sam Legvold was a graduate student of mine working on another of my projects in a room next to the computer. Much later, he told the federal court in Minneapolis of JWM having his coat off and working with CEB on the machine, when I was otherwise employed. JWM took the manuscript to my home with him and he took notes on white bond paper which I gave him, at his request.

JWM and I had a most cordial relationship while he was at Ames, and after he left we still corresponded, though at less frequent intervals. On September 30, 1941, he wrote a letter to me that contained the question, "Would the way be open for us to build an "Atanasoff Calculator" (a la Bush analyser) here?" In my answer of October 7, I had to tell him:

"Our attorney has emphasised the need of being careful about the dissemination of information about our device until a patent application is filed. This should not require too long and, of course, I have no qualms about having informed you about the devise, but it does require that we refrain from making public any details for the time being. It is, as a matter of fact, preventing me from making an invited address to the American Statistical Association."

(According to Mollenhoff)*

At the time of the trial Honeywell's attourney Halladay after days of quibbling over semantics, had finally persuaded Mauchly to admit the following:

1. He spent from 13 June 1941 to the morning of 18 June 1941 as a quest in Atanasoff's home in Ames.

2. During this period as Atanasoff's guest he spent uncounted hours in discussions of the Atanasoff-Berry Computer and computer theory with John Atanasoff and Clifford Berry.

3. On three or four days he accompanied Atanasoff to his office in the Physics Building and observed the Atanasoff-Berry Computer in the company of Atanasoff and Clifford Berry.

4. He had seen demonstrations of the operations or some phases of the functions of the Atanasoff-Berry Computer and might have engaged in manipulation of some parts of the machine with Clifford Berry.

5. He was permitted to read Atanasoff's 35-page manuscript on the construction and operation of the Atanasoff-Berry Computer from cover to cover and probably did read it. Atanasoff and Berry had willingly answered questions and entered into discussions with him about the machine and the booklet, but Atanasoff had refused to let him take a copy to Pennsylvania.

6. Immediately after his visit to Iowa State in June, Mauchly had written letters to Atanasoff and to his meteorologist friend, Helms Clayton, expressing enthusiasm about the Atanasoff-Berry Computer and had taken a crash course in electronics at the University of Pennsylvania.

7. On 15 August 1941 he wrote a comprehensive memorandum on the difference between analog calculators and pulse devices that incorporated some ideas that were almost identical with those in Atanasoff's 35 page manuscript on the Atanasoff-Berry Computer.

8. On 30 September 1941 he had written to Atanasoff suggesting a cooperative effort to develop an Atanasoff computer and had asked if Atanasoff had any objection to him using some of the Atanasoff concepts in a computer machine that he was considering building.

On December 7, 1941, the Japanese bombarded Pearl Harbor, and the United States was involved in that terrible holocaust. The future of everyone had to be adjusted to meet this emergency. Soon it became

* Mollenhoff, C.R. Atanasoff: Forgotten Father of the Computer.

evident that CEB would be drafted unless he were engaged in a war – related project. Our computer work did not have such a preferred status, and although I did what I could to get him deferred, the draft board had never looked for a position for which he could be deferred. He was so able that he quickly found a suitable position with Consolidated Engineering Corporation of Pasadena California. He married my secretary. Jean Read, and on July 1, 1942, he left ISC.

During the spring and summer of 1942, I continued to work with ISCRF and Trexler to get the patent under way. There always seemed to be some reason why it should be put off, however, and off it was.

U. S. NAVAL ORDNANCE LABORATORY (1942–1948)

I began work at the Naval Ordnance Laboratory (NOL) late in September. NOL was the research laboratory of the Bureau of Ordnance. It had responsibility for depth charges, mines, and various other projects, as assigned. Historically, it had been located in the US Naval Gun Factory, beside the Anacostia River, and there it remained until the war was over and a new laboratory was constructed north of Washington at White Oak, Maryland.

Although acoustics had not been one of my particular fields of interest, I was a theoretical physicist, and so I was put in charge of acoustical testing of mines.

My first objective was to get acquainted with the subject of acoustics; my next objective was to acquire a staff. I was able to get the services of David Beecher. He had not been my major student there, but I knew him well, and on occasion he had worked on the ABC. Later, I was able to get both Herman Ellingson, who was on the staff of Luther College in Decorah, Iowa, and my former major student, Sam Legvold. The rest of my staff came from various other sources.

I do not have the exact date, but I think that early in 1943 I was seated at my desk in my noisy, dirty space in Building 184, when I felt someone approaching me from the right. It was John Mauchly. By some means, he had become employed by the NOL, his security clearance was satisfactory, and he attached himself to my staff. I knew the exact basis of his employment with NOL, and Royal Weller, my superior, had no more knowledge than I. I did not know how much money JWM received for his consulting services, and I was too busy to find out. He said he was still employed by the Moor School, but he came back once or twice a week. At first, I planned various things for him to do; later, I attached him to Ellingson's statistical group. I do believe, however, that every time he came in, he stopped by to see me briefly. On one such occasion, he told me that he and J. Prosper Eckert (JPE) had devised a new way to compute. I remember that I was very busy, but I paused and asked him to tell me about it. His reply was simple: "I cannot, the subject is classified."

The visits of JWM continued sporadically until the end of the war. On August 30, 1944, both JWM and JPE visited me in the Gun Factory. I believe that JPE did not have security clearance for the area, and so they were both escorted. Through some military procedure they had obtained army and navy agreement that I should help them with quartz transducers. I agreed to help them, but presumably their needs elsewhere.

In the period from September 1942 until the war ended, I was in Ames every few months. At each visit I took the time to see some member of ISCRF and discuss the prospect of filing a patent application on our work on computers. At various times, I also wrote to Trexler and to ISCRF. During the first year or two, I really believed that a patent would be applied for. Much later, Trexler said he had never been authorised to proceed.

I have in my files an ISC inter office memo concerned with the patent situation.It has no signature, but was written, I believe, by R. E. Buchanan, dean of ISC. It is dated June 26, 1948; I did not see it for perhaps 20 years. The author speaks of seeing me at NOL; I do remember seeing Buchanan at about that time. He speaks of my saying that our computer was "probably largely obsolete." This was clearly incorrect; I spoke, instead, of the need for moving rapidly if anything was to be salvaged from our work. The memo gives contract between ISC and me.

About September of 1945, while I was attending a staff meeting at the gun factory, my superior, Lynn H. Rumbaugh, told us that the Bureau of Ordnance was going to build a computer. Of, course, the Research Department would do the work. It was over three years since I had left computing at ISC, and I had not spoken much of this part of my history; it was known, however, and so I was selected to head the project.

While we were in this dilemma, JWM came to see us for the first time in several months. In the last years of his life, he claimed that on this occasion I asked him how to build a computer. I do not remember doing this and do not believe I did; in any case, I do remember that as always we talked of many things, but I heard nothing from him about computers.

The computer project seemed to be doing well except for understaffing, but in a short time my superior and I were called to the office of the chief of research of the Bureau of Ordnance, and we were told that the bureau wished to discontinue the project. As is usual in such cases, no basic reason was given.

After the conclusion of the computer project, LWM no longer came to NOL; I saw him again only once, at a much later date, when he came to my house with Laurence B. Dodds (see Section 13).

THE ORDNANCE ENGINEERING CORPORATION (1952–1961)

Early in 1952, I was thinking of the types of experience I had encountered. I was 48 years old, and I knew that if I wanted to be involved in private enterprise, the time had come; one of my friends, in fact, had told me that I was already too old. With a few firm friends, however, I incorporated The Ordnance Engineering Corporation (TOEC) in the state of Maryland.

During the first years of this corporation, we rented space in Rockville, Maryland.

On June 15, 1954, we received a visit from A. J. Etienne, who was a patent attorney for IBM. As soon as I learned that we were going to discuss patents, I called David Beecher, our vice – president, into the conference. Etienne announced his purpose by saying in substance, 'If you will help us, we will break the Mauchly – Eckert computer patent; it was derived from you. "I hesitated to reply to Etienne. I was looking back over the years that had passed since JWM had told me (in 1943) that he and JPE invented a new method of computing, different from yours," and I had believed him. This was the first substantial item to the contrary that I had encountered. I did not know of the patent to which Etienne was referring – that is, the Memory System patent 2,629,827, issued in 1953. (The ENIAC patent, applied for in 1947, was not issued until 1964.) I remember wondering if Etienne was correct…

In 1956, we sold the corporation to Aerojet General Corporation (AGC), with principal offices in Azusa, California. After our incorporation entered into AGC, we were called the Atlantic Division. In 1959, I was made vice-president of AGC and managed the Atlantic Division.

As the United States changed to peace condition after the Korean War, I used my experience in computers to shift the activity of the Atlantic Division toward the invention and manufacture of automatic equipment for parcel handling and sorting. By this time, I had found being a "corporation man" not to my liking. Accordingly, I resigned as vice-president of Aerojet General Corporation early in 1961.

During these years, I was well aware of the growing interest in computing. Even before Etienne's visit, I knew that certain companies with an appropriate background were making inquiries of anyone skilled in the art, including Berry and myself.

From time to time during the 20 plus years that had elapsed after CEB had left Ames, I visited him and Jean in their home in Altadena. During, say, the first two – thirds of this period, I was told of his interest in and success with his work, and of his rapid advancement in his company. I have verified this success with others in his field, and it was truly phenomenal. I do not know exactly when this picture changed; perhaps by 1960, though, Clifford, while still excited with his work, was less satisfied with the position he held with his company. I also noticed a slight cynicism in his general attitude, which I took to be a natural consequence of aging. Late in 1963, I was overwhelmed to get a letter from Jean Berry, saying that Clifford had resigned his position, taken a place with a company in Long Island, and died one night at his apartment.

In late 1967, still feeling unhappy over his death, I made a personal investigation of it. I located his apartment and talked with the man who had first found him. I also visited the police of the county. CEB's death was not natural; he had been found in bed with a plastic sack over his head but with his bedclothes smoothly over his arms, which were by his sides. An autopsy revealed that his brain plasma had 0.12 percent alcohol content, which would have permitted him to drive a car in some jurisdictions. He had been taking Dilantin because of recent epilepsy, and so his blood and brain were carefully examined for this and other drugs; none were found. Suicide, said the authorities.

PRELIMINARIES OF LITIGATION

On April 26, 1967, I was visited by Allen Kirkpatrick, a patent attorney of Washington, who represented Control Data Corporation (CDC). He had learned of me by reading a book, Electronic Digital Systems, by R. K. Richards (1966); Richards had seen our computer with Clifford Berry in 1941, I think. Sperry Rand Corporation (SR) was suing CDC, and I was given a quick summary of the issues. Later, Kirkpatrick furnished me copies of the patents involved and suggested that I scan their clams to find any that were developed in my own work.

During his April visit, Kirkpatrick also told me that SR was going to sue Honeywell (H) (my notes say that the H suit was begun on May 26, 1967). More specifically, H was to be sued by Illinois Scientific

Developments, Inc. (ISD), a subsidiary of SR, but for our present purpose, we will refer only to SR. Kirkpatrick gave me some information on the H suit as well. At about this time, I was also contacted by Henry Hanson, D. Dennis Allegretty, and Charles C. Call, patent attorneys, and Henry Halladay, trial attorney, all of whom represented H in the case. I agreed to do consulting work for both CDC and H.

Not long after Kirkpatrick came to see me, I was approached by attorneys George Eltgroth, Norman Fulmer, and H. Mial Dustin of General Electric.Fulmer had been at ISC and had actually worked on the ABC. He initiated a meeting with me for communicating general information. I had partially read the ENIAC patent, and I knew that certain claims were derived from my work. Eltgroth, who had at one time been counsel for Mauchly and Eckert, said to me, "I had never heard of Atanasoff then. If I had, I would have protected them [in formulating both patents]." I must assume that the other patent counsel had not heard of Atanasoff, either. (As it happened, General Electric was not sued by SR, so I was not needed as a consultant for them).

I conclude this introduction by saying that I did not realise how long a period of study, analysis, and training lay ahead, before the preparatory process was finished and the trials began. Nor have I ever had associates and co-workers of such skill and ability as those who represented Control Data Corporation and Honeywell Incorporated throughout the whole procedure, and in the trials themselves. Our sojourn was arduous to the extreme, and counsel often had good cause to be irritated with me – and the reverse – but these men were gentlemen of the first order.

REASONS FOR SR SUITS VERSUS CDC AND H.

Law is not my specialty, although I had spent some 2000 hours studying patent law over the years, and I append the following from hearsay for those not otherwise informed. SR, having acquired certain patents from JWM and JPE – in particular the ENIAC patent 3,120, 606 and the Memory System patent 2,629, 827- felt that it had a basic patent control of the computing machine field, and sought to levy royalties on other companies in violation of the claims of its patents. I have heard these royalties at one billion dollars, all told. To begin this legal process, SR chose to sue CDC over the memory patent and H over the ENIAC patent, since both CDC and H had resisted paying royalties; H countersued for antitrust violation and became the plaintiff in a combined ENIAC suit. The memory patent had been applied for in 1947 and was issued in 1953. The ENIAC patent had been applied for in 1947 and issued in 1964. For some legal reasons and/or the desire of judges, the suit of SR versus CDC was to be held in Baltimore and the suit of H versus SR was planned for Minneapolis.

It was soon clear to everyone that these lawsuits would become monumental in computing-machine history and would take some years before coming to trial.

(From the Unknown Lawsuit*)

There was plenty for everyone to do. I had been chosen to participate, in part because at the beginning I knew more of the basic facts; so it was left to me to outline these facts. The following indicates some of the topics on which I wrote.

1. Evidence from the foundations. Contacts were made with the foundations to which I had sent my manuscript of August 1940 to verify its authenticity.
2. List of names, addresses, and connections of various individuals involved with our computer project.
3. Atanasoff – Mauchly relations. Recapitulations of all direct contacts between these parties.
4. Testing procedures and demonstrations of ABC.
5. Comments by JWA on JWM deposition.
6. Further exposition of ABC details.
7. Simple exposition of ABC for courtroom use.
8. Demonstration material for use in courtroom.
9. Last days of CEB.
10. JWA telephone conversation with JWM, November 10, 1967.
11. Visit to Atanasoff by Mauchly and Laurence B. Dodds, December 16, 1967.

Several of these topics have been discussed, and others need only be mentioned; the last two will be covered next.

I had not expected to hear from JWM but when both contacts occurred, they seemed important enough to record them immediately afterwards, from memory. My wife, Alice, and I made notes, as follows.

Call from Dr. John W. Mauchly, 1967 Nov. 10, 15:50–16:30.

Alice: You have a call from John Mauchly. [She remained on the extension phone]

* From **Джон Атанасов, Неизвестният процес, в. "Антени", 1985, бр. 23–26.**

A [JVA]: Hello, is this John W. Mauchly?

M [JWM]: Is this John V. Atanasoff? It has been a long time.

[The next few sentence are intended to be illustrative, and no great effort was made to make this part exact.]

M: What have you been doing? I've been hearing your name quite frequently of late.

A: You mean since the ACM meeting? [The Association for Computing Machinery's history session in Washington, D. C., in 1967.]

M: Yes. Before that Richards called me before he wrote his book and I told him I had no knowledge of what happened to you.

A: You know, Clifford Berry was a boyhood friend of Richards. Well, I finally left the government service, started my own company, sold out to Aerojet General, and became a vice-president of that company.

M: Well, this is more than I ever heard before. What has happened to your children? [We discussed our children at some length. His son James was actually living in Frederick.]

M: I have been asked by a patent attorney to arrange a visit with you.

A: Who is the attorney?

M: Dodds.

A: What is his first name?

M: Come to think of it, I don't know.

A: Who does he represent?

M: Sperry Rand. He represents them in a case involving Control Data.

A: When does he want to come?

M: On the 20th if that is all right with you. Of, course, if you do not want to see him, that will have to be that.

A: Well, I do not know why I should not see him. Of course, I do not know if he will be happy about the visit; that depends on what he says and what he wants to know. Also, I am very busy until after Thanksgiving.

M: Very well, I will try to arrange a date after Thanksgiving, one that is satisfactory to you and to me and to him. I think you will like him. He seems to be a very nice man. To be blunt, however, I thought Mr. Kirkpatrick [He called him Kilpatrick] was a nice man, he seemed so at first. Then later he put on the thumb screws, and then he tightened them. Perhaps all good attorneys have to be this way, so I am not sure of Mr. Dodds. Then, too, I remember that I was with Bill Hall when he tried to reach you. Did he ever get in touch with you?

A: No, someone who said he was Hall of Washington called when I was away on the West Coast but he did not call back.

M: Very cloak and dagger, isn't it? But what is this? I thought you were retired, and you were on the West Coast and now you are busy.

A: Well, when you retire you will find that you have just as much to do as before. That is one of the secrets of retiring. [Then he described his deposition in the CDC case, but he did not use that word.]

M: They gave me a subpoena in that suit between CD and SR, I was asked to bring all correspondence up to 1949, and I assumed that meant Moor School. So I tried to find all I could. To my surprise I was shown correspondence with you, and of course, I identified them although I had completely forgotten their existence. Thinking later about my copies, I think I may have turned them over to Sperry Rand. They had me in a room in Philadelphia asking questions. That is where I met Kilpatrick. When they do that your answers run into pages.

A: Maybe I should get a copy and read this.

M: Maybe you should if you have time to waste. Maybe you will be mad at me when you see what I said. [I started to overlook this, and then I thought, better not.]

A: What did you say to make me mad?

M: Several things; perhaps the worst was that when you got into administrative work you lost interest in computers.

A: Well, maybe I did seem to, perforce.

M: Well, yes, maybe perforce.

Throughout, the conversation was friendly to the extreme. At first Mauchly seemed embarrassed, but later he seemed well at ease. Some other points we noted at the time were the following.

1. He asked me if I had been to the ACM meeting. I told him that I had not [I was not invited], but that I had talked with several who were Cal Moers for instance. He then said, "I did not know you know him. Oh yes, I did; you introduced him to me when he worked for you at NOL." (I did not, but he did know him at NOL.)

2. Mauchly told of seeing a lot of witnesses in another case with Honeywell in which, of a long list of names, fully half were from Ames. I said, 'This Ames business interests me. Something seems to have happened out at Ames. "He said, 'Something must have."

3. Mauchly said that Mrs. Berry was on this list and not Clifford, and so he assumed that Clifford is dead. He said that this must be recent since he saw a letter which Clifford wrote to Richards saying that Mauchly had been the only one told of the machine in full and that Clifford seems to have forgotten about Caldwell. I told him that Clifford died in late 1963. I also told him that many people had been told something

of the machine, as was Caldwell, who is also dead, but that very few were given a full disclosure.

4. Mauchly asked if Warren Weaver had funded the machine. I told him no, but that he had once considered giving assistance. He said that he had seen his name on the list above mentioned.

5. He mentioned a Berry Holberton, now at the Bureau of Standards. She did the first data processing on the ENIAC, and [according to JWM] the poor girl has been subjected to endless questioning by patent attorneys.

6. He mentioned that Dodds was assisting Technitrol in a suit against the US Government for $30 million but that SR approved since they had a license from that firm.

7. Mauchly said he left SR in 1959. Since that time they only called on him in patent matters, but this is the first time he has been called by an opponent of SR.

8. He mentioned that he was called on at the time of the IBM investigation, but that blew over and they made a separate deal.

9. About Kirkpatrick, Mauchly said aggrievedly, "He practically accused me of plagiarising everything I've done."

VISIT BY MAUCHLY AND DODDS, SATURDAY, DECEMBER 16, 1967

JWM had called and made the date for the visit; he and Dodds were to arrive at 10 A.M. He arrived at 10:05, and we sat and visited until about 11 A.M. Dodds arrived soon thereafter. The following are notes Alice and I made soon after the meeting.

I told Mr. Dodds that I was perfectly willing to talk in general about the case, but I would not merely go over the information that I intended to give on deposition.

As a result, I was able to answer certain questions with the statement that it was properly reserved for the deposition. Then I made the following general statement on when I said we should have to base our discussion:

Dr. Mauchly came to Ames (approximately 1941 June 15), he spent considerable time with the machine, he understood it fully, and in substantially every detail.

I said, "If you don't like it, that is just too bad because those were facts. The courts must decide if this is derivation."

Dr. Mauchly did not deny that those were the facts but merely said, "You are taking a very positive posture which I cannot take. Your memory must be better than mine." A little later in the conversation, Dr. Mauchly asked, "Do you contend that I read the booklet?"

I said that the detailed discussion of this should be reserved for deposition.However, the answer is yes, and also you asked me if you could take a copy home with you. I denied that request, and so you did not take a copy away.

Mr. Dodds asked, "Will you treat us well as our opponents?"

I said "I do not see why I should place you and your opponents on exactly the same footing. It is obviously to your advantage to prove that there was no development of a computing machine at Ames, Iowa. Your opponents contend the contrary, and my interests must lie in that direction."

Dodds: "Do our opponents know exactly what testimony you will give on deposition?"

JVA: "They may know some testimony that I will give. In part I will have to say a great many things that they know to be true. However, in general they do not know what I will say on deposition, and to some small degree my own mind is not completely made up as to what happened. It will require research and refreshment of my memory to determine what is said in deposition. In other cases I have not told them what I will say at the time of deposition and so they do not know."

Dodds: "Are there other people alive who read the manuscript at the time at which it was first issued?"

JVA: "Well, you know that the manuscript was not only sent to the Research Corporation, but was also sent to the Scientific Aids for Learning, a subsidiary of the Carnegie Corporation, and to the Natural Sciences Division of the Rockfeller Foundation. The official of both of these organization presumably read the manuscript at that time and they may have reffered the manuscript to other persons who read it. I have tried to retrive files from these other two places and would be happy if you could succeed where I could not. I did not know what was contained in the "827 patent and in the ENIAC patent untill this last summer. I must admit that when I read these patents I was somewhat appalled to find that these patents duplicated my own efforts in their claims. In particular, the "827 patent almost exactly described my own apparatus in its specifications."

Dodds: "Well, specifications do not matter, it is what is contained in the claims that counts. We contend that that patent does not touch upon the work that you did in its claims, that its claims are much more specific and much different from what you actually accomplished."

JVA: "Alice, get me a copy of patent '827." (She complied).

Mauchly said, "You see how bad my memory is. Which patent is covered by '827?" (He was told).

JVA: " Lets us read the first claim together."

He read it aloud, Mr. Dodds following his copy.

JVA: "That is exactly what I constructed. What is the difference between that claim and what I had in my material possession at the time Dr. Mauchly visited me?"

Mr. Dodds was somewhat deflated and gave no answer to this query. Somewhat later Mr. Dodds asked, "Do you also contend that your work bears upon the ENIAC patent?"

JVA: " I have worked upon the ENIAC patent a number of days, and I do not pretend to understand it."

Dodds: "I do not understand it either."

JVA: "The answer to your question is yes, I really believe that there are claims in there related to the work which I did."

Dodds: " I belive that there was no regenerative memory in the ENIAC patent."

JVA: "Yes, but there was interaction of logic circuits in the computing elements, and that is an item which is derived from the work."

Dodds: " Yes, there are logic circuits in the ENIAC patents."

During most of the questioning, Dr. Mauchly was sitting to one side and not particularly participating in the conversation. Occasionally he would want to tell a story, probably irrelevant, whereupon Mr. Dodds and JVA would listen courteously. Mr. Dodds had arrived so late that it was soon time for lunch. Alice provided a simple repast. During the course of the lunch I asked Mr. Dodds if he would be hard upon me on deposition. After a moment's hesitation, he said, " Oh no." I have found him a rather intelligent, quick-witted individual; in fact I rather liked him. I liked him well enough so even tried the following question: " Mr. Dodds, in face of the facts, how do you expect to win this case?"

At this question, Mr. Dodds was somewhat irritated. "There are some things which are not contained in your 2000 hours [of study of patent law]. You don't know anything about how federal judges are likely to act. They may decide that question upon their own impulse instead of on fact, law or reason." There were a few moments of quiet while I continued eating and digesting this episode, and in a moment Mr. Dodds thought better of the situation. "However I should say that the judge at Baltimore, Judge Watkins is a very learned and able judge and I do not believe that will happen there." So basically the question of how

Mr. Dodds is to win the case remained unanswered… JVA said he would be willing to bet a small sum, say a dollar each, to the gentlemen present that they would lose the "827" suit. Mr. Dodds asked what he was betting on the ENIAC [trial], and JVA said perhaps the percentages would vary somewhat but the outcome would probably be about the same.

I have no doubt that he will think of something and probably it will be an attempt to controvert the testimony which I will give. At one point he stated, "There is no testimony except yours." I let it pass without mentioning the written material which exist, or Sam Legvold's testimony that Mauchly had been working on the machine for two days with his sleeves rolled up.

In the afternoon, considerable time was spent in a discussion between Dr. Mauchly and myself, concerning the subject of his employment by the Naval Ordnance Laboratory during the years 1943 to 1946. He seemed very anxious to establish the truth here, since he had always thought he had worked for me, and this is one way [Dr. Mauchly tried] to find out why his memory is so bad. Dr. Mauchly continued to support his testimony that he had worked for me and that I had hired him. I was equally vehement that nothing of the kind happened. I might not have argued the matter so strongly if I could not remember my amazement on his first visit to the laboratory. My memory of that instance is so vivid that I remember exactly where I was sitting when he first arrived.

Toward the end of this discussion Dr. Mauchly commenced to remember that he had a talk with some personnel people. He started that in that period he had considered shifting his employment from the Moor School to NOL. This fact was previously unknown to me. After talking with the personnel people he had come to the laboratory and had an interview with a large raw-boned man who was an expert in spectroscopy. After a moment or two we both agreed that this must have been Dr. Lynn Rumbaugh.

JWM did spend some time around my division and did some consulting on a variety of problems. Except in the matter of who hired whom, JWM's memory seemed rather good. He recalled the names of two or three of my men with whom he was associated while he was around my division.

Mr. Dodds and Dr. Mauchly expressed an interest in the house and they were given the usual tour. Dr. Mauchly made no effort to leave as Mr. Dodds drove away. He stayed and we talked in a desultory fashion. Alice and I both felt that he must have some objective in staying. He seemed to speak freely of his relations with Sperry Rand, whom he called a bunch of_____s. He gave a rather complete account of the time when he hired Mr. Eltgroth to act as patent counsel for the Eckert-Mauchly Corp. This was at the time that Mr. Eltgroth had contracted polio. He complained that Mr. Eltgroth had filed him in formulating certain contractual relationships, though he also blamed himself and Eckert for using him as a legal advisor outside the patent field. Previously in Mr. Dodds's presence, he stated that he had told Mr. Eltgroth all about my work. Mr. Dodds reminded him that Mr. Eltgroth had not originally drawn the "827" patent although he may have later had something to do with it, that it was really drawn by Mr. Smith all about our previous work.

Dr. Mauchly spoke of his corporation having received half a million dollars at the time at which IBM settled with Sperry Rand for the sum of 10 million dollars. The particular fault in drawing up the contract with Remington Rand by the Eckert-Mauchly Computer Copr. was that it was so drawn that all the royalties which they received had to be regarded as reimbursement for personal services so that Remington Rand could charge it off as an expense, but this meant that Mauchly and Eckert had to pay taxes on all this money they received as ordinary income instead of payment on a capital gain basis.

I told Dr. Mauchly that I had discovered that he gave his paper at Philadelphia in 1940 and not in 1939. This closes a year gap in the correspondence between Dr. Mauchly and myself and he was satisfied with this explanation. By way of reference I should explain that I obtained this information from the files of the American Association for the Advancement of Science, AAAS as it is commonly called, in Washington, D.C.

Dr. Mauchly was smoking continually and I felt friendly and easy with him, and of course gave him my "quit smoking" lecture. By the time all this had happened it was growing dark. Dr. Mauchly would start to go and then hesitate, over and over again, so I suggested that Alice prepare supper and I took Dr. Mauchly for a walk down to the lake and back. Evidently Dr. Mauchly's constitution is rather poor for he suffered more severely than Eltgroth had previously in making this trip. As we were coming up the hill he repeatedly stopped and rested. When we arrived back at the house, Alice had supper ready and we ate a somewhat more generous meal, all that Alice will allow me in my present state of calorie counting, also consistent with Dr. Mauchly's slight diabetic condition.

Again Alice and I expected Dr. Mauchly to make some statement. We waited courteously and gave him every opportunity. Alice would on occasion absent herself from the room so that he could speak to me privately if he so desired. As he left, Dr. Mauchly said he would seriously consider discontinuing his three packs of cigarettes a day. When he finally left, about 6:30, to drive to Philadelphia, he expressed his pleasure at the hospitality he had received. He seemed genuinely to have enjoyed himself. Perhaps he had. I had the uneasy feeling that somehow I had been taken in by the pair of them, but if this occurred, I do not know how. I got the impression that Dr. Mauchly was genuinely pleased to find that he had not entirely deprived me of living substance. During the day a great deal of the talk was about children and grandchildren and in a particular his relation with his son (who lived in Frederick).

ADDITIONAL ITEMS DISCUSSED

1. **Fulmer.** Dr. Mauchly and Mr. Dodds were told that Mr. Norman Fulmer, who is now a member of the computing machine patent staff of General Electric Co., was from Iowa State University and was formerly employed in connection with the ABC. This information seemed to disturb Mr. Dodds. It seemed to give the whole project of that time some substance in his mind to know that a present patent man had formerly been connected with it, although of course he did know Mr. Fulmer. They both did know, however, and immediately stated that Mr. Eltgroth was head of GE's patent division and that he must be Fulmer's superior.

2. **Trexler-Patent Application**. Mr. Dodds asked about the attorney who had been associated with the early computing machine project. He was given Mr. Trexler's name. He asked if Mr. Traxler had patent application. I explained that this depended on what was meant by a patent application; I started that the material had been written which was suitable for inclusion in specification. He then asked if a set of patent claims had been drawn and I started that they had not to the best of my knowledge. I however told Mr. Dodds that the patent attorney had been acting under the direction of Iowa State University and may have written some claims.

3. **Other Applications.** Mr. Dodds asked if we had other applications in mind for the ABC. I started that we did have other applications in mind and that this machine could be applied in many other situations. I pointed out that it is only the control system that was special and as far as the computing elements themselves, the regenerative memory and the circuit logic and the computing mechanisms, these could equally be applied to many other purposes.

4. **Completion of ABC.** Mr. Dodds asked how nearly complete the Atanasoff-Berry Computer was at the time it was left at Iowa State University. He was told that the machine was substantially complete, but that the data-in data-out base-2 apparatus was not performing in a completely satisfactory manner. He was told that this was the result of an occasional failure to read after the card had been punched by electric spark. We had expected to complete this by a material which would be more favorable to reading the card punchings. This had not been done at the time the machine was left at Iowa State University.

5. **Comments on Mr. Dodds**. At one point in the discussion, Mr. Dodds said to JVA. "I just have one piece of advice to give to you. When you are giving testimony, stick to exactly what you know or remember. Do not use your imagination or speculate in any way." I will of course take this advice to heart.

The following alternatives occur to me (a) Mr. Dodds thought my imagination was too vivid and I was extending my memory by my imagination; (b) Mr. Dodds felt that his only solution was to whittle away at my testimony and he intended to do it on deposition.

I cannot underrate or underestimate Mr. Dodds as a practical, hard-hitting trial attorney of great sensitivity, great aptitude, and with a very quick and agile mind. He seemed always to keep before his eyes the feeling that he was going to win the case, although I think this was somewhat affected by my confidence that nothing like this was going to transpire. Since I had somewhat disassociated myself from counsel for Control Data and for Honeywell, I could claim to be ignorant about any specific plans which they might have had. Of course no information of this type was disclosed, I gained the impression from Dr. Mauchly that Mr. Dodds was in complete charge of both of these cases and that Mr. Hall was only a lackey used to perform certain specific things. Mr. Dodds told me that he was a lone man, working alone, having no associated or assistants. I am concerned about his going into trial without a deeper backlog of supporting talent, but this is a casual concern and I will not exert myself further in this direction. Probably house counsel for Sperry Rand will give him support.

At various times during this discussion, Mr. Dodds would explain some point in patent law. At such times his verbalisation was quick and easy and he gave a graphic representation of the facts of law in a way that enabled me to understand what he said very quickly.

6. **Dodds to Mauchly**. After Mr. Dodds had left, Dr. Mauchly stated that his instruction from Mr. Dodds had been not to concern himself about attempting to reconstruct any details about his visit to Ames but just to remember casually what he could and otherwise state that he had forgotten. (He had mentioned this once in Mr. Dodds's presence.) At this time Dr. Mauchly was expressing regret that his memory was not in better shape, and this remark was made in explanation of it. He stated that he had made no effort to remember various things which had happened during the visit to Ames. Dr. Mauchly professed to be taking this as exhibiting a rather casual attitude on Mr. Dodds's part. I am not at all sure but what this really represents an invitation to Mauchly fully aboard because he was openly stating that Dodds had invited him not to remember. I cannot believe that there is a very close understanding between Dodds and Mauchly.

7. **Mauchly Compensation.** At one point Dr. Mauchly stated that he was being compensated very well for his time which was used in connection with preparation for the Sperry Rand case. He gave me a chance to ask but I did not ask the amount of his compensation, since I hoped not to disclose the corresponding information to him.

8. **Dr. Arthur W. Burks.** The following items were obtained from Dr. Mauchly in this connection:

a. Dr. Burks was the first to publish about ENIAC while Dr. Mauchly and Mr. Eckert were refraining from publication for patent and possible security reasons. Dr. Burks went ahead and openly published the first information about ENIAC.

b. Dr. Burks has obtained panels of the original ENIAC for the University of Michigan museum, thus putting this museum in a better position than any other original computing machine.

c. Dr. Mauchly stated that Dr. Burks has the best file of original work on ENIAC of anyone. He believes that Burks was very careful to maintain this file in a good state, and he does not believe that Sperry Rand has a good file of the original documents on this subject as Dr. Burks.

9. **Dr. Mauchly's Memory.** Although it has been previously mentioned, one point that was very evident was Dr. Mauchly's embarrassment about his bad memory and of having forgotten so much of what happened in 1940 and 1941. He repeatedly explained that he had made no effort whatever to recall or reconstruct what happened, on instruction from counsel, and he used this as an excuse.

10. **Berry Letter to Richards.** Perhaps it would be useful to mention that at least twice Mr. Dodds pulled out the Berry letter and asked questions from it. I believe the actual material has already been discussed.

CONSOLIDATED ELECTRODYNAMICS CORPORATION
360 SIERRA MADRE VILLA, PASADENA, CALIFORNIA
A SUBSIDIARY OF BELL & HOWELL COMPANY

March 22, 1963

Air Mail

DR. R. K. Richards

1821 Allen Avenue

Ames Lowa

Dear Dr. Richards:

I have often regretted that the work in which I assisted Dr. Atanasoff during 1939-42 was never publicised, and I certainly support your effort of retrieving and storing for historical purposes what information still exists. I have suggested this to Dr. Atanasoff on several occasions when we have met during the past few years.

Unfortunately, my own records are extremely scanty; I have only two newspaper clippings (one based on the copy of the press release which you included with your letter), a few photographs, and a copy of my Master's Thesis. The latter, entitled: Design of Electrical Data Recording and Reading Mechanism" (1941) should be on file in the Library. I am enclosing the photographs and one press clipping; since these are my only copies. I trust you will treat them with care and return them promptly.

As to other sources of documented information, Dr. Atanasoff may have forgotten to tell you that(1) we wrote a series of detailed reports to the Research Corporation, which funded much of our work, and (2) prepared several patent application (which were never filed) with the aid of a firm of patent attorneys in Chicago.

Copies of these may still exist.

An interesting sidelight is that in 1940 in 1941 we had a visit from Dr. John Mauchly who spent a week learning all of details of our computer and the philosophy of its design. He was the only person outside of the Research Corporation and the patent counsel who was given this opportunity, and he may still have notes of what he learned from us.

I am not sure what Dr. Atanasoff told you about the machine so I will describe it briefly. The machine was designed specifically to solve sets of linear simultaneous algebraic equations up to 30 x 30. All internal operations were carried on in binary arithmetic; the size of the numbers handled was up to 50 binary places (about 15 decimal places). Initial input of data was by means of standard IBM cards, with five 15-place numbers per card; the machine translated these numbers to binary numbers. The machine's "memory" consisted of two rotating drums filled with small capacitors. The polarity of the charge on a given capacitor represented the binary digit standing in that position. A: "clock" frequency of 60 cycles per second was used, the mechanical parts of the machine being driven with of a special binary card punch, with which 30 binary numbers, each 50 digits long, could be punched on one card. The mathematical method employed to solve sets of equations was that of systematic elimination of coefficients through linear combination of pairs of equations.

If I can help you in any further way please let me know. I shall be very interested in reading your book when it is published.

Very truly yours,
/s/
Clifford E. Berry
Director of Engineering
CEB: sr
Encls, 6 snapshots, 1 newspaper clipping

P.S. For the utmost importance of this letter for the result from legal disputes, John Atanasoff included a facsimile from it in his memoirs.

PREPARATION OF JVA AS A WITNESS

After learning from the attorneys of H and CDC how seriously they regarded the litigation, I made a careful search of my papers. I had just moved into a new house and had a collection of boxes that had not been opened for many years. Some had been with me, and some had been in storage. In two boxes, I found my files for the computing machine. There were hundreds of items, which were later used in the litigation. The lawyers expressed joy with each scrap of paper.

I was interested, but slightly amused, that I had found myself in the mesh of the federal court system of our nation. I have always been intrigued by the law and our patent system, but jurisprudence is far removed from the fields in which I have laboured. Watching these two cases unfold in our federal courts gave me a little deeper feeling of how man gets along with man.

Contrary to the experience of JWM, I was encouraged to recall what happened in the early days of our computing, and two item of my memory was ever suggested or suppressed. These counsellors-at-law paid particular attention that my memory should be extended to the earlier possible date and the most remote circumstances. As a consequence, I came to remember events that happened back to the age of two, and many others that followed. As each event of memory came to mind, I tried to verify it. Thus my memory at the age of two was of the birth of a sister; she was born late in the afternoon and I could and did check my memory of this fact with my mother. I could refresh my memory with my notes and 1940 manuscript and with other published material, and sometimes other important material would come to mind.

I had never before experienced the attention trained legal counsel give to such matters, but the gentlemen in question took it all as a matter of course. I have always had a good memory, but I soon learned that a careful verification of memory is most worthwhile, particularly if you bear the responsibility of being a witness in important litigation.

Counsel for H also gave me extensive training in answering questions on the issues under litigation. Counsel did not know all of the answer and where gradually adding to their own knowledge of the subject, while I, on the other hand, was learning how to give an answer in court. After two or three tries, counsel found what answers they could expect, and I gradually became skilled in giving complete answers to the questions. During the process, no one objected to the answers that I gave on any subject; I suppose that each knew I was doing my best and I could not easily have my mind changed. In a few cases, they did expose me to other information that they thought would refresh my memory; I was sure, though, that the final answer was always up to me.

FORMAL LITIGATION

We use the term formal litigation for the two processes, deposition and trial, by which evidence is produced for the judge (or jury) to use in reaching a verdict. This part of litigation is the major pert; in important cases, the records become voluminous. In the matter of computer litigation being considered here, there were only two cases at that time, the Memory System case and the ENIAC case; even so, the legal documents numbered in the thousands.

In the early years while the trials were pending, there were many depositions, including those of the principal witnesses and of many other witnesses who would not attend the trial. I was deposed once for each of the two trials. My first deposition, on the Memory case, was short; the second, on the ENIAC case, lasted approximately two weeks, beginning on November 11, 1968. In both cases, Dodds was counsel for SR.

Among the witnesses deposed (of personal interest to me) were JVA (both trials), JWM (both trials), JPE (both trials), Lura M. Atanasoff [JVA's wife in 1941] (both trials), and Sam Legvold (both trials), as well as many other people. CEB was not alive at the time of deposition, but in a way a letter (Figure 9) he wrote to R. K. Richards on March 22, 1963, quoted again in trial, served as a statement by him of the situation when JWM came to Ames.

On October 11–13, 1967 JWM's deposition was taken on behalf of the defendant, CDC, in the suit by SR on the Memory patent 2,629,827 and certain other patents.

JWM spoke of a visit to see our machine. He spoke of being cordially received, but hinted that no one was willing to tell him all about the machine. He claimed that nothing worked except the motor. There was no demonstration of the action of machine, he asserted.

He said he had no time with the machine – perhaps 1 hour.

He saw one cylinder or condensers, he said. He learned that memory was relained by the use of regeneration, but said he was not told how the regeneration worked.

JVA and Legvold. On deposition and in trial testimony, stated, under oath – and CEB in his 1963 letter to Richards corroborated – that when JWM visited the computer laboratory at Ames, he was given the full details of the project and he was given much more than any one else; that he was given the complete current operational test of the computer; that he spent a length of time with the machine in excess of 16 hours, took his coat off to work on the machine in his shirtsleeves, and held certain parts of the machine in his hands; and that he saw our current manuscript (August 1940) on the machine and took notes.

The reader is reminded that at this time there were two legal actions taking place, both involving my work at Iowa State College, since certain litigants held that divers claims of each were derived from my computer and computing principles.

HONEYWELL VERSUS SPERRY RAND

The H-SR trial was held in federal court at Minneapolis, with Judge Earl R. Larson presiding. It began June 1, 1971. Knowing that I would be an early witness, I went to Minneapolis on June 7. I spend my time listening to the court testimony and having private briefing by counsel for H.

This being my first testimony in a federal court, I took it seriously. The total record associated with my presence on the witness stand was 1338 pages long. Of this, the major portion was material I have already covered here in describing the computer; one of the last parts related to the period when JWM was working for me at NOL, and I have covered that in my historical summary of the case.

It was late on Friday, June 25, 1971, and I was through testifying, after nine days on the witness stand. I took time to say goodbye to some of the staff including the court reporters who had stood by and given good copy in spite of technical words and low tones.

Then I looked over at the table for the defense and there was Ferrill, alone, picking up some papers. I do not like to be lacking in manners, and so I advanced with my hand extended to say goodbye to him. For the next few seconds, I felt that I was looked over in minute details. In the end, he reluctantly took my hand. He did not look happy: perhaps he knew better than I did the effects of my testimony.

After the trial ended, the judge took some time to reach his decision. The trial in the ENIAC case ended in March 13, 1972; it had taken 135 days or parts of days. A total of 77 witnesses were heard.

The total trial transcript was 20,667 pages.

Larson signed his decision on October 19, 1973. The decision should have received major coverage, but the press was occupied with other matters: October 20 was the date of the "Saturday Night Massacre" of Watergate fame.

The decision comprised 248 pages of legal-cap paper, with an appendix of 60-plus pages. The judge found 17 specific claims on the ENIAC patent invalid on a variety of grounds, including two claims taken to be representative of the subject matter derived from me by Mauchly and Eckert. He found the entire patent invalid on three grounds unrelated to inventorship: public use, on sale, and published disclosure, all more than one year prior to the ENIAC patent filing date of June 26, 1947. Of greater significance for the purposes of this paper, however, is the fact that he also found the entire patent invalid on the ground of derivation from my prior electronic digital computer.

After thus spelling out the conduct of Mauchly and Eckert in regard to me and my work, Larson presented the other side of the picture, including a lack of action by me, and found Honeywell not entitled to antitrust damages for wilful and intentional fraud on the Patent Office.

In addition to his finding on the derivation of the ENIAC from me, Larson now ruled that the Memory System Patent No. 2, 629, 827 at issue in the CDC case in Baltimore – was derived from me.

* * *

Everyone expected that Larson's decision would be appealed, but it was quickly settled by the payment of money and an agreement between the parties that each would support the judge's decision of 1973. I have been told that SR paid $3.5 million – sufficient to reimburse H for the cost of the trial. Thus ended this important case.

As to the Memory case in Baltimore, I acted as a witness in it after the intervention and after the ENIAC trial was over. The trial in that case was active for only a few days; then it was abandoned from lack of interest of principals or counsel. In 1981, nine years later, a federal judge insisted that the case be settled, and so it too was settled by a contractual agreement, this time between CDC and SR. I was told that SR made a payment of money here, but the amount and other terms were not disclosed. The matter was moot, because the patent had expired. I feel that institutions such as the law are imprecise; I do not know, however, how we can get along without them, and I was interested in how they worked.

THE PROTOTYPE AND THE COMPUTER

Nicolay Bonchev

The desktop model dated from October 1939, the first in history Automatic Electronic Digital Computer, could be seen reproduced at the Computer Museum in Marlboro not far from Boston, MA. In the rear of the drawing is a disk of insulating material that rotated on the slow shaft at about 60 revolutions per minute. On each face of the disk were 25 condensers (2). Using the historical term, we called each circle of condensers (partly filled) an abacus. The near portion corresponded to the keys of an ordinary calculator, and so we called that it the keyboard abacus (ka); the other set of condensers was related to the wheels, or counters, of the Monroe, and so we called that part the counter abacus (ca). Actually these are two identical memory devices for writing, reading in which a cell, that remembers a binary number, resembles a condenser with capacity 1,5 n F. The model has an 8-tube add/subtract mechanism (3), which with the aid of one carry-over condenser (4), adds/subtracts the two binary numbers, stored respectively in one "counter" and one "keyboard" condenser (2) on the disk. The number 25 meant that the prototype was designed to operate at 25 base-2 places, or the equivalent of 8 base-10 places. A memory regenerating circuit is also used (5), but no provision for "shifting" was made in the ABC. Atanasoff and Berry completed the "black box", initially designed in Illinois, with an electronic circuit, with set rules for addition and subtraction of binary numbers. That is why the logic circuit (fig. 4) chooses the correct answer (the sum or the difference) and with this result replaces the content of the respective discharge in the "counter" memory. This electronic switch (commutating element) in the black box is Atanasoff's biggest achievement. It clears the path for electronic computation.

The laboratory model – the prototype – is very simplified. Nevertheless it opened up before the two inventors, the possibility of receiving a funding for the design of a big electronic computer, which could solve systems of 29 linear algebraic equations with 29 unknowns. They received such a subsidy from the Scientific Research Corporation, after Atanasoff completes his famous Manuscript – a description of the computer. The prototype was, of course, a crude device. "Nevertheless, CEB and I regarded this machine as a great success. It settled many doubts about how an electronic computer should be built".

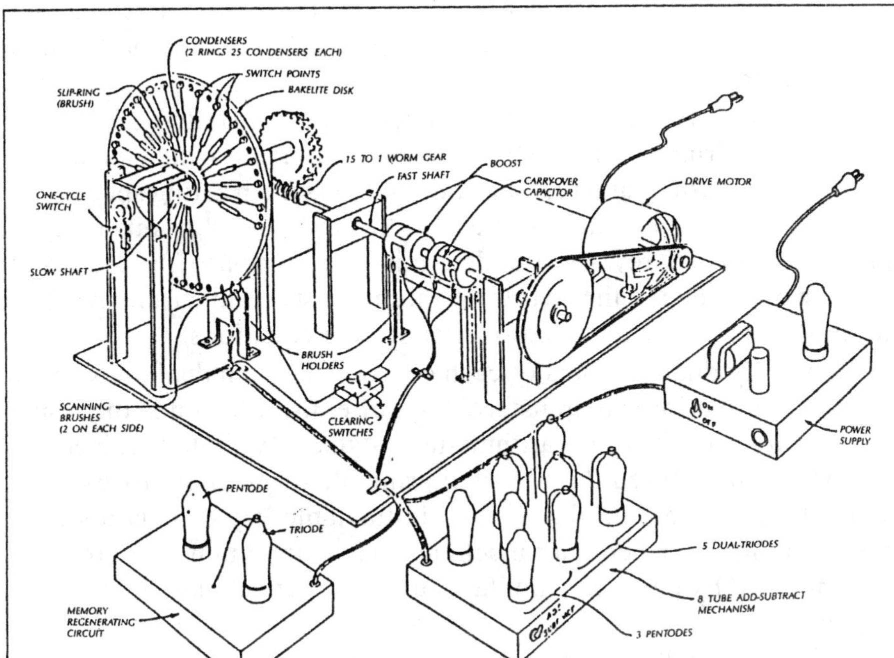

Fig. 1. Atanasoff digital computer prototype. (The operating model of the computer – 1939)
1 – memory disc (2 rings, 25 condensers each); **2** – slip ring (memory condenser); **3** – tube add – subtract mechanism; **4** – carry over/borrow capacitor (condenser); **5** – tube memory regenerating circuit; **6** – dual – triodes; **7** – pentodes; **8** – one – cycle switch; **9** – scanning (reading/writing) electric brushes (2 on each side); **10** – slow shaft; **11** – worm gear; **12** – fast shaft; **13** – drive motor; **14** – power supply; **15** – add – subtract switch; **16** – on – off switch

THE ABC COMPUTER

The Atanasoff–Berry computer was designed to solve systems linear algebraic equations with up to 29 equations including 29 unknowns. In the mid-nineteen thirties there were no Digital Electronic Computation Machines, thus the solution to such systems, required the use of electromechanical type table calculators. Gauss' method of elimination was widely accepted.

In this way the modification of the algorithm of Gauss' for consecutive elimination of the unknowns in a system linear algebraic equations set the pattern for ABC / fig. 2/. Two equally constructed memory drums 1 and 2 with 1500 small condensers each, situated on the inner side of the drums.

The contact terminals of the condensers are installed on the outer surface of the drums – these are the contact wafers on which the electric brushes for recording and reading slide. What is the rotating speed of the memory drums, which are installed, on the same axis? In this case, the selected speed of 1 rev/sec was determined by Atanasoff's decision to perforate on the dual punch cards the intermediate results from the elimination, i.e. the newly obtained smaller system equations.

The fifty dual numbers of each coefficient (each dual number carries 1 bit information) are transferred one after the other on to the respective discharges of the thirty arithmetical devices. With this project decision, Atanasoff refused the accepted principle of parallel processing of the numbers separate discharges and in the table key calculators of his time and in the punched-card machines the decimal numbers are added and subtracted by parallel /simultaneous/ arithmetical operation on their numbers.

Atanasoff called these abacuses i.e. the memory drums, respectively a counter abacus (ca) and keyboard abacus (ka). The counter abacus ca is drum 2 on fig.2 and the keyboard abacus ka is drum 1 on the same figure. For facility's sake, they are accepted in the same scheme as Arabic numbers. These two names are transferred automatically by the inventor from the decimal key table calculator to his own computer. These two names here do not correspond to the functions of the two abacuses, as little similarity of the analogous functions in the respective devices of the calculator exists.

Neither of them has anything in common with counters, or with keyboard. In fact, these are only two memory devices for recording and reading. In contrast to the memory of the other machines at that time,

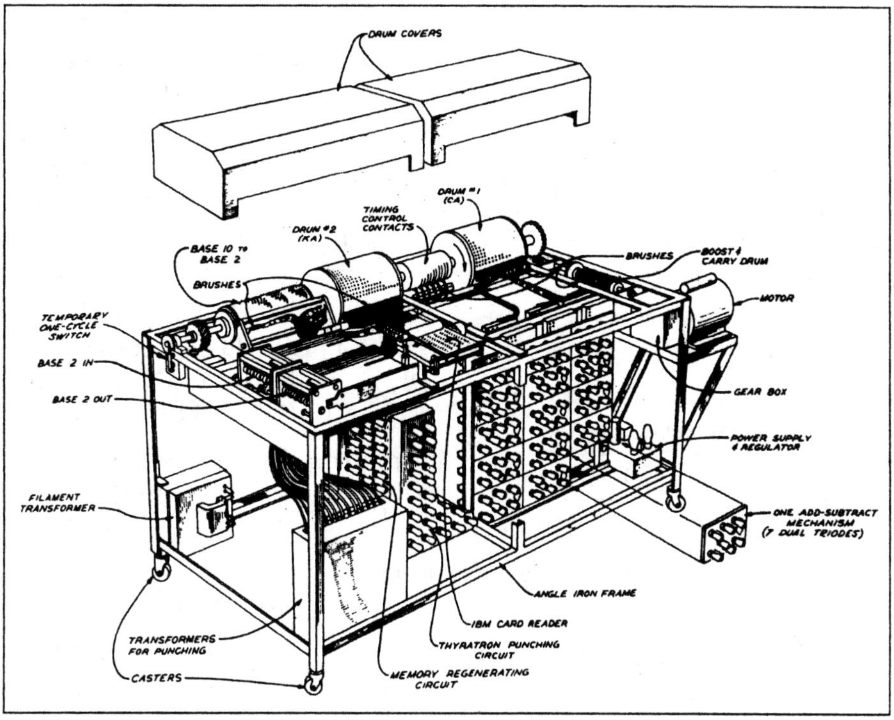

Fig. 2. Exterior of the ABC with the Roll covers removed.
1– memory drum ka; **2** – memory drum ca; **3** – logic device for adding/subtracting; **4** – transfer/taking drum; **5** – device for regenerating/displacing; **6** – device for reading of decimal punched cards; **7** – drum for modifying of the base of counting system (decimal–couple transducer); **8** – part of perforator for coupled [key] punch cards; **9** – electric part of the perforator for coupled punch cards; **10** – reading device for couple punch cards; **11**– power supply regulator; **12** – motor; **13** – timing control contact

these two devices only accept, store and transfer the numbers undergoing processing, but do not process them.

Why did Atanasoff change his intention of using the electronic controlling device and exchanged them with electro-mechanical ones? He has already devised elaborated keys, triggers and counters. If they are replaced with lamps, this will increase the cost many-fold, making them more expensive than the electric-mechanic control device. Besides, the constructive limitations of the machine (function capacity of this device is1/6 of the second) make high-speeding electronic control devices useless.

A series of peripheral devices are built into ABC. Inputting of data is achieved through a specially constructed device for reading of stan-

SIMPLIFIED BLOCK SCHEME OF THE ABC	READING AND RECORDING MEMORY	
Drum for modifying of the base of counting system (decimal-couple transducer)	Drum *ca.* 30 remembering ring-shaped tapes	Drum *ka.* 30 remembering ring-shaped tapes
Reading memory modifying drum for counting system	30 device for adding/subtracting and transfer/ borrowing roll	30 device for regenerating/ isplacing
Reading of coupled punch cards device	SYSTEM FOR REGENERATING OF THE MEMORY AND FOR ARITHMETICAL OPERATIONS	
Perforator for couple punch cards		
Dial-plate for decimal output	Synchronizing drum and organizers for controlling. Manual device for controlling.	

Fig.3. Common scheme of ABC

dard decimal punch cards 6 while for output, a special accumulator (accumulating sumator) is used. For inner transformation of the data from decimal to base – 2 form and it's reversal original electronic devices are constructed – for perforation 8 and reading10 of dual punch cards. Modification of the base of the number system is done by a special drum 7, together with adding/subtracting devices. Initially the 30 coefficient of the system's equations are modified from the decimal into the base – 2 system. Finally the two dual coefficient of each equation with one unknown have to be transferred into decimal system. To determine the unknown, Atanasoff had envisaged these two coefficients to be divided with a table electronic-mechanic calculator.

The dual device for inner processing of the data from the punch cards (with intermediate result) allows an elegant diagram solution of the machine to be achieved – coordinating (on a dual principle) between input-output, memory and arithmetical devices. This gives some undisputed advantages to the electric-mechanical version. For the solution of the system for the later one are needed 30 simultaneously perforations to be performed (30 parallel rows for punch cards with 50 consecutive columns).

The recording and the reading of the dual punch cards also becomes elegant. For synchronizing the frequency of supply voltage (60Hz) – the ignition of tiratrons in recording, and the breaking of the position in reading, occur during the peak values of the supply voltage. The solution, of course has its own shortcoming – in this way the work frequency of the machine is being restricted, and can not completely make use of the greater abilities for faster computation that the electronic arithmetical device allows. The electro-static memory drums could be made to rotate at a higher speed, as well, while preserving their reliability.

The Atanasoff's manuscript dated August 1940 contains the two electronic methods – for calculating and for recording (reading) of punch cards. The problems appeared in the summer of 1942 with the test trials of the machine for its basic purpose – solution of large system of linear algebraic equations. The test show 1 mistake to10 000 or 100 000 dual discharges on the punch cards. This, in effect means, that if the equations are more than three, the systems solutions are not reliable enough. The material (dielectric) appears to be the critical factor from which the punch cards are prepared. Unfortunately, the inventors have exhausted the material that gave them the best results, and their tests do not find the supply place. Both of them – Atanasoff and Berry, lack Edison's patience, to be able to try out thousands of materials, until they find the best one. They were short of time in their search for the optimal relation between the materials available and the peak voltages at which the perforation was obtained (by an electric discharge) of the dielectric, i.e. perforation of the dual punch card. The wartime conditions also contributed to the shortage of time and materials as the greater involvement with research on war-contracts limited the potential of the inventors. Summons for military service were sent to the scientists and were appointed to military labs. So, the Second World War forced Atanasoff and Berry to abandon their arduously created invention – the ABC.

The ABC surpassed three fold the speed of the most widespread calculator machines of its time. From today's point of view, this is not a major leap, but its revolutionary importance is fundamental. But it proved, that it was possible to perform automatic electronic digital calculations, while demonstrating successfully the capacity of the logical arithmetic devices, the electronic keys, the regeneration of memory, and a great many other essential principles of the computers of the future generations.

From the book **Джон Атанасов. Изобретателят на компютъра**

30 YEAR PATENT WAR

Nicolay Bonchev

The law suit for the patent of the ENIAC (Electronic Numerical Integrator and Computer – a universal (DECM), created in the University of Pennsylvania (1943–1945), could really pretend for a place in the Guinness Book of Records. Only the procedures in issuing the patent, preceding the law suit took the USA Patent Service Office 17 years. 157 witnesses were called for the lawsuits and their interrogation took another 6 year for the Federal Court in Minneapolis. The original appetites of the Philadelphia Company "Sperry Rand" to collect royalties from the possession of the basic patents of the whole computer industry were estimated to be several billion dollars. The documents, presented to the Court, could only be processed with the help of a computer, as the total number of documents and material evidences is 32,654, the number of pages amounts to 50,000, and only the records of the proceedings comprise 20,667 pages. The Testimony and deposition of the chief witness John Atanasoff are recorded on to 1338 pages. Another 76 witnesses testified, and from another 80 were taken affidavits during the preliminary period of the law suit.

Destiny gave John Atanasoff the opportunity – to prove his priority in one of the greatest innovations of the 20th century – the computer. And he brilliantly made use of this opportunity, as the predominating part of his 1338 page testimony describes with great accuracy the principles, constructions and action of the first computer in the world. This together with the great amount of factual material from the recorded proceeding and the evidence provided, represent an invaluable source material for research into the computing technologies. It is also, really an unprecedented case in the history of patent process. If this law suit had not been started, what would subsequent generations have learned about the real inventor? Virtually nothing. Only a few decades later, no eye-witnesses would be left, who could remember to tell us about the functioning of the computer ABC, dismantled and forgotten after the war – and mentioned only in three newspapers from the 1940-ies and three scientific technical books. The historical truth, about the developers of the modern computer, would be irrevocably lost. Atanasoff, himself until the lawsuit in 1967 – 1973 had not published anything about his computer, the ABC. Because of bad management, the State College of Iowa (later University) had not patented it.

Indeed, in August 1940 he described in 31 pages his project, whose most-important innovating principle had been tested by their prototype a year earlier. This document, manuscript, had great significance during the law suit, and is written as a report – a fundamental basis for his request from the management of the College to grant him an insignificant sum – several hundred dollars for the completion of his computer. The description, along with the enclosed photographs showing the finished electronic-tubes centers of the computer remained unpublished until 1973, when B. Randle published in London a collection of classic works on the pioneers in the computing technology. "Origins of Digital Computer Machines. Selected Works." But, we can't find any mention from the extensive detailed material collected as evidence for the trial, noting that the fundamental principals of the ENIAC computers were derived, and borrowed from the very first computer – the Atanasoff and Berry, ABC computer.

On 19.10.1973 when the Federal Court Judge, Earl Larson, announced in Minneapolis, Minnesota, his verdict, he actually put an end to a nearly 30 year patent war between the two giants of the American computer industry. It was a war for the right to manufacture computers, and respectively, to collect royalties derived by the basic patents in that field. The patent of the "innovation of the century", as is the ENIAK computer US Patent N3 120 606 sometimes called, was applied for by the electronic engineer Eckert and the physicist Mauchly in the Patent office as early as 26.06.1947. It was issued on 4.02.1964. The reasons for these astonishingly slow proceedings were due to the patent war, which the buyer of the patent, Sperry Rand waged in order to gain a dominant position on the market of the promising computer industry.

THE BACKGROUND

The first computer manufacturing company – Electronic Control Company was established by Mauchly and Eckert after they left the University of Pennsylvania and existed until 1947. It was then transformed into another smaller company – Eckert-Mauchly Computer Corporation.

Mauchly explains their business undertaking with their desire to overcome their financial difficulties, resulting from the development of the computers. In fact, Eckert – and "the electronic genius" Mauchly, were Vice-president of these companies and their Chief Engineer, whose technical ideas were always replaced with newer and better ones. As his collaborators share, that extremely capable "universal engineer", until recently the Chief Engineer of the ENIAC project, changed the constructive decision of the current project literally every second day: undoubtedly, that such an approach cost money, which the new businessmen could not afford. After refusal of the American Research and Development Corporation to grant them a loan, they found themselves nearly bankrupt, and offered their company for sale to the big companies in the field – IBM, National Cash Register (NCR), Remington Rand, Philko, Burrows, Hughes Aircraft and others. IBM was ready to appoint them to work, without buying their company, because, it would risk being sued for breaching the antitrust laws. Besides this, "the head" of that big company – Tomas Watson Senior – seems could not get rid of his prejudice, that DECMs have no future (that is why, ten years earlier he had refused to finance Atanasoff's work).

Only NCR and Remington Rand showed some interest in buying Eckert and Mauchly's company. They were so desperate at that time, that they sold it to the first company that offered fairly acceptable conditions.

At the beginning of 1950 Remington Rand bought them out. As a major corporation with a solid industrial position, it showed an interest in the fast developing computers, and apparently began receiving some commercial importance.

The Company American Totalizator, holding 40% of the share capital of Eckert-Mauchly Computer Corps, received $ 438,000; Eckert, Mauchly and other workers holding share capital of 6% were paid $ 100,000. Besides that both innovators were guaranteed an $ 18,000 annual salary for a period of 8 years. Their company would continue to function as a special department of Remington Rand. With the sale of the company Eckert and Mauchly, precluded further projects from their monopoly over the manufacturing of "the innovation of the century". In the memoirs of their collaborators they are “brilliant technicians and lecturers, but naive businessmen”. And, as the weekly Business Week noted, commenting on the Remington Rand transaction, only a few companies at that time would buy a computer like the UNIVAC it was mainly those working with massive quantities of numbers data or with sophisticated mathematical formulae.

If we look back, for a moment, at the beginning of the 1940-ies, this is what the young Atanasoff wrote in his letter to the Remington company: “I have made and I make some elaboration in the field of computing machines, which could be of interest to you, as they are related to tabulating machines. I think, that my elaboration will give a possibility of creating a computer, which will perform all operations of the standard tabulators and a large number of other operations with a much higher speed and at a lower construction cost.” Then, Remington makes a mistake by not assisting Atanasoff.

Ten years later (it proves, that this is a usual term for an innovation to receive recognition and large market share) Remington Rand does not repeat its “parental” mistake, i.e. the improvidence of its Remington predecessors. A representative of Remington Rand contacted, asking Atanasoff to submit his documentation to the company, but he refused. For the company as a buyer, making the deal is a “coup”. Indeed, that is a strategic move to controlling future multibillion-computer industry: Shortly after (1951) Remington Rand marketed the first ever serially manufactured computer – the UNIVAC 1. It is also the first computer, which can process both digital and alphabetic information. UNIVAC is a DECM with a program memory and consecutive action, it has an input device with magnetic tape and memory with mercury delaying lines.

At that time, in its glory days, the Chairman of the Board of Directors for Remington Rand is Gen. Douglas MacCarter. Given its market niche and the growth of the computers markets, in 1952, Remington Rand incorporated the Engineering Research Associates, which produced computers for scientific needs.

With the developing potential of its new acquisition, Remington Rand developed and marketed a new model series of UNIVAC.

In 1955 Remington Rand bought out Sperry Gyroscope, which became in turn, its department Sperry UNIVAC. Its founder (of Sperry Gyroscope Corp.) is the innovator of the autopilot, Elmer Sperry. It is said that his gyroscopic devices had no rivals until the onset of the airspace era. The “dowery” that Remington gave for the “marriage” between the two companies to Sperry Gyroscope, were the basic patents for the Remington Rand manufacture of computers (issued patent for regenerative memory and the application for ENIAC). At that time, and nearly 10 years before the ENIAC patent was issued, Sperry Rand continued attempts at collecting royalties from other manufacturers. But at that time, IBM emerged ahead of its rivals, by implementing new principles, knots and elements for the computers and thus increased their commercial market share. IBM had already left its rivals well behind in the mass production of computers by the mid of the 1950's when it produced the first semi-conductor DECM. The company's operations were on a scale incomparable to Sperry Rand. Until 1957 IBM, rarely sold any patents. But then IBM sold no computers either. The corporation leased them with the obligatory service and maintenance clause. IBM, fast developing and occupying the first place in the computer industry, was closely followed by Sperry Rand. The two companies, leaders in their industry started litigation dealing with the patent rights.

A.J.Etienne, IBM's patent attorney paid a visit to Atanasoff's Research and Development firm, called Ordnance Engineering Corporation, located at Rockville, of Maryland on June 15, 1954. As the subject of discussion dealt with patent Problems, Atanasoff brought in David Beecher – executive vice-president to the meeting. Years later, when the 1967–1973 litigation began, he had acquired an important future witness A.J.Etienne has declared straight all to Atanasoff, that if he agreed to help, IBM will make Mauchly and Eckert computer patent invalid. But Atanasoff hesitated, according to Beecher, who was surprised, because the chief executive officer always acted decisively. Atanasoff remembered that in 1943 believed Mauchly, when he informed him, that both Mauchly and Eckert had invented "a new method, different from yours". And now, more than a decade later, he found out that he has been duped, at best, at least regarding the patent for the regenerative memory, issued to Mauchly and Eckert in 1953.

Atanasoff was not aware of this patent. Etienne kept his promise to send it to him only within six days' time. Atanasoff was flattered by this meeting for the honor, rendered to him for his computer development. He replied to Etienne, that he would like to help him, but his time was entirely occupied running the company. He did not know where the computer archives were. Atanasoff began the search but as the allocated time was short, he could not locate them. Atanasoff promised to continue with the search. Someone could regard this as a failure on the part of

Alice and John V. Atanasoff are greeted according to the old Bulgarian custom, by offering of a special bread and salt, by the villagers of Boyadjik, December 1970

Alice and John Atanasoff moments from their visit to the family village Boyadjik, December 1970

Among the relatives
of the Atanasoff clan

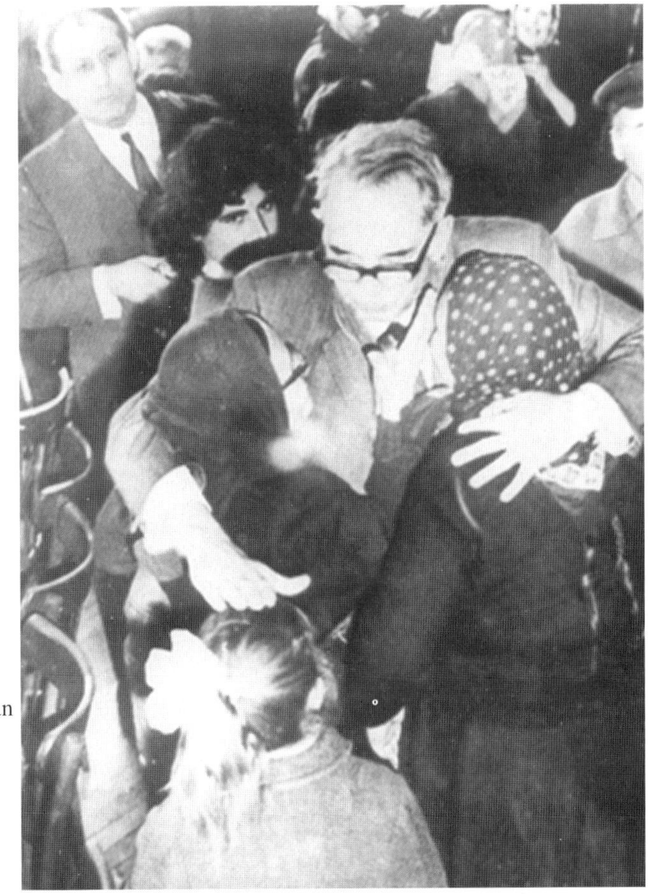

Six of the seven children born to Ivan and Iva Atanasoff,
along with the 88-year old Iva Atanasoff (Frederick, Marilyand, September 1969). Left to Right: Margaret, Avis, Iving, John Vincent, Theodor, and Ethelene-Zorka

John V. Atanasoff
with Bulgarian colleagues

Facsimile of the letter written by
John V. Atanasoff to the villagers
of Boyadjik, May 1985

George Jordanov awards John
Atanasoff with medal People's
Republic of Bulgaria, I[st] class
17 May 1985, Sofia

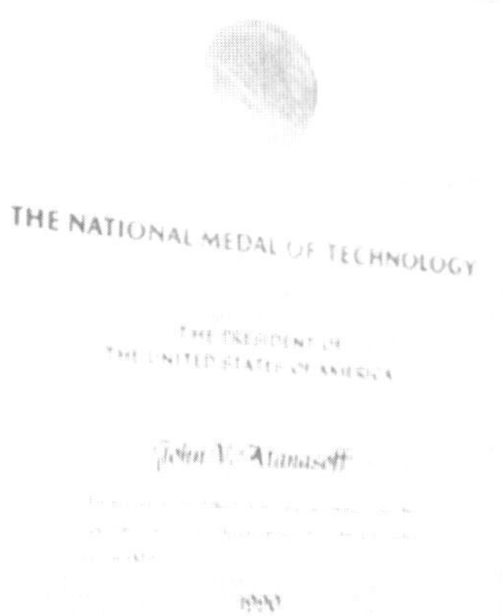

THE NATIONAL MEDAL OF TECHNOLOGY

THE PRESIDENT OF
THE UNITED STATES OF AMERICA

John V. Atanasoff

John V. Atanasoff receives an honorary medal
for Achievement in Science
from Acad. Blagovest Sendov, 1983, Iowa

1985 May 14

To the Library of Boadjik, Bulgaria for the people of that village

It commemorates the death of my grandfather, Atanas Ivanov; my father went to the USA in 1889 at the age of 13 with his uncle Constantine and was left alone at the age of 15. He graduated from Colgate University at Hamilton, N.Y. about 1900.

This record also commemorates two journeys made by John Vincent Atanasoff in Dec. 1970 and May 1985 to the town of Boadjik.

John Vincent Atanasoff

The inventor in his Maryland workshop - 1867

John V. Atanasoff with his famous invention

John V. Atanasoff and the rebuild breadboard of the Atanasoff-Berry Computer at the Digital Computer Museum in 1980

IBM to prove through Atanasoff's documentation the invalidity of the ENIAC patent – the small revenge of an inventor insulted by the company. Many years ago IBM had refused to help Atanasoff with the completion of the ABC, had it not? And even earlier, it had treated Atanasoff and his tests with the tabulators with suspicion. Or perhaps fate had played a part, by preventing him in helping IBM, but saving the documentation for later evidence, that would irrevocably prove his priority in the patent. Three years later, in 1957, some USA government circles were disturbed by the very real tendency shown by IBM in monopolizing the whole branch of the American computer industry. That is way the anti-trust authorities intervened in the law suit brought between Sperry Rand and IBM for patent rights. It is then, that both computer giants signed a confidential agreement for their technological merger (the so-called cross license agreement). Later, Atanasoff understood that the information regarding his computer, obtained by Etienne, had been used as a trump card by IBM, to compel Sperry Rand to agree to and sign the cross-license agreement. On the strength of this confidential agreement both companies exchanged their patents and patent applications. Thus IBM became obligated in the future, to continue to sell its patents and manufactured machines. The cross-license agreement made their law suit irrelevant.

IBM than filed another yet untenable claim against Sperry Rand, which was dropped by the court and the dispute was over.

During the ENIAC (1971–1973) litigation the confidential cross-license agreement became exposed, which made Judge Larson declare, that both companies have known it, all along, and that their legal action at that time have been simulative.

Mauchly had been questioned during the investigation. Some years later he complained to Atanasoff, that at that time IBM had paid Sperry Rand $ 7 millions as a compensation for the great value of the ENIAC patent application, which in the future would be jointly owned, while to the Department – Mauchly and Eckert's former company, Sperry Rand had given $500 thousand, instead of the promised $5 million.

As a result of the signed agreement IBM retained its leading position as an economic power in the USA computer industry. While second place in that peculiar "tandem" was held by Sperry Rand. Both companies held 95% of the USA computer industry. During the period of 1957 IBM has installed large computing machines for $ 200 million, while Sperry Rand – for $ 90 million.

At that time 68% of the powerful computers in USA, and 87% of medium powerful were manufactured by IBM. During the following year the total IBM manufacturers and laboratories came to one square million meters with 86,736 workers. During approximately the same period, Sperry Rand had a total of 100,646 employees in various countries. Its department, Remington Rand, at that time produced 30 % of all computing machines in the world. Every day, one DECM was manufactured. The company's sales in 1958 were about $ 864 million. Both companies began implementing, at the same time, triodes semi-conductors (transistors) in the computers and diodes instead of vacuum electronic tubes used in the first generation computers. Of course, IBM left behind all others in 1956 with all IBM 608 series, while Sperry Rand followed suit in 1960 with the models UCC of UNIVAC, working with punch-tapes peripheral devices.

In 1961 Sperry Rand concluded a similar agreement with Western Electric Company. Like the IBM confidential cross – licensing agreement, both companies were now obliged to share all their current know-how in the field of punch-card and electronic data processing. Other corporations emerged alongside the two leading corporations like General Electric, Burrows, NCR, RCA, Control Data Corp., Philco-Ford and Honeywell, that began manufacturing computers. As soon as Sperry Rand was granted the patent it established its own branch called Illinois Scientific Development (ISD) in order to sell the ENIAC patent rights. It was then that ISD began making demands that it be paid licensing fees by all made in computers manufacturers, contending that the ENIAC patent's rights spread over all electronic data processing devices, manufactured by Sperry Rand over the past 17 years, spanning from the date of the first application until the date of issuance of the patent. Honeywell countered that Sperry Rand should include, as part of the negotiations, a package of other interesting patents. Realizing, that following the issuance of the patent, IBM has paid to Sperry Rand only and additional $ 1.1million, the other computer manufacturers rejected Sperry Rand's demands (which were $ 250 million from Honeywell and $ 150 million from the remaining six manufacturers). Later, Sperry Rand "came-down" in its pretensions, requesting up to $ 20 million from Honeywell, which still countered that this did not correspond to the real value of the patent package. Inspite of every thing, Atanasoff should be grateful to the Sperry Rand action. If that company had not been this greedy, there would not have been any law-suit, and the inventor would not have received any official recognition. The adherents to Eckert and Mauchly, on occasion cite a legal verdict of 1962 given, on the instituted by Sperry Rand against Bell Telephone Laboratories, law suit. During the trial proceeding (which lasted less than a month), both companies contracted a "cross license agreement". As a result the defendant no longer had interest in declaring the ENIAC patent invalid.

Federal District Court Judge Larson reached this opinion in the subsequent trial.

Following the meeting with the patent attorney Etienne by the end of the 1950's patent attorneys from other companies also visited Atanasoff. In 1957 Henry Henson, the Datamatic attorney visited him. In 1959 he was cross-examined by two representatives of Sperry Rand. During the same year, Ch.Bradly from Burrows also came to visit him, and questioned him about his progress in the computing technologies.

"I found out, that Clifford Berry has also been interrogated by these and other teams" – writes Atanasoff in his memoirs.

Electric Digital System by R.K.Richards authored in 1966 is published, where he forwards information regarding the first DECM created by Atanasoff and Berry. The passage that subsequently played a major role in the trial, and served as the initial impetus for the process, recognized Atanasoff's priority, reads as following: "It seems, that the genealogy of all electronic digital systems begins with […] the computer of Atanasoff and Berry".

R.K.Richards, a childhood friend of Berry's, had studied at the State College of Iowa and had seen the ABC in 1941. He holds a Ph.D. from MIT and had worked several years for IBM. He is the author of more than 25 patented inventions, most of which are connected with the computer systems and is author to four books dealing with computer technology and its history.

In 1967 Richards published the books Electronic Digital Computers and Schemes and Elements and Schemes of Digital Computive Machines, in which he said: "It is considered, that the first use of digital electronic schemes in the so called computer or "digital system" has been matarialized in the computer of Atanasoff and Berry – 300-tubes machine for solution of systems linear algebraic equations, constructed at the State University of Iowa in the period 1939–1942". While writing the first of the forementioned books, Richards asked Atanasoff and Berry for information about the development of the computer. At the end of March 1963 Berry replied.

During the 1960's computer manufacture and implementation increased at a very fast rate. Thousands of computers were implemented in industrial enterprises, the government offices, airports, and also in the armed forces at the cost of hundreds billions dollars.

On 26.04.1967, Alen Kirkpatrick – a patent attorney for Control Data Corporation who had heard about the ABC from Richards' book, arrived from Washington to meet with Atanasoff. He informed the inventor, that Sperry Rand had began a claim against his company demanding compensation for breaching its patent rights on the bases of patent 827 dealing with the regenerating memory (applied for in 1947, and issued 6 years later – on 31.10.1953). The trial was to be held in the town of Baltimore, Maryland. Kirkpatrick arrived at Atanasoffs' with the proposal to have him become a consultant in connection with the law-suit. As a first step Atanasoff had to study patents, brought to him by Kirkpatrick, and to determine which of the Eckert and Mauchly's authors' pretensions referred to as computer knots were in fact developed initially by him for the ABC.

The Honeywell patent attorneys made a similar request of Atanasoff as did their trial lawyer. The latter dealt with the ISD – a Sperry Rand Subsidiary Honeywell Henry Halladay. It is about the other lawsuit – regarding the ENIAC patent, of the branch of Sperry Rand ISD versus Honeywell. The trial was instigated on 26 May, the same year in Minneapolis, Minnesota. According to the company in possession of the patent, the subject of the ENIAC patent is "invention of authomatic DECM". The patent itself, N 120606 of the USA is an enormous document with – the description of the separate knots of the machine and their action principles are spread over 232 columns of text, accompanied by 91 pages of drawings, and the author's claims are numbered in 148 points. The exceptional value of this patent is in its unique controls – the basic principles of computing with electronic digital devices. That's why in the claim against Honeywell through out in the court proceeding the following statement was made: "Today in the USA, not even one computer for processing of data of whatever importance [...] is being manufactured, without utilizing the inventions, subject of this patent.". The law-suit against Honeywell is instituted as an initial test of the Sperry Rand strategy one of the selection of a large manufacturer of computers for "a target practice ", prepared for the munificent "hunting" of hundreds of millions of dollars. In other words, this first law-suit is a test of efficacy for the scenario of the unprecedented by its volume operation ...

Atanasoff accepted the offer to become a Consultant to Control Data and Honeywell in their respective law-suits. "I am not a legal specialist – he said – inspite of the fact, that over the years I have devoted about 2000 hrs to studying patent law ... I had no idea the long period of studying, analysis and rehearsal in store, until completing the preparatory work for the ENIAC law-suit and began the proceeding of the trials, nor I have had in the past so good and qualified collaborators as those, which represented the interest of Control Data and Honeywell. The time, we spent together, has been strenuous up to the most and the lawyers often had right to be angry with me, and the reverse, but these were gentlemen of the highest probe".

THE ENIAC PRE-TRIAL PREPARATION

Initially for the ENIAC patent, two lawsuits were simultaneously instigated. One in Washington D.C. at the Federal District Court, District of Columbia, ISD brought a suit against Honeywell for compensation of the patent. The second, Honeywell court case began in Minneapolis at the Federal District Court, in the State of Minnesota, accusing Sperry Rand in breach of the Sherman anti-trust law, namely "For monopolizing of the industry for electronic processing of data through fraud and putting into effect an invalid patent". With the passing of this bill in 1890, the beginning of the antitrust legislation in USA was established. Its purpose was for the goverment to exercise control over the monopolization of an industry. While during the first decade of XX century after the Sherman Anti-Trust law came into effect, the Supreme Court of the USA had heard only several suits for its breach while during the second half of the twentieth century, violations of this kind had become something common.

In the first case, ISD as plaintiff, claimed Royalties over 17 pretentions from Honeywell (defendant) who is accused in violation of the ENIAC Patent. On 5.03.1968 for the the Federal District Court District of Columbia transferred the trial against Honeywell to the Federal District Court in Minneapolis. There on the 1-st of May, judge Nordby united it with the trial Honeywell had against Sperry Rand and ISD. Both sides claimed royalties.That was then to became John Atanasoff's trial!

In his corrected claim dated 01.05.1968 Honeywell expands its antitrust accusations by pointing out the agreement made between Sperry Rand and IBM for monopolizing the electronic data industry processing. In 1969, Honeywell submitted a second corrected brief regarding the 30A patents package of Sperry Rand, 25 of which are crucial. For instance, the regenerating memory, for the three consecutive dual summators and the BINAC and UNIVAK patents. Some of the patents were issued on Eckert's name, but most of them, – were issued jointly to Eckert and Mauchly's names. According to Honeywell, the obtainment of these patents is also a violation of the Sherman's anti-trust law.

Atanasoff had already studied the ENIAC patent and found that some of the basic author's pretentions were derived from his computer, the ABC. While contemplating over the patent, it became obvious, that the most worthy pretentions made in the ENIAC Patent, as far as he remembers, were included in the documentation of his computer, which a quarter of century earlier, he had discused with Mauchly on his visit to Ames. Which is why Atanasoff decided to clarify the whole matter regarding the contributions of the ABC. He was pushed towards this decision not so much by his personal ambition, but by the feeling for justice and especially in the memory of Berry.

Honeywell's attorneys were faced with an unimaginable complex and voluminous task – to study in detail, the scientific and technical essence of the ABC and of the ENIAC, as well as the related circumstances and facts, and they formulated aiming to prove that Mauchly has been acquainted with the construction and principles of the ABC operation, before beginning work on the development of the ENIAC together with Eckert and a large team of specialists. The actual events that had proceeded three decades earlier have to be reconstructed. Atanasoff mentioned in his memories: "It was soon clear to everyone, that these lawsuits would become monumental in computing-machine history and would take some years, before coming to trial".

Initially, Honeywell's attorneys – the plaintiff, acquired only one basic document – the description of the ABC in the Atanasoff's manuscript addressed to the board of the College of Iowa dated 1940. Subsequently, they were lucky in finding the patent application for the first computer, the ABC, prepared by Atanasoff and Berry. After studying these extremely well documented papers, the lawyers were convinced, that the ABC is a significant invention, preceding the ENIAC. But as to finding evidence that the ENIAC originated from the ABC, it is necessary to travel around the country, and as well as be separated from their families, for more than a year, during the time allocated for the pretrial hearings. They traced out all the available evidence of direct contacts that had taken place between Atanasoff and Mauchly, as well as contacted live witnesses of these meetings and demonstrations of the ABC.

They examinated the research and development materials to the construction of the ENIAC, University of Pennsylvania, and impartially compared the structure and functioning of this giant machine with the principles of its predecessor, namely the ABC. All this, in order, to prove not only their common features, but to prove as well, the direct derivation, made by Mauchly from the Atanasoff-Berry computer.

In executing these difficult tasks, Honeywell's defense very much depended on the co-operation of their consultant, John Atanasoff. And indeed, he helped a great deal with his documentation of the ABC acquainting the patent attorneys with its details. He prepared detailed descriptions of his machine for the legal proceedings and monitored the preparation of a set of drawings and schemes, as well as models to be used in for demonstrating the computer "in person" in the Court room. Atanasoff recalled the names of all people, that had been connected with the computer project at Iowa – quite a difficult task, as decades had since passed, and some of the most important witnesses, like Clifford Berry had in the interim passed away...

Atanasoff remembers, that during the time of his testimony in Court, the lawyers to whom he was a Consultant, had not protested to any of his answers. But the testimony provided by the second in importance witness, – namely Mauchly, are contradictory. That has already been ascertained at the time when he testified before the depositions.

According to the American legal procedure the so called testimony under oath as deposition is a legal procedure, during which the witness is examined and crossexamined by the lawyers of both sides, in the presence of one or more court reporters, but without the presence of the judge. Very often this procedure, called depository is necessary in the initial stages of a legal process, in order to determine and preserve the testimony of witnesses that could not be heard at the trial, and to provide the lawyers with the subject matter about the testimony that will follow at the hearing of the trial itself. Every single evidence during the time of trial is with equally evidential power, just like the testimony of the regenerating memory witnesses present in Baltimore. The defendant of this trial – Control Data Corporation has also invited Atanasoff to testify, but it was very brief. Kirkpatrick, Honeywell's lawyer, had summoned the Mauchly depository from 11 to 13.10.1967. The proceedings of his testimony comprises 33 pages! The defense counsel, Kirkpatrick's purpose was to determine to what extent patent 827 for the regenerative memory is related to the development of the Atanasoff and Berry memory device for the ABC.

His questions were directed especially to the so-called principle of regeneration (or refreshing) of the memory, implemented for the first time in the computive technology by Atanasoff himself.

During the second day, Mauchly answered Kirkpatrick's questions, while Dodds objected from time to time. Mauchly stated, that inspite of the cordial reception, that he was given at Ames, nobody had wished to reveal to him all the information about the machine. Its operation had not been demonstrated to him. Mauchly insisted, that only the electric motor of the computer worked. He has seen a cylinder with condensors and understood, that the memory stores its contents, due to regeneration, but the principle of operation had not been explained to him.

All these statements were refuted from the testimony under oath of the two witnesses to his long experiments with the computer – Lura Atanasoff (John Atanasoff's first wife) and Samuel Legvold – a post-graduate, who at that time was working in the adjoining room. Berry's letter to Richards dated 1963, also served evidence at the lawsuit. The testimony stated that Mauchly had spent a week (and not an hour and a half, as he maintained) in studying all the details of the computer and the concept of its project. Atanasoff's clear memories and Legvold conformation of the events indicated, that at that time Mauchly was given all details of the project. A full working model of the computer had been demonstrated in front of Mauchly. Mauchly had taken his coat off, in order to work a whole 16 hours with the machine. He had also taken some notes, but he considered them as insufficient. Atanasoff remembered, testifying in court: "He asked, if he can take to Philadelphia (one copy) of the Manuscript, written in August 1940, holding it in his arms, but I refused, and he wrote down a lot of things from it". Contradicting all witnesses Mauchly stated, that at Ames, he had not taken any notes. Iva Atanasoff testified that at the time of his one-week visit Mauchly and Atanasoff had held discussions about the computer at home, even during meals.

Mauchly's testimony contradicted not only other witnesses' testimony – they were at variance with his own, he maintained. On one hand, he testifies to the availability of the regenerative principle in the memory of the ABC and maintains, that he has not made a patent application that could prevent Atanasoff from using this principle while in fact, patent 827 contains author pretention for exactly the same principle. At another point of his testimony Mauchly says, that he and Eckert had used this principle in the EDVAC and BINAC computers.

Again, in contradiction with the other witnesses, Mauchly maintains, that some electronic lamps had been seen, but their action was also not explained to him. They had told him only that the machine worked with numbers in the binary numerical system. Instead of discussions of the ABC, the larger part of the time during his visit to Atanasoff, they allegedly spent talking about his – Mauchly's, analog analyser and about the harmonic (sinus) components of the oscillations, also called the Furie analysing device. It later became clear, in court, that this analog apparatus was not an original construction of Mauchly's, but a reproduced one, from a literary description.

Until 1967 Atanasoff considered the jurisprudence to be an inaccurate science. But having been involved as a witness in the legal patent disputes, again (and not for a first time) he showed a distinguished feature – his striving to always penetrate deeply in the matter. He did not tolerate the position of an amateur, who used some specialists as middlemen. Just as during the last decade before his retirement – as a businessman, he himself learned the details of accountancy to such an extent in short stance, that he provoked the delight of the experts, auditing the company, which he had offered for sale. He, himself, studied patent law. That's why in 1967, although the labyrinths and paragraphs of the American patent law seem to him very annoying, Atanasoff concentrated and succeeded in understanding the juridicial details of the complicated patent lawsuits. And what is more he, having been deprived by his University 25 years earlier, summoned the courage for something that no one, not even he himself, did not even imagine until then. Understanding, that Mauchly had construed a great injustice toward him, Atanasoff entered the role, similar to that of "Gulliver against the giants" – he made the unbelievable transformation from a witness to a plaintiff.

The idea to become plaintiff came to him in January 1968 in Chicago, when he sat with Honeywell's lawyers, for the preparation of their trial versus Sperry Rand. Atanasoff answered the endless questions posed by the lawyer Henry Halladay. The other Honeywell lawyers, Alegretti and Call are also there. At the legal discussion, Atanasoff felt as if he had found himself in another, strange, world. But following a half an hour break, and Atanasoff rid himself of depression. His thoughts were freed, his mind began scrutinizing all sides of the juridical situation... and then an idea was born, that the witness, could become a claimant in the legal disputes and institute an additional trial to the already started lawsuits! Atanasoff overcame his feeling of inconvenience and that very hour he expressed his pretensions before the lawyers. It was as if a bomb had exploded in the cabinet. The three lawyers looked at him dumbfounded. After a pause, they recovered from the surprise, asking him to leave them alone in order to consult each other. Some minutes later, they told him about their decision: "We ask you to forget everything we have told you, we should tell you nothing. We cannot act as your lawyers, you have to use your own head!" Indeed, over several years they had carefully built their strategy and tactics in an exceptionally complicated and unprecedented in scale and importance legal situation and they could by no means afford to destroy all that was so strenuously built, only because an ordinary witness has decided to "shuffle the cards". And despite their well-meaning, for, Honeywell's lawyers refused to give Atanasoff advice, which he needed so much. Who but the State University of Iowa could help him, whose board had regreted harming the inventor in 1940? The significant financial benefits, which the University itself could receive, were also not to be neglected, despite the enormous legal expenses. The inventor suggested they think over a new contract – sharing the amount, allocated after winning the case, with which he will demand through the court to be recognized as a co-author of the invention of ENIAC (Atanasoff undertook this move considering this a safer way for succeeding, than hoping that federal courts will gladly rule invalid the ENIAC patent, only because Mauchly and Eckert had eliminated him as a co-author). Early the next day, he found himself in Iowa. At first, the University's board doubted, that the inventor of the ABC could defend his rights, but the lawyer defending the University's interests were convinced in the irrefutability of his evidences and recommended to proceed with the case. Atanasoff feared, that his case would be given to a State Judge. That would mean the case will fall under the jurisdiction of the Supreme Court, and knowing, "the speed" with which they proceed there, he might not live to see the final verdict. Luckily for him, the University decided to authorize its scientific research foundation to proceed with the case for the ABC's patent rights. The lawyer of the foundation tried to avoid taking any risk with huge expenditure for legal fee and that is why they rejected Atanasoff's proposal to indulge in the lawsuit for the basic ENIAC patent. Instead, in order to reduce expenses, they decided that foundation would join the smaller, Baltimore based lawsuit, which dealt with the regeneration device.

And so, at last the application for joining the legal dispute in Baltimore was filed. Judge Watkins gave the foundation permission to participate in the lawsuit on 24.08.1968 but only for "particular decisions". The lawyer appealed this restriction to the Court in Richmond, Virginia. This court allowed the foundation and Atanasoff to state their case in the Baltimore lawsuit. But there, the foundation stingily did not hire lawyers, as judge Watkins had suggested and decided to withdraw from the Baltimore case. Its Iowa board ventured to join the promising Minneapolis lawsuit, but it was already too late. The Sperry Rand Corp. rightfully objected and judge Larson rejected the application. The deadline was missed. For a second time, in the history of the first computer the State University of Iowa, because of hesitation and indecisiveness, had harmed Atanasoff as well as itself. Financially the balance was also negative. The foundation has lost for court procedures about $40,000 while the inventor, $8,000.

THE COMPUTER ASSISTS JUSTICE

Before Judge Earl R. Larson had begun the trial hearing on 01.06.1971 in the Federal Court of Minneapolis, Honeywell's lawyers, Dennis Allegretti and Charles Call, had computerized the whole information, gathered through the four years of preliminary research on the lawsuit. The huge mass of data was processed with electronic means, thus making it readily available, coordinated and generalized for fast and convenient use at a certain moment of the court sittings.

It might be interesting to learn how Honeywell's lawyers had managed to organize the thousands of documents and other Court exhibits. It would have been impossible without the use of a computer which enable the creation and maintaining up to date various lists for verification.

The plaintiff's computerized legal file consisted of a list that had "only" 4500 pages and was composed of "evidential statements". These statements were usually accompanied by the following information:

1) Plaintiff's reply (objection), which often disputed the validity and the importance of the statement (or both of them).

2) Claimant's comments on that objection.

3) Additional, much more detailed argumentation of the claimant with extensive referred to witness's testimonies and exhibits.

4) The claimant's response to additional arguments.

5) Last arguments of the defendant – also very detailed.

6) List of exhibits of the claimant with a short description of their contents together with a reference to the number of all pages of the proceedings of the lawsuit, where that evidence is mentioned.

7) Summary of the evidences of a witness from the claimant's side, in support of the mentioned statement, again with a respective reference page in the proceedings.

It was in this manner, that the pertinent information was electronically processed and ordained, grouping into clusters the situations the proceeding of the legal dispute. Other simply constructed indexes were the result of the tedious legal process of the computerized summarizing and analysis, which the lawyers had to undertake. One such example is the main KWIC (key-word-in-context) index. It shows every appearance of a given key word in the text or group of texts together with the surroundings of the word. The documents' summaries – plaintiff's sources (7500 pages) and the number of smaller versions of KWIC indexes, made for the summaries of the witness's testimonies, and the description of each exhibit for the lawsuit is also shown on the same basis. Computerized lists of the exhibits were also created, in alphabetical order, sorted by different criteria, which together with more than 150 000 pages of the court proceedings today, are placed in 200 microfiches.

At the beginning of June, Atanasoff was already in Minneapolis, expecting his turn to testify and listening to the interrogations of the other witnesses. He, had to as well, study the lawyers' private files, created by Honeywell's lawyers. To support its case, the company has also hired some experts from the Philadelphia Consultancy Company in the computer field – Auerbach Associates. Nevertheless, Call's ability to understand not only the intricate legal cases, but also, the details of the complicated scientific matter was of invaluable importance.

DIRECT EXAMINATION OF THE WITNESS ATANASOFF

The testimony provided by John Atanasoff in the courtroom began on 17.06.1971. The concept "directed examination" in the American legal system refers to the examination conducted by the Plaintiff. Already 700 pages from the proceedings of the ENIAC trial, comprise records of the direct examination of the witness Atanasoff, conducted by the lawyer Henry Halladay, at the time of the court proceeding, Honeywell' was assisted by another lawyer, Charles Call. But the task of Honeywell's defense was incomparably more difficult than the task of the opposition as side, as it has to prove its central thesis, that the basic principles on which ENIAC was constructed were obtained from the ABC. After several months of argumentation, and attempt at refuting this thesis, Mauchly, Sperry Rand's witness was powerless in fighting the foregoing thesis, became confused and contradicted himself numerously during his testimony. As the ancient writer Apooley says, "it is possible to blame an innocent, but to expose – only the guilty".

The main witness of the plaintiff namely John Atanasoff, was convincing in his defense of Honeywell's thesis. The investigations of the proceedings of the litigation indicate, that with his professional competence, punctual and clear explanations and demonstrations of the stages of his former elaboration, professor Atanasoff passed brilliantly the most important test of his life. The good systemization of information, which was made possible with the use of the computer, proved to be invaluable assistance to Halladay.

To prove Atanasoff's competence, the lawyer presented before the court, the educational background of the witness, and ending up with his Ph.D. in theoretical physics (1930). For example, after presenting documentation of the research conducted by Atanasoff, Halladay asked him to explain to the court an aspect of his master's thesis on mathematics, aquired in 1926, namely – the principle of Clausious. In a laconic, but in an easily understandable language, John Atanasoff explained to the court the concept in question with the help of visual aids. The witness underlined that the mathematical equations are models, which can successfully replicate and explore the processes in the real world. As an example, he poited out, by means of mathematical expressions how the growth curve of a bacterial culture can be analyzed.

In the same clear and concise manner, Atanasoff described his research dealing with the physical phenomena of the quartz crystals. Despite protest by Sperry Rand's defense, Halladay succeeded in having the court make note of the long list of research and research manuscripts, undertaken by John Atanasoff as part of the proceedings in the testimony. The court accepted the list as a proof of the theoretical depth, to which the witness had mastered the art of these sciences. Halladay did all he could to prove Atanasoff's expertise as a distinguished specialist in the field of applied research. Consequently, he thoroughly interrogated

Atanasoff on his direct examination on the construction device for monitoring of the anti-aircraft artillery, developed in Iowa. Halladay questioned in detail about the scientific tests that Atanasoff conducted during the two atomic explosions, exploded in the Bikini atoll (Marian islands in the Pacific Ocean) in 1946. It was pointed out in court, that the seismic monitoring following the explosion of the German depository for explosives in the island of Helgoland, carried out in Europe, lay the foundation of the remote detection of atomic explosions.

Halladay in the direct examination proceeding raised the issue of the nine groups of equations from various aspects of physics, which during the 1930-ies spurred Atanasoff to explore the construction of a principally new computer.

The opposing lawyer, Ferrill, tried to trip the witness into stating that his ride to Illinois, during which the general concept of the future computer has crystallized in his mind,had taken place during the winter of 1938 and not during the winter of 1937. But Atanasoff did not hesitate, remaining constant on this point. First, he testified that was absolutely sure, that he had thought over the new computer as far as 1935 – 1936 while developing other devices. And secondly, the practical result of the decision made at the end of 1937 resulted in his applications to the College requesting a grant required for the development of the logical schemes for the addition/subtraction devices. Halladay supported Atanasoff's testimony by providing an exhibit namely Atanasoff's letter dated 10.07.1940 to the President of Research Corporation, with request for allocating a sum of $5 thousand. Here, the inventor writes, that he had started exploring the possibility of a mechanized solution of system linear algebraic equations "seven (7) years ago".

Here is what he confessed later: "I did not keep a diary. But I knew how much time I had spent in designing the logical scheme for calculating and to clear my mind about the remaining knots of the machine, before being ready to ask for a financial assistance. But Ferrill underestimated the difficulty of this hole process" in the mid of 1933, and that "three (3) years ago" (i.e. in the mid of 1937), the ideas arose as he would say later: "They gave me the possibility to design a calculating mechanism".

Atanasoff remembers very clearly the circumstances in which he and Berry created the so-called "prototype", i.e. the laboratory model of the new computer, composed of the most important knots. The first time

Atanasoff explained, its construction took place under the direct examination, conducted by Halladay: "I was constantly worried if a vacuum electronic tube could be installed in a computer, to do calculations, so, our first effort was in that direction. I had already elaborated on the drawings of the logical scheme, when Berry started working with me, and we immediately assembled the experimental model, that would help us evaluate the problems and convince ourselves, that the vacuum electronic tubes in a computer were not castles in the air."

With the help of a large visual aid, a drawing of the model, made according to the instruction given by Atanasoff and the counsel Call, Atanasoff scrutinized each of its details, and described its operation of addition/subtraction. The work of the model was demonstrated in front of trusted people, invited to the Physics Department building. One of them was Samuel Legvold, who at that time (the autumn of 1939) was working with Atanasoff on the project of anti-air missiles monitoring device.

"It was the end of 1939 – November or December, when the model took its shape, shown at the drawing […], it worked for some time in November and performed the functions it was intended to […], Atanasoff testifies. Legvold also testifies, that "in October or November 1939 he has seen the model at work".

Afterwards during the hearing Atanasoff demonstrated to the court, how the ABC worked. More specifically he demonstrated now the regeneration of memory materialized, and also the shifting of the numbers in the memory so that the arithmetical operations of multiplication and division could be performed; and how the computer solved systems of linear algebraic equations. Explaining how the logic system worked was the hardest part of the elaboration. There were many successive steps in the process, and an error, in one part, would make the whole explanation invalid – says Atanasoff. By means of charts, illustrated with colored stickers, he succeeded in explaining, in simple words, the work of the very first electronic computing machine. He had prepared a full electronic demonstration of how the various elements of the logic systems worked, guided by the original manuscript dating from August 1940. The original electronic tubes were used in this reconstruction. For convenience and the facilitation of the demonstration, a contemporary device for power supply, was used.

CROSS-EXAMINING ATANASOFF

The cross-examination was conducted by Tomas Ferrill. Atanasoff's impression was that he is a very able attorney, who must have had some experience in the field of computing or electronics, who has as well minutely studied the history of the witness. A highly competent scientific assistant further aided Ferrill. This assistant never said a word, but passed notes to his boss on any error Atanasoff made. Atanasoff wrote of those days: "I remember the most traumatizing events in my life and though this cross-examination does not have a lead position, however it is surely on that list. Most of the questions asked at this cross – examination which took four days, of course, were not of a great importance, but the hurt caused by some of them, and the banality of others was such, that even rereading of the copy (from the proceeding) necessary for the writing of this article, has moved me very strongly." The situation, in which Atanasoff was placed, could not be considered comfortable. First, because he had no advanced knowledge exactly what question would be asked – Atanasoff had only the most general idea about the nature of the cross-examination. And second, by the backache he suffered partly due to the witness chair, but partly as early warning symptoms of the spinal vertebral disease, which he later successfully cured through surgery, but which at that time was made bearable by liberal doses of codeine. Thus the cross-examination conducted by the Sperry Rand's lawyers. Atanasoff was harassed hours on end with the conclusions drawn from his answers to insignificant questions, like the details from the time when he was working in NOL. Or, for example, with whom, when and where he had had lunch. Not until later would Atanasoff understand, that these tactics were intended to create confusion in the witness. The questions used and the details that the counsellor provided, were extracted from the diary of one of his subordinates who had worked at that time in the laboratory. It is not difficult to guess how Dodds got a hold of this diary, keeping in mind that at that time Mauchly had maintained some secret contacts with Atanasoff's staff from the laboratory, and had even made preparations to transfer some of Atanasoff's lab assistants to work with him.

Perhaps the most emotionally difficult question for Atanasoff arose when Ferrill questioned how he had got along with Prof. Warren Weaver, who on an occasion had made a negative remark pertaining to him, and when that statement had become known to the court. Atanasoff explained, that he knew the professor from the time, when he was preparing his thesis at the University of Wisconsin, where Weaver has been one of the senior members of the faculty. He also remembered the highly responsible position held by Weaver during the early 40's on the governmental committee, monitoring and coordinating scientific research of the military contracts. At that time Atanasoff had worked under a military contract at the State College of Iowa. In fact, that project dealt with the development of the firing of anti-aircraft artillery. Through the recruitment of mathematicians for those projects, Weaver had ensured many battle victories in the air, on land and in the sea. As an example of their research was the conducting of statistical analysis in correcting the direction of the anti-aircraft firing against a swooping bomber. One other example of the successful research dealt with the Japanese ship carriers when torpedoed. The research groups dealing with these operations exploring the problem solved it by creating "flexible firing". It became especially important in the defense of the bombers for "flexible shooting".

Atanasoff had joined that project, together with his work on the ABC, and the other obligations in the college, as the Second World War was raging. It was expected that USA will soon join. During the proceeding, Atanasoff succeeded in convincing the court, that his relationship with Weaver was not of significant importance to the legal dispute. Recently, he had even received a cordial letter from Weaver. Here is what Atanasoff remembers several decades later, "Yes, Weaver was a great man, but I could remember the time when he sat in a chair in a classroom in the Physics Department, sobbing that no one felt his ideas important, while I was telling him that we all honored him greatly".

During his pleading, Halladay tried to point out Atanasoff's positive qualities. While the lawyer Ferrill, on the contrary, directed his efforts to challenging those qualities. To the great displeasure of the opposing party, Atanasoff's behavior under oath served as additional evidence that would gradually confirm judge Larson's understanding of the veracity of his testimony.

One of Ferrill's strategic aims was to cast suspicion on the reliability of Atanasoff's memories. Despite his attempts at inducing confusion, with the use of a large number of questions dealing with details events and occurrences dealing decades, Atanasoff astonished the court room by his excellent memory. In his childhood memories everything connected with mathematics and techniques had engraved themselves on his memory. He spoke of the Dietzgen slide-ruler given him by his father, supplied with a valuable application – a logarithmic table. So, that he had been introduced in his early years to an analog computing device introducing him the marvelous and interesting world of calculations. He remembered when electricity had entered his home. How he, the young boy, had installed the electrical wiring of the house... His first two books from England on radio technology and radiotelephony were also unforgettable. Even now, before his eyes emerge the black numbers of their price in pounds sterling printed on the light-green covers...During his cross-examination, Atanasoff gave further evidence about his early studies on mathematics as a self-education. He shared that, in contrast to languages, which did not come naturally to him. He had always had high marks on physics and mathematics in school.

It was not difficult to discern the motives, which made Ferrill question the essence of the model and its date, i.e. the time when it had started operating. These questions directly affected the dispute, namely, who had invented the first DECM. Atanasoff succeeded immediately in discovering all doubts that it was possible to construct an operating model in a time span of two or three months by testifying, that he has developed the "mechanism of adding and subtracting" as early as the spring of 1939. That's why the model was constructed that fast and successfully by that November, when faultless and accurate functioning had been demonstrated before the College officials.

Then Ferrill tried to refute the dating given by Atanasoff, by moving it three months later and by presenting a quotation from the Manuscript of 1940, in which Atanasoff wrotes: "An experimental assembling of an abacus and mechanism for adding and subtracting and alternator was made in January 1940. The device had worked perfectly and held promise in performing real experiments of different components under working conditions".

For same time he yielded to Ferrill's suggestion and was ready to confess "his mistake", but Halladay paid attention and pointed out, that the word "alternator" was the key to eliminating that misunderstanding. This word suggests, that it does not refer to the elementary arithmetical operations, as the experiments in November, but to experimenting the combined work of the arithmetical device, the memory and some other devices. Atanasoff recalled, that "the alternator has been in fact a contact appliance", additionally designed by Berry for "input of numbers in the machine, while was rotating". He reproduced before the court the device and the action of the appliance. Halladay finally "defeated" Ferrill in that dispute by presenting written evidence – a dated letter written by Atanasoff to the company manufacturing the condensers used in the model.

Feeling, his efforts in questioning the witness' testimony were in vain, Ferrill attempted at "catching any straw at all". For example, he began his cross-examination with such insignificant questions like what material is used for the contact buds on the outer surface of the memory drums. This refers to the electric outputs from the memory condensers, installed in the interior of the drums. Atanasoff remembers clearly, that these had been pieces of metal rods flattened out at both ends. Ferrill took a whole day (100 pages proceeding) insisting, that the buds were made of small brass tubes, in "support" of which showed an invoice for the delivery of such small tubes. Atanasoff replied that those tubes had been slated for other details, they were to be used as brush holders. By the way, the subject of the dispute itself was located in the court, the only preserved knot of the ABC – a roll with memory condensers. That's why Atanasoff suggested to simply take a bud out and to examine it. Then, the question arose as whether the owner of the drum would not eventually object. The situation was used by Ferrill to forward a "new confusing" question, whether anybody had tried to construct a computer with the same drum, or at least, had intended to do so. Atanasoff categorically rejected the existence of such a fact. Nothing remained for Ferrill except to renew the dispute with the material of the contact buds. Atanasoff even remembered, that the material of the rods, from which the buds were manufactured consisted of a hard zinc alloy. The provision of the material evidence followed suit. At the time of second direct interrogation, Halladay presented as evidence the document mentioned by Atanasoff, dated five months prior to the supply end delivery of the small brass tubes. This document contained both the rods and the matrix for forming the ends of the contact buds as well, which had been developed in the mechanical workshop of the College. That is how, the "storm in a tea cup" blown up by Ferrill ended. At the end of that court sitting, Atanasoff in detail and understandable manner reveals the stages involved in the construction of the memorizing drums.

Ferrill even resorted to inadmissible scientific technical sophisms, in order to refute the Atanasoff' authorship regarding the electronic performance of the computations of the ABC. Describing the construction and the way of action of the machine Atanasoff says, that all its calculations are performed electronically, although the tack generator is a mechanical one. At this time Ferrill immediately made the questionable conclusion, that the ABC is a mechanical calculator, and continued to maintain it "ad infinitum".

But, as David Beecher – a former student and an Atanasoff colleague successfuly pointed out later, that if we view things in this manner, a large number of contemporary electronic devices would be ranked to the mechanical ones, only because the stability of their working frequency is maintained by the high frequency of the mechanical oscillating of a quartz crystal. Ferrill spent an entire day cross-examining Atanasoff regarding the algorithm by which the ABC would solve the system of five linear algebraic equations with five unknowns. And the witness very accurately, step by step "works through" this algoritm, writing on the large scheme of the ABC and the magnified electronic-lamp scheme of the 1940 Manuscript, in which the principles of operation of the central devices of the computer are exposed. Atanasoff played a leading role in that "scientific spectacle". Of course, from time to time he used other schemes and photos of the basic knots of the machine, and with the authentic memory drum, as well.

Analyzing the whole operation of the machine on the algorithm, Atanasoff allowed only one mistake – in the morning sitting he said, that the add-subtract mechanisms, perform the second of these operations, using some supplement to the numbers. In the afternoon he corrected himself, indicating that these devices subtract, by "borrowing". When in some minor details of the description he could not exactly remember how it was really done, he gave several possible alternatives.

Ferrill's insistence on using the five equations and five unknowns as an example during the cross-examination he succeeded in showing, that the speed of computation with the ABC (Atanasoff-Berry) computer was not hundred times higher than that of the current tabulator (mechanical) calculator, as maintained by the witness. Atanasoff objects, that the machine is more effective in solving a system with greater number of unknowns, for which indeed it had been designed. Then Ferrill concentrates his "fire" on the speed of the add-subtract mechanism. Earlier, at the time of the direct examination, Atanasoff demonstrated, through an operating model the work of that exceptionally important knot of the machine. The description, he makes of that knot, comprises 56 pages of the proceedings! Now, during the cross-examination by the defence, he examines the principles of its operation with the help of an expanded figure from his Manuscript. Ferrill's aim was to prove, first, that the speed of ABC was quite slow for a Digital Electronic Computation Machine and, secondly, that Atanasoff was wrong in the quantitative estimation of the speed of the add-subtract mechanism, which he gave during the direct interrogation, saying that this device uses for processing from input to output "only a few 1/millionth" of a second, or "one 1/millionth' or "half/millionth' of a second". In the beginning Ferrill asked, if the entire computer possessed such fast action (about one microsecond). Atanasoff replied, that he has not analyzed the speed of the scheme. A little earlier Ferrill has asked suddenly a particularly provoking question – if the witness has at any time designed a Digital Electronic Computation Machine. Atanasoff used this opportunity to stress upon the fact, that although the ABC was for a special purpose, it could be used for other purposes as well.

Ferrill insisted for the witness to calculate, once again, the speed of the add-subtract mechanism. After a number of calculations, it was shown that the real working time of the device is about 25 msec. Atanasoff explained, that he had not made any similar evaluations of the speed at that time, because the processing of the remaining knots of the machine was much slower. "I made numerous tests to find a direct and easily applicable method, to avoid the use of mechanical moves in the machine, and I failed to find methods, that were of practical use for their work, and so, the mechanical movement determines the speed of the computing. Indeed, this machine has thirty parallel channels for calculation and the speed increases in times, but on the other side, the speed of the computer (as a whole) is restricted by the mechanical commutation, connected with the rotation of the given drum." By the way, the peripheral devices set in motion electromechanically, during the next decades after ABC and in our days restrict the successful fast action of the "lightning" electronic – computation machines.

Furthermore, Ferrill "grabs" the duration of the impulse of the add-subtract mechanism, which is 1/60 from the second, i.e. about 16,666 msec and finds contradiction in Atanasoff's testimony from the direct examination, when the witness had mentioned only a few microseconds. Atanasoff explained that they had agreed to talk about the speed of the machine – it adds two dual number for a second. On Ferrill's request, he calculated, that the time needed to carry out one elementary addition is about 24 msec. On the question for the interval between them, the witness replied, that according to him, it is not more than 250 msec, although, he thinks that it is much less, "but this is a relative thing". By the way, at the time, Atanasoff and Berry had used an electronic-ray oscilloscope, on the screen of which, (calibrated time units) they could detect the time-intervals. That is how the second attempt of ISD's defense (i.e. Sperry Rand) to underestimate Atanasoff's achievements in ABC is stopped. Of course, today's researchers clearly see, that it is from the ABC, from where Mauchly learned, to use the electronic keys needed for the construction of the ENIAC. And the summator, with consecutive operation, in the EDVAC is also borrowed from the ABC.

Ferrill maintained, that Atanasoff, had chosen the wrong approach, avoiding addition by counters and prefering instead his own method with the logical schemes.

Atanasoff explained, that at about 1936, he has installed, using literary data, some dual schemes for counting of cosmic rays, but instead used them for adding. "There were some difficultes with instability. They were then constructed, to work with cosmic rays, but were very sensitive to the kind of impulses, which were sent to them, and also to the form of the impulses and [...], the few experiments carried out made me take a gloomy view of that approach."

Ferrill succeeded in convincing Atanasoff, that if he had used a ring counter in the ABC, it would not have been necessary to rotate mechanically the memorizing devices. Two days later the attorney come back to the question, underlining it as a shortcoming of the ABC, for its reliance on the rotating condenser memory. Atanasoff replied, that at that time he had experimented various solutions, keeping in mind the idea, that the magnetic drum could rotate much faster. But because of ABC's purpose, he should have installed 30 separate amplifiers for the elements of the magnetic rotational memory, which would mean a significant power increase, consumed by the machine.

Ferrill insisted, that the solution used in ENIAC is preferable – calculating by counters, which are not separated from the memory as the logic Add-Subtract "mechanisms" of ABC. By the way, Mauchly and Eckert transfer, the consecutive dual sumators from the separated memory of ABC into the next computer after ENIAC – EDWAC together with the memory-regenerating circuit – also borrowed from the ABC, which Ferrill does not consider at all. He does not like seeing, that Atanasoff's first electronic digital computation machine with the unusual, for its time, capacity of the memory and with the excellent coordination of its successfully operating complex devices is a great achievement.

Atanasoff's cross-examination ended with questions concerning his preliminary relations with the patent attorney Trexler, at the time they were preparing to file the Application for the patent of ABC. As the experts on the lawsuit state, it becomes clear, that the materials supplied by Atanasoff and Berry to Trexler, "were more than adequate as a base for issuing that patent".

The so-called, in the American legal terminology, "redirect examination" of Atanasoff was conducted by Honeywell's attorney – Henry Halladay, and the recross examination from the defense – again by Ferrill. To the particular ticklish question about what Mauchly learned from his visit at Ames the witness replied convincingly, to both attorneys, that Mauchly had understood the most specific particulars of the computer. "I also pointed out, that I had been a college professor for a large part of my working life and that I knew whether or not someone understood me. I recall that the judge smiled broadly at that".

Atanasoff's nine-days testimony ended on 25.06.1971 and he took time to say good-buy to everyone including the attorney of the opposing party and with the "court reporters", who had stood by and given a good copy in spite of technical words and low tones. When reading them over Atanasoff finds it hard to believe he had done as well as he actually did on the witness stand. As a matter of fact, it should be noted down that when Atanasoff indulges in superfluous details, the attorney Call, was there to focus him to say only the most important for the particular disputed situation.

This trial, which lasted for 135 days, had just started and a lot was going to happen before its closing on 13.03.1972.

THE WITNESS MAUCHLY

The direct examination of John Atanasoff, conducted by the attorney Delone, started on 08.11.1971. Gradually, before the court, the high points of Mauchly's education through his obtaining the Ph.D. in Physics, were outlined. Because of exceptional capabilities that degree has been conferred on him at the University of John Hopkins, Baltimore, in 1932, without defending any bachelor or master's thesis.

Following the instruction of Sperry Rand's attorney, Mauchly tried to forget as much as possible about his contacts with Atanasoff. Delone's questions are to launch a false thesis: that as early as when he was a lecturer at the Earsinous Collegeville, Pennsylvania (1933–1941), he had ideas of constructing a Digital Electronic Computation Machine. The aim is to underestimate the influence of the principles, appropriated from Atanasoff's ABC computer, on ENIAC.

But he did not give any evidence in support of that contention during his testimony. Exactly the opposite, he then confessed, that he had shared similar ideas with colleagues at the Moor School only in the autumn of 1941, i.e. soon after his acquainting with the ABC. An additional material evidence can be found as well in his letter to Atanasoff of the same autumn, in which he expresses his intention to work out, at the Moor School, the idea given him by Atanasoff in a recent letter – using the ABC as a base for construction of a machine for integrating of differential equations. At the same time, in order to keep up with modern electronics, Mauchly starts attending courses in the Moor School, which is another indication of the time, when he began to launch ideas about a Digital Electronic Computation Machine, briskly changing his plans to become a lecturer.

Mauchly gave detailed testimony about the development of the ENIAC and the EDVAC. Afterwards, the attorney Delone, pointed out the large number of scientific distinctions and grants, with which Mauchly and Eckert have been honored as "inventors of the computer".

The Detronation of that myth in the history of the computive technology begins with the experienced conducting of Mauchly's crossexamination by the attorney Halladay on the 10th of November. When he testified in court on the ENIAC trial, Mauchly does not admit as to what he had already admitted at the regenerating memory trial (patent 827). Besides, he deliberately shifted with a whole year backwards his first meeting with Atanasoff, when he learned of the development of ABC, namely instead of the end of 1940, at the end of 1939. All manipulations with the dates have one transparent aim – to dispute the derivation of essential principles in ENIAC from the ABC. By the way, as the court found out that at that time, Mauchly worked on an analogous and not on a digital computing device. The main trump here are the so-called "Mauchly's devices with neon glow lamps" constructed by him as if for "calculations". On another occasion he admits, that they were meant for "indicators of counters". At the end, the truth emerges and it is proved that these notorious devices represent a part of a toy's "rail-way", imitating the signaling of the rail-way stoplight. Another "digital" eleboration of Mauchly's at the end of 30-ies is a device for ciphering (but without calculation), which he had offered to a military service but to no avail. In fact, in that specific field called criptoanalysis, the English held the lead in 1943, when at the Research center in Blechly, a Digital Electronic Computation Machine Colossus, successfully started working. For a quarter, of a century it has even been considered to be the first computer. And while the ABC and ENIAC had not been used in military service, through the computer, the Colossus and its "follower" Mark II Colossus elaborated by the schemes of the mathematicians Turing and

Neuman, the engineers Flowers, Chandler, Brodhurst, Kumbs, etc., the English succeed in deciphering the system ENIGMA from secret German codes. This influenced the progress of the Second World War.* As a result of that, the transport ships, supplying the troops of Romel in North Africa were destroyed. The traffic of the German submarines was discovered, as well as the radio-transmissions of the German army during the landing in Normandy. Unbelievable, but true – so that decoding of the German codes through ENIGMA can not be discovered, Churchill did not warn the population of the town of Coventry for the German bombing, it was not evacuated and thousands of people died.

Mauchly and Eckert were left behind once again, this time by English researchers. A Digital Electronic Computation Machine with a memorized program EDSAC of Prof. Moris Wealks (holder of the medal for a computer pioneer of IEEE) is completed before EDVAC, in Cambridge, England at the academic "temple" of Babbadge. An interesting fact is that in 1978 Prof. Wealks, inspired by the trial of his great predesessor, writes a quite successful play on Babbage presented at the Computer Museum in USA.

Coming back once again to the examination conducted by Halladay, we should note, that Mauchly's testimony is contradictory. On the question what he has seen in Atanasoff's computer laboratory in 1941, he replies "almost nothing", but in his answers to other questions, he describes in detail, the principles of operation of the separate knots of ABC.

Sometimes in his testimony Mauchly avoids giving a straight answer, but in other cases, he even makes insinuations diverting from the essence of the question. For example, once, instead of replying to a particular question about the regenerating memory, he tosses without any connection, that he does not know what is the participation of Atanasoff in the development of the ABC and that of Berry. In fact, at the lawsuit in Baltimore, he could not say from where he has learned the principle of regenerating memory, inserted in the EDVAC computer by Eckert and Mauchly only in 1953. Eckert, in an article states, that an earlier elaboration of the development of the regenerating memory is made in the Atanasoff's computer. That is why, "electrostatic rotary memory" is literally plagiarized from the description of ABC. Contradictive was also Mauchly's statement, that because of the nature of his work in NOL,

* See Hodges A., Alan Turing: The Enigma of Intelligence, London, 1983.

Atanasoff had lost all interest in computers. But, it is in this same laboratory that Atanasoff had conducted for a time the development of a computer, hadn't he? He has seen Eckert only once in his life, without knowing, that both of them – Eckert and Mauchly, after their meeting with him, went to the Patent Office, filed for a patent, whose scope of action included his own inventions! But Eckert and Mauchly actions are revealed before the court. They were obliged to inform the Patent Office of the Atanasoff and Berry invention, despite the fact that no such patent application has been filed for by the College of Iowa, as the contract with the inventors required. No remorse from both Mauchly and Eckert! Mauchly even blames Atanasoff as responsible for the losses, which he himself had caused because of the patents, issued on the names of Mauchly and Eckert, declaring, that Atanasoff "has not displayed zeal in defending his own patent interests"!

Later in his turn, Eckert's testimony, with general phrases answers the question asked in the court-room, and resorts to beating about the bush, when asked about the borrowings from the ABC, implemented by him and Mauchly in ENIAC, EDVAC and the next computers.

Day after day, Halladay patiently overcomes Mauchly's refusals to admit to of a whatsoever borrowing of computer principles from Atanasoff. To the question, if he could present schemes of an electronic digital computation machine designed by him before his first meeting with Atanasoff, Mauchly answers, that he could not find in his archives neither schemes nor other documentation.

For a long time he also avoided giving a direct answer to the question whether the harmonic analyzer of Furrier, constructed in 1940, is his own work, until judge Larson compels him to answer. It became clear, that it is a modification of a development by MIT, to which he had added voltage divisor manufactured by General Radio Company.

The interrogating attorney succeeded in pointing out in an article written by Mauchly, immediately after his visit to Atanasoff, and the borrowing of the analog and impulse type computing devices concepts.

Mauchly confesses, that he had read Atanasoff's manuscript, but maintained, that at that time he was interested in the developments of an electronic digital computing machine, only for his own calculations, and not for construction intentions, i.e. with the direct hinting of the idea for a universal Digital Electronic Computation Machine, Atanasoff had stimulated him in constructing the ENIAC. In order words, it appeared something like the fable about the Fox, the Raven and the Cheese.

Mauchly's confessions came slowly, one by one, provoked by the numerous purposeful questions made by Halladay, asked with patient insistence, registered in the court proceedings: that Mauchly who "had learned nothing from Atanasoff", had in fact, understood from descriptions and demonstrations, especially performed for him by Atanasoff and Berry, the operation of electronic tubes as computing elements, the principle of binary calculations performed by the logic arithmetical device of ABC, of its component electronic lamp logic schemes, and also the principle of the regenerating memory, realized by means of condensers.

The results from Mauchly's cross-examination exceed all expectations. They confirmed, in the end, Atanasoff's testimony and were a great victory for Halladay, unveiling the forthcoming successful conclusion of the case.

Besides these main witnesses detailed testimony was also given by other pioneers of the computing technology, and some great specialists in the field of physics and mathematics: D. Auerbach, P. Klipinger, S. Dash, A. Dikinson, K. Francle, Ks. Goldstain, J. Mark, H. Metropolis, K. Moors, F. Moom, B.Felps, J. Reichman, E.Teller and S. Ulam.

THE FEDERAL COURT'S DECISION

On Friday 19.10.1973, Judge Earl Larson announced his decision on the ENIAC case. The patent, considered until then as belonging to Digital Electronic Computation Machine was ruled invalid. But during that Friday night something happened, something which occupied the first columns of the morning newspapers. The proper place of the inventor of one of the greatest scientific achievements in human history was taken over by the Watergate scandal. President Nixon fired the Special Watergate prosecutor the Vice District Attorney, and the District Attorney resigns himself. At the end of the same week, the OPEC countries imposed a petroleum embargo. The decision of that court should have received greater news coverage, but was stifled by all this news*. The recognition comes actually later, mainly due to the professional scientific and detailed studies of A. and A. Burks.

Of course, Watergate was not the only reason for the press silence. Only after three months the Washington Post, published an article about the lawsuit by D. Gardner – a journalist from the Datamation magazine, followed also in January by the article of Clark Mollenhoff in De Moines Registers, published in Ames, from where the citizens of Iowa learned about the lawsuit.

* According to Mollenhoff

What are the reasons for this extraordinary delay of 40 years, before Atanasoff's achievement was honored? Prior to the onset of the law-suit they are as follows:

First, the war put an abrupt halt to Atanasoff's efforts on the ABC, just as he had reached the brink of the triumph. The confusion during the first war years is the reason why the State University of Iowa did not apply for a patent, with which it could ensure its priority.

Second, there was no organization, or a private person, interested in clarifying that priority.

Third, Atanasoff himself did not exert any efforts in studyng the importance of his contributionn or of its dissemination. As an inventor, he was completely absorbed by the problems of the moment. His efforts and interests in other fields, including merits during the time of war, the establishing and management of his own company, as well his numerous other inventions, had not left him with time to go back and contemplate over his first achievements in the computer world.

Fourth, the State University of Iowa, a higher educational institution, having for example one of the best centers on material sciences in the world, was not very influential in the academic world. Had Atanasoff completed his work in Berkley, Cambridge, Harvard or Copenhagen, he would be recognized as the inventor of the computer much earlier.

The reasons after the lawsuit are two:

First, the sophisticated scientific matter, exposed in a voluminous verdict and in a large number of documents, and Secondly, the myth about the inventors priority of Eckert and Mauchly, who even after the end of case, took advantage of the informational vacuum, to bring confusion, ignoring the trial and went on to praise themselves, without even mentioning Atanasoff 's name. Luckily, the achievement of Atanasoff was largely recognized in the literature and he received many honorary rewards and degrees, among which is the medal in the name of Holly, the highest reward, given by the American Institute of Electrical Engineers "for pioneer research, invention and construction of the first digital computer, the basic concepts in using electrical and electronic means, the use of dual numerals and of the logic for computing without counting out, as well as the use of regenerating memory – all of them used in modern computers."

SECTION 3 LEGAL VERDICT OF THE FOURTH DEPARTMENT OF THE USA FEDERAL COURT, MINNESOTA STATE 19.10.1973 (Judge Earl R. Larson's decision in the legal dispute of the companies Honeywell Inc. versus Sperry Rand Corp. and IDS /28/)*

3.1. The subject matter /the essence/ of one or more claims /author's pretensions/ of the ENIAC was derived from Atanasoff /the computer ABC/, and the invention /applied for with the ENIAC patent/ claimed in the ENIAC was derived from Atanasoff.

3.1.1. SR and ISD are bound by their representation in support of the counterclaim herein that the invention claimed /against/ in the ENIAC patent is probably "the invention of the Automatic Electronic Digital Computer."

3.1.2. Eckert and Mauchly did not themselves first invent the automatic electronic digital computer, but instead derived that subject matter from one Dr. John Vincent Atanasoff.

3.1.3. Honeywell has proved that the claimed subject matter of the ENIAC patent relied on in support of the counterclaim herein is not patentable over the subject matter derived by Mauchly from Atanasoff. As a representative example, Honeywell has shown that the subject matter of detailed claims 88 and 89 of the ENIAC patent corresponds to the work of Atanasoff which was known to Mauchly before any effort pertinent to the ENIAC machine or patent began.

3.1.4. Between 1937 and 1942, Atanasoff, then a professor of physics and mathematics at Iowa State College, Ames, Iowa, developed and built an automatic electronic digital computer for solving large systems of simultaneous linear algebraic equations.

3.1.5. In December, 1939, Atanasoff completed and reduced to practice his basis conception in the form of an operating breadboard model of a computing machine.

3.1.6. This breadboard model machine, constructed with the assistance of a graduate student, Clifford Berry, permitted the various components of the machine to be tested under actual operating conditions.

3.1.7. The breadboard model established the soundness of the basic principles of design, and Atanasoff and Berry began the construction of a prototype or pilot model, capable of solving with a high degree of accuracy a system of as many as 29 simultaneous equation having 29 unknowns.

* Published in **Mollenhoff, C.R. Atanasoff: Forgotten Father of the Computer.**

3.1.8. By August 1940 in connection with efforts at further funding, Atanasoff prepared a comprehensive manuscript that fully described the principles of his machine, including detail design features.

3.1.9. By the time the manuscript was prepared in August 1940, construction of the machine, destined to be termed in this litigation the Atanasoff-Berry computer or "ABC," was already far advanced.

3.1.10. The description contained in the manuscript was adequate to enable one of ordinary skill in electronics at that time to make and use an ABC computer.

3.1.11. The manuscript was studied by expert in the art of aids to mathematical computation, who recommended its financial support, and these recommendations resulted in a grant of funds by Research Corporation for the ABC's continued construction.

3.1.12. In December, 1940, Atanasoff first met Mauchly while attending a meeting of the American Association for the Advancement of Science in Philadelphia, and generally informed Mauchly about the computing machine which was under construction at Iowa State College. Because of Mauchly's expression of interest in the machine and its principles, Atanasoff invited Mauchly to come to Ames, Iowa, to learn more about the computer.

3.1.13. After correspondence on the subject with Atanasoff, Mauchly went to Ames, Iowa, as a houseguest of Atanasoff for several days, where he discussed the ABC as well as other ideas of Atanasoff's relating to the computing art.

3.1.14. Mauchly was given an opportunity to read, and did read, but was not permitted to take with him, a copy of the comprehensive manuscript that Atanasoff had prepared in August, 1940.

3.1.15. At the time of Mauchly's visit, although the ABC was not entirely complete, its construction was sufficiently well advanced so that the principles of its operation, including detail design features, was explained and demonstrated to Mauchly.

3.1.16. The discussions Mauchly had with both Atanasoff and Berry while at Ames were free and open and no significant information concerning the machine's theory, design, construction, use or operation was withheld.

3.1.17. Prior to his visit to Ames, Iowa, Mauchly had been broadly interested in electrical analog calculating devices, but had not conceived an automatic electronic digital computer.

3.1.18. As a result of this visit, the discussions of Mauchly with Atanasoff and Berry, the demonstrations, and the review of the manuscript, Mauchly derived from the ABC "the digital computer" claimed in the ENIAC patent.

3.1.19. The Court has heard the testimony at trial of both Atanasoff and Mauchly, and finds the testimony of Atanasoff with respect to the knowledge and information derived by Mauchly to be credible.

* * *

Then in more stately legal terms Judge Larson almost said that Mauchly had lied under oath as a witness. Larson rejected Mauchly's vague, contrived, contradictory, and uncorroborated contention that he had learned nothing of consequence from the Atanasoff-Berry computer, from his talks with Atanasoff and Berry, from Atanasoff's Manuscript he read and from his observations of the work of this computer.

The fact that Judge Larson did not call Mauchly a liar, but rather used the word "derived", for stealing from Atanasoff the concept for the computer ENIAC, should not blunt those who consider themselves researchers and computer historians. Larson was kind to Mauchly for not castigating him as a willful liar and falsifier and in accepting the possibility that his incredible and uncorroborated testimony might have been a result of a bad memory and confusion.

According to Larson, who deemed, that the evidence provided in support of Atanasoff, as well as Atanasoff's behaviour and testimony, confirmed his conclusion, that Atanasoff was a credible witness with a trustworthy testimony. Therefore, inferring that Mauchly has not been an honest witness and his testimony is not reliable.

Atanasoff: "After my talks with Theodore Syordsma, I came back home and went through the articles from 1974 about Larson's verdict. These articles included a short description of my conversation with Mauchly at that time. I decided that it is time to write a book with a documentation to clarify the question. The facts were stranger than a fairytale."

Abiding by the American legal norms, on 19.10.73 LEGAL VERDICTS Larson issued the Court Conclusions and Verdict, a total of 420 pages. It is stated in the Verdict: "With the present Verdict, the ENIAC patent – USA patent number 3 120 606 of the Illinois Scientific Developments (ISD) is ruled invalid and with no legal power. The counterclaim of ISD against Honeywell is disallowed. In this 248 page verdict, and the 60 page enclosure, the judge rules invalid the author of 17 pretensions of the patent. Two of the pretensions are used in the verdict as representing the established truth, that Mauchly and Eckert have derived the subject of their invention ENIAC from the description of the first DIGITAL ELECTRONIC COMPUTATION MACHINE – ABC (the Manuscript of Atanasoff dated August 1940).

In his verdict Larson gave his approbation of the memory and conscientiousness of the witness Atanasoff, stating : "The Court has heard both the testimony of Atanasoff and of Mauchly and finds the testimony of Atanasoff with respect to the knowledge and information derived (from the computer ABC) by Mauchly to be credible."

And in his comments regarding Larson's verdict of Atanasoff states, accordingly that, the judge has displayed a vivid interest in this complex case and had represented the legal profession at the very height. "In two findings however, I am obliged to argue just a little" – states Atanasoff in his memoirs – "These are p. 13.25 and 13.25.1., in which Larson states, that Mauchly might not have understood the relationship of the ENIAC to the ABC. I am sure, on the other hand, that the judge was quite right in citing p. 13.20.5., in which he says that neither Eckert nor Mauchly informed their attorneys of my work (on the ABC). Without such information, any patent counsel would do just what was done in the ENIAC case, and also the memory case: take what the principals had done, extend it, and draw the broadest possible claims in jargon of "patentees". In p. 13.25 Larson rules: "Mauchly may in good faith have believed, that the monstrous machine, he helped create, had no relationship to the ABC of Atanasoff", and in the next p. 13.25.1., we read:

"Mauchly may in good faith have believed, that he did not derive the subject matter claimed in the ENIAC patent from Atanasoff." In September 1944 Mauchly wrote a summary of the situation, as he then saw it: "I thought, his /Atanasoff's/ machine was very ingenious, but since it was in part mechanical (involving rotating comutators for switching), it was not by any means, what I had in mind." Mauchly did not explain – exactly "what he had in mind", he did not explain to Atanasoff either. In any case Atanasoff couldn't accept p.13.25 and p.13.25.1. from the verdict, because, according to him Mauchly and Eckert have been aware, that they directed deriving the principles of the ENIAC from the ABC. A good example, as he points out, in his memoirs is the author's patent of the ENIAC, a claim covering the electronic version of the no restriction method of division. This method was first implemented by Atanasoff in the ABC, which he had described in his Manuscript of 1940, for which Larson had ruled in his verdict, that Mauchly had read it, while visiting Atanasoff in 1941: "I find it hard to believe, that my concept of nonrestoring division could have inadvertently become claim 100 of the ENIAC patent. I find it just as difficult to believe that in the case of the Memory patent, Mauchly and Eckert, did not know they were employing my principle of "jogging" or regenerating ("refreshing") the memory – a principle also explained in my 1940 manuscript and a conspicuous feature of the machine. They used this principle in both the specifications and the claims of the patent. Atanasoff also notes the pretension 190 only after the case!

Larson rules, that Eckert had learned about that principle from Mauchly, but Mauchly was at a loss to explain the difference between the "jogging" principle of Atanasoff and their (with Eckert) principle of regeneration. Eckert, himself, in his article of 1953 writes, that the regenerating memory in the machine of Atanasoff precedes the corresponding memory in their computers.

In his comments to other points made in Larson's verdict Atanasoff clarifies, that the Research Foundation of the State College of Iowa did not uphold its end of the Agreement with him, namely obliging it to file for a patent of the ABC invention. He had believed for quite some time, that such an application would be submitted. Only to find out years after that the College had not authorized the patent attorney Trexler to file the matter with the Patent Office.

Atanasoff, reproached judge Larson's decision as with regards to part 13, entirely devoted to addressing the issue of fraud on the U.S. Patent Office – in the context of any damages Honeywell might deserve on the basis antitrust and not to the issue of fraud per se, as against any part other than the Patent Office: "Although I believe my ideas were taken and used to claim an invention that was rightfully mine, I must content myself with the court's finding that the ENIAC patent was invalid on the basis of derivation from my prior research, and with the court's stress on the great extent to which fraud must be proven in an antitrust case. The full text of the judge's decision contains numerous citations of law in this latter instance, and several references to derelictions on the part of Eckert and Mauchly, including their failure to reveal knowledge of my work."

As to the other three reasons for ruling the ENIAC patent invalid, they are connected with the violation of basic rules of the USA patent legislation. The applicants are required to keep from the public the essence of their invention, to have not sold, and to have not publicly used it. But the three requirements in the USA have an only one-year tolerance period. In other words, violations of these requirements are admitted in the period of one year prior to applying for a patent. The motive for that tolerance is to safeguard the interests of the society; the development of technologies and techniques. To Sperry Rand's great disappointment for the ENIAC patent, the application for which was bought by Mauchly and Eckert, the Court rules, that the violations of the three requirements were done before 26.06.1946, i. e. More than one year before submitting the application.

Sperry Rand's attorneys and the witnesses of the team, that had constructed ENIAC, maintain that the blame for using the computer in public practice, in fact refer to the cases, at which ENIAC has been in experimental exploitation with the aim to remove any defects, because in November 1945, the machine had not yet been completed. But in its Verdict, the Court declared, that since December 10th of the same year, ENIAC has entered the nonexperimental practical use for in solving equations in the elaboration of the Hydrogen bomb in the first nuclear Center at Los Alamos. This decision was reached, following the testimony of Edward Teller ("the Father of the Hydrogen bomb") and following the examination of thousands of documents, presented by uninvolved sources. And after the announcement of Larson's verdict, researchers from Eckert and Mauchly's team, continue to receive published, in books and articles, containing "refutations" of ENIAC's entering in normal exploitation. They explain, that at that time, the Legislative Act dealing with the thermonuclear weapons had been stopped, in order to collect the necessary information for the accuracy of the bomb's concept.

That is why, the Los Alamos scientists had been in a great rush, due to the need to make massive calculations and their only solution was ENIAC. They had agreed with the University of Pennsylvania, that the computing in the nuclear center would be performed as an "improvised testing" of ENIAC. Although, ENIAC's memory was found to be insufficient for solving their task, nevertheless the scientists from Los Alamos had decided to use it, by reducing the tasks to simpler computation. They had considered, that by studying the separate solutions to the simple tasks as a whole, they would be able to solve the large task and thence, the problem regarding the appropriateness of the concept chosen for the hydrogen bomb. And so, on 10.12.1946 the date pointed out by Judge Larson as the beginning of the practical use of ENIAC, the nuclear computation at Los Alamos had already begun. The first two days, the computer was programmed. It was done manually, adjusting the code–selecting pulleys and a great number of commutation cords were placed into the jacks. To check the validity of the solutions given by ENIAC, among the actual steps of the computing procedures, the scientists made calculations with known results. The solution, obtained from the computer, confirmed the appropriateness of the chosen method for creation of the thermonuclear bomb. To solve this first task, ENIAC processed about one million IBM punch–cards!

Larson's opponents maintain, that in the ENIAC diary documenting these computations, repeated mistakes were registered, which necessitated some corrections in the machine. But the judge's verdict refuted these allegations – it was settled, that during the computing, 99% of the capacity of ENIAC had been used for computing of differential equations at Los Alamos, where the mistakes were made by mathematicians, and not by the machine.

In addition it was said in the verdict, that with the completion of the machine's computing in February 1946, the task of the scientists had been solved, thus they obtained a reliable confirmation as to the concept of the Hydrogen bomb.

After solving the task at Los Alamos (still under security clearance today), Mauchly and Eckert organized a demonstration of ENIAC at a press conference and an official Ceremony for the implementing of the machine in practice. They also invited Atanasoff, but Mauchly does not even mention his name in his address! The event is filmed for the newsreels and was shown on the screens throughout the country. During these demonstrations, conducted by Arthur Burks, ENIAC solves a large number of small tasks. But what 'holds the breath' is, that the computer calculates for 20 sec the trajectory of a shell, which reaches its target in 30 sec.! (For a comparison we will point out, that the table calculators calculate that trajectory in three days, while it takes the differential analyzer – to reach it in thirty minutes). Throughout it all, Mauchly and Eckert assured for themselves "publicity", i. e. advertising, without which, as correctly noted by Ilf and Petrof, there is no "prosperity". The world should be taken aback "astonished, from the achievements of the "first" computer with giant dimensions. In vain, the representatives of the Artillery Management, whose contract financed the construction of the

ENIAC, in vain, warned Mauchly and Eckert, that their actions would damage the patentability of the machine. Judge Larson had found many other cases, at which ENIAC had been publicly used. For example H. Huskley had used it, on April 1946, to produce sine and cosine signals. The violation "disclosing of the invention by the public use" had provoked the instituting of proceedings even before the issuing of the ENIAC patent, but then the authors succeeded in staying.

According to the American patent laws, the forbiddance for public use of the invention is also valid for its sale, if done before the one-year term. Mauchly and Eckert kept silent before the Patent Office for this violation as well. From the official reports that are now made public and the memories of participants in the development of ENIAC, before the final stage of developing the machine had started, it was decided, that it would be tested through a double – accumulator model. Under the accumulator, it should be understood "accumulating register", i.e. digital device, for these purposes, which can memorize 10–digit numbers together with their sign, and also to add to the memorized number or to subtract from it another number. In ENIAC such a register was composed from 10 decimal counters and two triggers for the sign of the number. The 20 registers of ENIAC have been its "real heart".

In June 1944 the decisive testing of the essential processes in the computer – adding, subtracting, memorizing and management had been completed successfully. The model, called "the little ENIAC", has been sold immediately to the Artillery Management. (The sale helps Mauchly and Eckert to sign a contract for the development of EDVAC). On 11.04.1946, with an aim to sell ENIAC they demonstrated it before the Bureau of Census (the same bureau, that six decades earlier gave a powerful impetus in the development of the electromechanical calculating techniques, which opened the flood gates to the powerful flow of the Holerit tabulator machines). As a result of this demonstration, the newly formed company Eckert–Mauchly Computer Corp, signs a contract for the development of UNIVAC. By that time both co-authors had already left the University of Pennsylvania, after cleverly using one of its shortcomings. According to the main contract, the University agreed to give the ownership of ENIAC to the American Government, i. e. to Artillery Management and the rights to receiving a percentage of the income from the computer. But, as it was omitted in the contract to demand both designers to transfer all their rights to the University, in order for the agreement with the Government to enter into effect, it is necessary to obtain their agreement. That's why the University is compelled to transfer to both designees all rights to ENIAC, without the ones envisaged in the contract. But Mauchly and Eckert had developed the computer, not with their own means, but with government funding, had they not! Furthermore they were released from conscription, to fight in the Second World War, becausc; they were working on a military project – Artillery Management had signed a contract with the University for the construction of an electronic computer for the computation of ballistic tables.

It is due to that contract for performance of a military research and development (top secret) that Mauchly and Eckert received privileges, which would be impossible for a civil or peacetime project –free entry to the developing laboratories of the big American companies manufacturing electronic apparatuses and electromechanical calculating machines. The Court finds and notes in its decisions, that the inventors of ENIAC had received reports pertaining to electromechanical devices from Williams at Bell Telephone Laboratories and from Reichman from the RCA Corp. and permission to install and modify devices for input and output of data of the IBM Company. Judge Larson also points out in his verdict, that author's three pretensions to ENIAC were borrowed from the electronic multiplier developed by Brian Phelps from IBM, and successfully tested in 1942.

The verdict finds, that Sperry Rand "has provoked numerous patent disputes, by copying author pretensions from patents for devices, developed by competitors". Out of 156 such pretensions from 1951 to 1957 the Patent Office has rejected 147. Thus delaying the issuance of the ENIAC patent with a whole 17 years. Sperry Rand portends a dual purpose – on one hand, to claim for compensations for more years, and on the other hand, for saving negotiating time for reaching mutual license agreements, like the ones realized with the IBM and BTL companies. In 1952 Sperry Rand institutes a patent dispute against BTL dealing with the Williams patent application. As the Patent Office rejects Sperry Rand's application, it appeals the decision in Court, but the trial is prolonged for another 6 years, so that the claimant can gain, as to Larson's expression "profit from his comprehensive mutual license agreements for technological incorporating". In 1962 the District Court of South New York reached a verdict in that lawsuit, concluding, that ENIAC has not been publicly used before the legal term! Obviously the reason that BTL did not succeed in declaring the ENIAC patent invalid is rooted in the circumstance, that it was no more of interest to the company – plaintiff, which meanwhile had signed a mutual license agreement with Sperry Rand. Furthermore, and on an occasion, Mauchly and Eckert's supporters use this wrongly, maintaining, that in fact there was no other lawsuit, authenticating the validity of the ENIAC patent.

As with regards to the verdict dated 1962, Larson states, that, “If the one or two months” long litigation, undertaken in the spring of 1962, had been conducted by BTL, it would have probably made the 9 months’ long lawsuit for ENIAC, conducted between 1971 and 1972 unnecessary”.

And so, the verdict on the lawsuit declares, that although the undisputed creative contribution of the several participants of the team that created ENIAC, in the construction and in the patent of that computer, Mauchly and Eckert had implemented essential principles of devices, developed by the inventors – predecessors, Atanasoff, Phelps and Williams. Naturally, the question as to whether other participants from the team besides Eckert and Mauchly have to be acknowledged as co-inventors arose before the court. First of all, why was not Atanasoff declared a co-inventor of ENIAC ?

The explanation is extremely complex due to mutually reciprocal transfer from ABC to ENIAC. They had been identiful and clarified in a six year, step by step process, that took thousands of pages, documents and litigation, in order to be summarized by the paragraphs and points of the Court’s Verdict that contained over than 200 pages.

During the Court proceeding, Mauchly, Sperry Rand’s defense, and Judge Larson as well, noted that for a long period Atanasoff was uninterested in the defense of his invention. Coming back to the explanation of the question, as to why in spite of the recognition with which he renders to the priority of Atanasoff, the Court does not declare him as a co-inventor of ENIAC. We must note, that besides the exceptional complexity of the borrowings from the ABC, a certain “contribution” is also contributed by the company – claimant, Honeywell. All these pleas, and its preliminary research are aimed at the one goal, refutation of the pretensions of ISD (Sperry Rand’s branch) to pay the percentage compensations for violating the patent rights. And among the 17 author pretensions, the ones that were connected with the borrowings from Atanasoff were not included! No comment.

The opponents of the decision resort to sophisticated skills. For example they blame Judge Larson, that he “contradicts” himself, concluding, that the decisive part of the invention of ENIAC is derived from the ABC and on the other hand, that Mauchly and Eckert have no co-inventors. Perhaps, the reader has already grasped, that between the concepts “inventor-predecessor” and “co-inventor” exists not only a logical, but juridical deference as well. It is found undoubtedly, that Eckert and

Mauchly had sped up the development of the ENIAC. They had made use of the research conducted by of other researchers besides Atanasoff, namely Williams and Phelps. The input-output system of the ENIAC borrows the resistor matrix, invented by P. Crauford and I. Reichman (independently from each other). Atanasoff's trustfulness and the beginning of the Second World War help Mauchly. He, himself in a letter, dated 1941 wonders, why Atanasoff did not relate his work on a project for device, monitoring the anti-air fireing, to his computer development. But, probably his astonishment surpassed any limits when instead of doing so, after his work on the ABC was interrupted, but instead joined the NOL. Many facts give ground to suggest, that the development of the computer in that laboratory by a team under Atanasoff's guidance had been stopped not without the Mauchly's interference. In other words, the Court and Mauchly are not right, when saying Atanasoff was not interested in his own invention. Mauchly gladly welcomed the inertia shown by Atanasoff and other proved co-inventors from the team that developed ENIAC. Similar to Atanasoff, they received a delayed recognition in the legal verdict, but on the grounds of the mentioned reason, Larson refuses to recognize them officially as co- inventors of ENIAC. They are Arthur William Burks, Tomas Kite Shaplis, Robert Show and also John Davis, Frank Murel and Geophrey Chuan Chu. According to Prof. D. Branard – the former manager of the project – at least nine people have made "important contributions" to ENIAC.

Larson is also convinced, that for the designing of the separate knots of the ENIAC "inventor contributions have Burks, Sharplis, Show etc.", but still underlines, there are no exact characteristics of the individual contributions.

"I am inclined to believe, that the work on ENIAC was a team or group effort of a group or a team, and that inventor's contributions have also Burks, Sharplis, etc." – states Larson.

Naturally, the reader would ask: with that strong engineering team that had developed ENIAC, what is the personal contribution of the applicants of the patent – Eckert and Mauchly? Mauchly appointed as research engineer suggested the general, system solutions of the preliminary design, participated in all discussions, continuously gave consultations to the whole team, performed decisive testing of the most important electronic knots. As a "spiritual father" of ENIAC he continuously instructed and encouraged the participants in that "exciting, very complicated and tenuous undertaking".

JOHN WILLIAM MAUCHLY

He was born on 30.08.1907 in Cincinnati, Ohio in a family of a physician, who moved to work at the Carnegie Institute in Washington and studied magnetism and the electricity of the Earth. John graduated from a Secondary Polytechnic School. After two years studying at the University of John Hopkins, following a post graduate and in 1932 defended a Ph.D. thesis in Physics, devoted to the spectroscopic exploration of Carbon oxide. For his physics-chemical research Mauchly received a grant. From 1933 to 1941 lectured Physics at the Orisons College, near Philadelphia and worked on scientific-research work, studying the implementation of statistical methods in elaborating data from scientific research. In 1936, he began exploring the influence of the solar spots on the earth's climate, and together with the team under his guidance analysed a large amount of meteorological data for composing the long-term weather forecasts. As a result he became interested in methods and apparatuses for automatic performance of voluminous computing work. In 1939–1940 worked out a manual calculating device, the so-called harmonic analyzer, which speeds up three times his calculations as compared to the table calculator. Leaving the College in 1941 as Associate Professor, Mauchly is appointed as a lecturer at the Moor School, his work being connected with the training of personnel for wartime activities. In 1942 he proposed the construction of a digital electronic computing device, which would sharply increase the ballistic computing that he was currently doing. In 1946 the machine ENIAC was completed–the first universal purpose DECM and is demonstrated in public. For the development of ENIAC Mauchly and Eckert were honored in 1949 with the Pot medal, a lifetime membership of the Franklin Institute and other awards. Mauchly is one of the founders of ACM and a former president. He died in 1980.

But the Chief Engineer John Prosper Eckert Junior – an exceptionally talented specialist in electronics who proceeded with his predecessors' developments with his unique inventiveness, undertook the he whole development and performance of the project.

JOHN PROSPER ECKERT

He was born in 1919 in Philadelphia. As a teenager he accumulated experience as a amateur–radio constructor, after which he graduated from the Moor School of Electronic Engineering, where he contacted Mauchly. He conducted the development of ENIAC. Eckert gave the idea for a computer with a memory program and after completing ENIAC, together with Mauchly developed such a computer called EDVAC. It was followed by the UNIVAC and BINAC models. He occupied high positions in the companies founded together with Mauchly, and later at Sperry Rand. He had personally and in co-authorship registered 87 patents for inventions. In 1969 is honored with the highest reward in the USA for achievement in the science mathematics and technology – National Medal of Science.

Eckert was a capable organizer. He dexterously formulated the electronic-schemes solutions, implemented improvements in the developments of the others and firmly maintained the whole development, control and management the performance of all subtasks. He worked out the "heart" of ENIAC – the accumulating register, assisted by Burks, Sharpless, Mural and Davis. He participated in the construction of the tact generator, and also of the manual programming desk of the tasks through commutation of the conductors, which ended with sockets in the jacks.

After the names of the key figures of the project – Mauchly and Eckert, in the memoirs of some participants from the team, the name of Arthur William Burks is often seen. He is a holder of a bachelor and a Ph.D. degree in mathematics. After his work on the ENIAC project, he was a collaborator of John Von Neuman. Burks knew the whole history of ENIAC from close, because together with his direct work on one of the most important knots of the project, he was responsible for keeping a diary on the progress. After dismantling ENIAC in 1955, he saved some computer panels, which today are kept by the University of Michigan Museum. For over than 20 years Burks was a consultant on the ENIAC patent disputes. He was an especially important witness to the lawsuit, because he had the most complete documentation for this computer, and his research to the history of the computing technology, published during the last ten years, added to the juridical conclusions and strict evidences of the scientific analyses dealing with the contribution of Atanasoff, Mauchly and Eckert.

During his visit to Atanasoff in 1967, Mauchly complained, that Burks, two decades earlier, has disclosed through his publications the essence of the ENIAC invention and with that had violated his patent purity. But the Verdict of October 1973 removed any blame from Burks in that connection. The two articles, for which he is blamed, do not represent any violation of the patent legislation. In fact, an actual violation of the same character was found by the court elsewhere. In the beginning of the summer of 1945, there is a large spread reporting the results from discussions on the concepts of the computer with a memory program EDVAC. The discussions were held in the beginning of 1945. Participants are Eckert, Mauchly, Burks, Goldstein, the director of the ENIAC project – Warren and the consultant John Von Neuman. According to the court verdict this "Report on the initial project of EDVAC", disclosed the novelty not only of EDVAC, but also of ENIAC. In this way the court received an additional reason to rule the patent invalid. Larson clarifies, that nine author pretensions about the ENIAC project are found in the report. After studying them the subject of the invention – "automatic DECM" is obvious. The report was written by Von Neuman, but it is H.Goldstein, who multiplied and spread it. But this was only the beginning of a number of injustices.

Judge Larson's conclusion, that the report has disclosed the novelty of EDVAC is disputable. In this report, the author did not give any information about Neuman and H.Goldstein while creating the computer in the institute for perspective research in Princeton and others. Besides being a Director of the group on logic of the calculating machines at the University of Michigan, he was a professor on computing and communication sciences and philosophy. He is a holder of the highest reward "University lecturer Henry Russel" for 1978 about the nature of the electronic schemes, and had described only the logic structure of the computer hardware. Obviously Neuman placed an accent on the logic structure of EDVAC, because its detailed development is one of the two great achievements of this project (the other being the creation of the first contemporary program language). Unfortunately, this narrowing of the report's subject, published with quite a general heading, proved incorrect as to remaining participants in the discussions of the memorizing device. The credit for the development of that device belongs to Eckert, in spite the fact, that his starting point is Atanasoff's regenerating memory principle, of which he had taken from Mauchly. On 29.01.1944 in three typewritten pages he presented his concept about invention of a magnetic computing machine – an office proposal about "a simplified method for construction of a DECM". In that machine on a rotating disc, tape or a drum with some magnetic film (combination of two constructive ideas of Atanasoff) can temporarily be recorded (i.e. erasable), numbers or signs, encoded through "electric signals, like the ones necessary for measuring the beat time /coordination in time/, control and start of the operations necessary for the computations". Further, he writes, that the use of the suggested system gives many possibilities for "automatic programming devices and the processes in them", and to obtain of a constant memory of the programs Eckert suggest engraving on discs. On these three pages we encounter other principles, known to us from the machine ABC – electronic-tube keys, binary counting system, etc. But Eckert's priority in the idea of a computer with a memorized program is indisputable. The word is only about a DECM with a saved program. The absolute priority belongs to Ch.Babbage, who had designed the first universal mechanical digital computation machine with a memorized program (the so called Analytic machine) one century earlier. Because, this document was classified this concept remained classified for a long time known only to a few specialists. And these seals " Top secret", which were carefully placed at the beginning and end of each page succeed in hiding the historical truth, even from the authors of historical references, who today impute the principle of the memorized program to Von Neuman. Of course, Von Neuman himself is to blame for that misunderstanding. It originates from the fact, that only he signed this report, and that is why most of the people consider, that he is the author of the whole development of EDVAC. During the last few years, Burks and Goldstein have objected, in some publications, to this misrepresentation of the historical truth. In fact, the other great contributions of John Van Neuman to the science, is sufficiently glorious, which by virtue of the psychological adjustment to the notorious names, overshadows the remaining talented specialists, that had worked with him in the field of computers.

A great part of the Verdict (more than 200 pages) is devoted to the violation of the anti-trust legislation. It should be pointed out, that the claim of the Sperry Rand branch, brought against Honeywell for compensation due to the violation of the rights of a valid patent was countered by the company – claimant with accusation of monopolization of the industry for data processing, i.e. in violation of the Sherman and Clayton anti-trust laws. As a result, the roles were reversed and as of May 1968 the litigation constituted a suit brought by Honeywell against Sperry Rand and ISD.

Judge Larson rejected part of Honneywell's accusations, because the allegations that it has violated section 7 of the Clayton–Sherman anti-trust act, does not correspond to the requirements of that law, which refers only to funds and companies, but does not cover the obtainment of patents from private persons. Furthermore, according to Judge Larson, Honeywell did not succeed in showing, that the obtaining of the patent by Mauchly and Eckert in 1950 by the company predecessor of Sperry Rand – Remington Rand, had expressed a wish for a monopoly. The court declared, that Sperry Rand did not succeed in the formation of a monopoly; in spite of its partner in the technological agreement, IBM, has succeeded in that direction.

The Larson's decision recognized as lawful, the allegation of Honeywell, that Sperry Rand has agreed with IBM with the aim, both of them to monopolize the computer industry and, that Honeywell has undergone some harm and damages, namely as a result of the agreement between its two competitors, and not because the existence of the patent for ENIAC.

To the plaintiff Honeywell, no damages were adjudicated, because it, in itself, has not acted zealously enough, in order to defend its interest on the market of the means for electronic processing of data and besides it unsuccessfully had tried to use for license purposes its own package of patents.

The court satisfied Honeywell's claim by ruling the ENIAC patent invalid and without legal power. When a given patent is decreed, without legal power, it means, that its owner, cannot look for his patent rights through the court. Concerning the 25 patents package and patent applications, instituted in the claim of Honeywell under number 30A, Larson paid great attention to its role in the licensed technological unions of Sperry Rand. He satisfied Honeywell's claim by declaring them invalid because of violations, similar to those of ENIAC. The judge also found as justified the accusation, that Sperry Rand has violated the Clayton–Sherman anti-trust law.

The counter-claim of Sperry Rand to receive compensations from Honeywell because they had violated the rights of the ENIAC patent was recognized by the court as legal, but compensations were not adjudicated, as the patent has already been ruled invalid.

In spite of the numerous dodges, which Sperry Rand applied in the undeclared patent war, in some of the cases it succeeded getting condescension on the side of the court. For example, the court's decision of not declaring the patent invalid because of illegal delays in obtaining it from the owner company, but only as deprived from a legal power. Its decision regarding Honeywell's accusation, that Sperry Rand has cheated the Patent Office of the USA is similar. In his verdict, Larson finds, that a deliberate fraud has not been proven, although he numbers some violations undertaken by Sperry Rand. Namely, hiding documents, refusal of information, providing written evidence by false witnesses, frustration of the competitors to receive the necessary documents from government offices, filing for patents despite the warning received, that they contain violation of the requirements and many other inappropriate activities. This long list of shortcomings, Larson accompanied with detailed examples, but in spite of this he stipulates, that the defendants Sperry Rand and ISD might have acted conscientiously. " For example Mauchly and Eckert may have not understood the term" on sale "or may be have really thought, that the demonstrating of ENIAC does not represent a public use".

Sperry Rand chose not to appeal the final decision to the Supreme Court. But it undertook decisive steps to prevent any appeals from Honeywell's side as well to which the requested release from court expenditures and compensations payment was not adjudicated.

That is why Sperry Rand in a secret agreement with Honeywell undertook the obligation of paying $3.5 million;enough to cover all its expenses for the trial. Besides that, both sides were obliged to accept the Judge Larson's verdict. In fact Honeywell came out as winner from that duel. By achieving the nullification of the ENIAC patents and 30A, it removed the threat of paying to Sperry Rand many millions of dollars worth compensation.

Larson's verdict could in no case be constrewed as in favor of Sperry Rand. But as John Atanasoff says: "It is a Salomon decision", because no fraud was found and no damages are adjudicated to Honeywell, in result of violation of the anti-trust laws on the part of Sperry Rand. It seems, that Larson consciously had wished to conclude the trial with such a moderate decision, which could not be appealed.

Following completing of the ENIAC patent litigation in March 1972 in Minneapolis. This time in Baltimore another trial was being conducted for the regenerating memory patent. After his unsuccessful attempt four years ago to intervene, together with the State University of Iowa as a separate party at that trial, Atanasoff was again called as a witness. Going back, we can note, that on 01.04.1964 Sperry Rand claimed for compensation from Control Data, accusing it of violation of patent 827 of the regenerating memory. Control Data instituted a counterclaim, that its patent has been borrowed from the ABC. The inventor of the first computer is called as a witness from the plaintiff (Sperry Rand), and Mauchly – for the side of the defendant (Control Data). We should further point out, that the evidence centers on testimony, given by Mauchly during his direct examination by Kirkpatrick contradicts his testimony in the other lawsuit. Kirkpatrick presented to the court numerous material evidences in support of the case of Control Data – photos, documents and the whole correspondence of Mauchly, found, although, he "had failed to find it". The destiny of the Baltimore lawsuit was already adjudicated at the ENIAC process. Judge Larson found, through the disclosures of witnesses, that the regenerating memory had been also derived from Atanasoff and it became clear, that its patent would also be ruled invalid, as was the case with the ENIAC patent. The sitting of the trial, conducted at Baltimore lasted only several days, because it was easy to predict its outcome and Sperry Rand lost any interest in it. The trial was abandoned until 1971, when on the insistence of a highly placed judge was stopped by mutual agreement by both sides. They signed an undisclosed agreement, which stipulated that Sperry Rand pays to Control Data a certain amount. Subsequently, the company Sperry Rand, changed its name to Sperry, and is presently a part of the giant Unisys

Corp., Detroit, presently assigned with the almost half billion dollars construction, of the Radar-computer meteorological system NEXTRAD for duly notification of hurricanes, floods and other calamities – one peculiar materialization of Mauchly's youthful dream.

According to Atanasoff, Larson's verdict is a Solomonic one, because it recognized the significant contribution made by Eckert and Mauchly in the development of the computer technologies after the ABC. ENIAC was completed in a record short time – two and a half years. Its main role in history was the successful introduction of the machine in operation, which provoked the immediate development of the next generation computers, from where the contemporary computer revolution began, spreading over all spheres of life.

And yet, the Atanasoff-Berry computer, whose acting model for electronic computation is demonstrated six years before the ENIAC, gives the initial push to that revolution. The direct impact of that computer in the development of the ENIAC, runs like a red thread through the thousands pages of the proceedings of the ENIAC lawsuit.

The verdict finds the direct presence of the principles of the ABC in the computers constructed under the guidance of Eckert and Mauchly following the ENIAC, and namely EDVAC, UNIVAC, BINAC. The same principle we discover in the most-advanced contemporary computers – from the personal laptops, the microcomputers to the super-computers, performing hundreds of millions of operations per second.

THE OPPONENTS AND THEIR ACTIONS

How do Mauchly and Eckert react to the Verdict? Encouraged by the lack of publicity around that verdict and of the widely social discussion on the outcome of the lawsuit, both of them made statements in the press and at scientific forums misrepresenting the truth, as at the lawsuit. In 1975 Atanasoff was invited to participate by presenting a report at the Conference on the History of the Computing Technologies, held in the spring of 1976 at Los Alamos. He saw this as a rare opportunity to clarify before the computer experts and scientific historians, the evidence documenting his priority, as brilliantly as he had done in the courtroom. But his health conditions prevented him from participating at that conference and Mauchly made use of it. In Los Alamos he read a report, in which he rejected the influence of the Atanasoff-Berry computer on the ENIAC, and ignored not only the testimonies of the witnesses, that had exposed his behavior at the lawsuit, but also the conclusions that Judge Larson made. With disappointment, Atanasoff read later in Mauchly's printed report, his allegations, that before he was acquainted with the ABC, he had already constructed "small models of experimental digital schemes, using gas-discharging tubes (neon lamps), and vacuum electronic tubes". We have already mentioned, that this version of Mauchly, was blown up like a soap-bubble. In the same report Mauchly "plays the hypocrite" maintaining, that in 1941 he had tried hard to convince Atanasoff, that the ABC did not implement the possibilities of electronics for fast calculations. Atanasoff clarifies, that all these statements Mauchly were made much later, but tries to impute to them as "backdate".

"His letters disclose, that he considered my computer quite fast, as it was indeed, in comparison to everything, developed at that time. Actually, he obviously considered, that my computer is simply wonderful". But the most insolent fabrication in Mauchly's report is the following : "When in 1941 I entered in the Moor School, I sent him (to Atanasoff) a letter, in which I alluded to him, that he could join us and could have a run of luck in the developing of his ideas, but he preferred not to do that". On this occasion Atanasoff states: "This allegation is devised from beginning to end. I have not heard at all about such proposal, until I read the report of John William Mauchly".

Eckert stands fast by Mauchly in his comments on the ENIAC lawsuit, even exceling him with his insulting phrases. For example, in the autumn of 1984 in the American magazine Data Processing Management Eckert qualifies Larson as a "crazy judge", who threatened to turn the whole trial in an anti-trust lawsuit against Sperry Rand, but he and Mauchly had already spent $ 1 million on that trial and did not like to be engaged in it any more. According to Eckert, Atanasoff "had not spoken the truth" – during the Mauchly's visit at Ames, Atanasoff " had no computer, but only schemes and descriptions of what is going to be constructed". "And something more – even had he completed the ABC, it would not be able to work". Eckert suggests, that Larson's verdict should be considered as "an absurd exaggeration" and "a shared joke", because credulance was given to Atanasoff's evidence, that he has constructed an acting computer.

He is the main speaker of the large celebration, organized on 13.02.1986 by the Computer Museum on occasion of the 40th anniversary of the inauguration of the ENIAC. In the announcement printed by the New York Times on the occasion of the celebration – "30 tons "mind" gives birth to the computer epoch" – there is not even a word about

Atanasoff. In the spirit of his previous statements Eckert also writes in 1986 in the weekly, Computer World, which tried to give a forum for both disputing parties.

But why did the myth about Eckert and Mauchly's priority for such a long time reign over the minds and hearts of the computer society in the United States, ignoring the memorable lawsuit? On one hand, throughout the 1970 only a few had heard something about the Atanasoff trial. While on the other hand, it could be explained with the psychological barrier. Mauchly and Eckert had spent the previous twenty years lecturing and printing their version and could not at once abandon it. In 1984, in the April issue of the trimestrial American magazine, Annals of the History of Computing, an attempt is made to question Larson's verdict. The article, entitled the "Early Years of John Mauchly", is written by Kathleen Mauchly the widow of the deceased in 1980 Mauchly.

Obviously, a direct reason for writing her article K. Mauchly stems from the published, in 1981, in the same magazine, article by Arthur and Allice Burks the ENIAC – the first universal DECM, in the nature of the ABC and his direct influence on the creation of ENIAC is analyzed in depth. The authors themselves were participants in the development of the ENIAC. And as we mentioned, Arthur Burks became a recognized expert on the Atanasoff-Berry computer following research into the documentation of the ENIAC lawsuit and crosschecking its conclusions through references with Atanasoff's manuscript from 1940 and discussions with the inventor himself.

Isn't it indicative of the fact that Kathleen Mauchly does not even refer in her article to the extensive investigation of the Burks family made in of 1981? A mathematician by education, she is included in the development of the ENIAC as its former operator-programmer. In 1948 she married John Mauchly. In the article, „The pre-history of creation of the ENIAC", is described according to the evidences of Atanasoff in the lawsuit Honeywell – Sperry Read. She publishes some selected paragraphs from the declarations of the defendants of both parties. Eckert is cited too – with his testimony on the patent lawsuit, which he and Williams Mauchly institute against Williams in 1954.

The main trump of K. Mauchly's are some letters and photos, so far not presented at the trial ENIAC, which at that time "have not been found". According to the author, they support Mauchly's thesis, that he has designed digital computing schemes before his meetings with Atanasoff during 1940 and 1941. Unfortunately, her touching attempt at posthumously to elevate her husband's reputation, harmed by the lawsuit does not stand to criticism. The deliberately selected quotes in no way could create the conditions of provoking any reverse moves at an eventual pre-hearing of the trial. In fact, it is John Mauchly's occupation after the lawsuit. The only result of that publication is, that she provokes temporary confusion instead of emphasizing on the actual achievements of Mauchly in the development of the first computer with universal purpose, the ENIAC, and also of the computer with a memorized program EDVAC.

What are the arguments, with which she tries to prove the main thesis of her article – that Mauchly has not been influenced from his direct predecessor Atanasoff in the development of ENIAC? K. Mauchly does not succeed in proving the allegation, that she possesses "the physical components of DECM, constructed by Mauchly at the time, when he had lectured in the College". The newly discovered evidences in support of Mauchly, in fact do not constitute any basic parts of the computing device, as the author tries to present them, but are instead slated for the use of other needs. They constitute elementary scheme combinations of electronic elements and certain laboratory gadgets-components, which not even a genius, but only a magician with a magic wand, could turn into the knots of a computer.

After the lawsuit, the Board of the State University of Iowa undertakes in honor of Atanasoff, certain actions, in order to perpetuate his historical invention. More ever, in the person of D.Lent – the director of the Information Office, the University regularly sends objections to the editions, in which, "mistaken accounts about the history of the computer" are allowed for instance the Wall Street Journal, as on 05.06.1979 the newspaper publishes a photo, in which Eckert is photographed next to the ENIAC, and the text points out, that this is the "first DECM". Errors of this kind appear on TV broadcastings of CBS, in publications of the Chicago Museum of Science and Industry, the World Book Encyclopedia, The magazine National Geographic, etc. But in 1983 the picture changed. Then Lent wrote: "From there, where we were accustomed to receivivg some short notes, that we are mistaken, now we receive polite apologizing letters, expressing interest. But the current of the computer history is from many years extensively contaminated and many years will elapse, before restoration of its initial purity".

From the book **Джон Атанасов. Изобретателят на компютъра**

Mollenhoff comments*: For the owners of the ENIAC patent and for the whole computer society, the Federal District Court Decision issued on 19.10.1973 "falls like a heavy aircraft bomb", destroying the myth, that Mauchly and Eckert created the first DECM. The verdict rules the ENIAC patent invalid and finds out, that Mauchly and Eckert have derived the essential principles from the invention made by John Atanasoff. Several hundreds pages disclose as well other violations of the applicants of the patent.

After the lawsuit, Mauchly and Eckert continued to misinterpret the informational vacuum about the concluded lawsuit. But gradually the truth about the priority of John Atanasoff began to emerge, penetrating into the scientific encyclopedias and the other specialized editions of the world. In 1985 Atanasoff, once again visited Bulgaria, his roots, but this time he came as a winner in the historical lawsuit, which ended with his official recognition as an inventor of DECM.

In spite of Judge Larson's findings and the massive court recordings, there are still writers of computer textbooks and some of magazines and newspapers, which refuse to recognize, that the first DECM had been constructed in the State of Iowa by John Atanasoff and Clifford Berry. Part of that misinformation remains in the texts, because the practice of the writers of textbooks is to copy from previous textbooks, without making any effort in checking the documents, or to analyze the court proceeding, or juridical discoveries, which contradict their point of view on computer history.

The chronicles continue to be confused by articles and statements made by Mauchly, and after his death emitted by his widow, which for the larger part are simply, repetitions of his „incorrect" testimony and the evidence given before the court, and which were then discredited. Provided, that Mauchly had the opportunity at the trial to present all kinds of documents, and witnesses, in order to support his statement that he had developed the DECM, before his meeting with Atanasoff in December of 1940 and his visit to Ames in June 1941, the decorated repetitions of these doubtful stories from others, are not very convincing.

While friends, relatives and business partners of Mauchly's believe, out of personal interest his statements, and most probably will continue to rely on his unlikely statements for personal benefit, even

* Mollenhoff C.R. Atanasoff: Forgotten Father of the Computer.

when Mauchly's statements sharply contradict his own letters, written to Atanasoff and others, during the period immediately after his visit to the State College of Iowa. These friends, relatives and business partners of Mauchly's, most probably will reject the proposal to make an objective analysis of the information from the massive court records, which support judge decision Larson's, that Mauchly has derived his ideas from Atanasoff.

But the opinions and conclusions of friends, relatives and business partners are immaterial, unless they are accompanied by inexorable written evidence, supporting the work of Mauchly on the DECM before his meetings with Atanasoff during 1940. It is impossible to find such evidence, provided, that the attorneys of Sperry Rand had spent millions of dollars for unsuccessful efforts to find such for the testimonies and for the trial before the Federal District Court with Judge Larson presiding.

It is time for the computer historians, to stop accepting the self-serving statements and unsupported new theories of what Mauchly might have thought in the 1937–1944 period. He had his opportunity to prove it in several depositions and in the trial, where Sperry Rand and Ilinois Development Corp. lawyers had the motivation and the financial support to produce every scrap of evidence and every bit of testimony that might support his contention that the ENIAC was the product of his intellect and was not derived from knowledge he gained from the Atanasoff-Berry machine.

It is time for those who argue that a record made in a court of law may not be as valid as scientific historical research, to come forward and point out where that court decision in the Honeywell case was in error. It is time, for those who purport to challenge Judge Larson's decision to do so in a manner that gives some indication that they have read at least the relevant parts of the testimony of the key figures – John V.Atanasoff and John W.Mauchly.

IN THE LAND OF MY FOREFATHERS

INTERMEDIA:VISIT TO BULGARIA

John Atanasoff

Towards the summer of 1970 the time of the two juridical inquires had been delayed, probably for adjusting the new court calendar. In the begining of the autumn I received a letter from Blagovest Sendov, the then Dean of Mathematical Faculty of the University of Sofia. He had said, that obviously I have a Bulgarian name – later I found out, that names coming from the root Atanasius, as Atanas, Atanasius or Atanasoff are much more common in Bulgaria, than Smith in our country, and that he has studied my work on the computers. Would I like to describe him my real situation? I wrote about my father, how my grandfather held him like a baby, while he had been shoot and killed in 1876 in the eve of the uprising against Turkey. My father had arrived in the USA in 1889 at 13 years age together with his uncle and was left alone at the age of 15. He graduated from the University of Colgate and married for my mother, who is a descendent of a typical mixture of English, Irish and French nationalities, which all of them have been for a long time in the USA. During all my life I have known only one Bulgarian – Boris Iliev : I met him, when he was a student on agronomy in the State University of Iowa in 1927, and I lost his traces during the war. Obviously, Sendov had been carried away quite a lot, as I received another letter: he has found my friend in Sofia and my father's native village – Boyadjic, Jambol district, where the 80-th elapsed years, have not errased the memories of the people about my father and his family. Could I come to Bulgaria? – Sendov asked.

In the beginning, I thought of refusing him, but things have developed with the speed of lightning: about 19 November 1970 I, together with my wife, hired a car from Wolvberg, FRG and set off for Berlin, and from there toward south-east, to Bulgaria. With our entering in Sofia (2 December) I realized, that I have no confirmation either of the place, nor of meeting. I realized too, that I have forgotten my language and alphabet as well. Nobody was around and no militzia man or other official person, so I approached the first man who got the team. He did not know English, but followed, that we speak that language: he entered our car, guided us to a big building, for which I was sure, it was government office. It happens to be, his own working place, from where he brought a man, who knew English. With his assistance I found my old friend, now retired, from the Institute of Agriculture, and after that I contacted Sendov. It was the first time, we were told, that we would be guests of the Bulgarian Academy of Sciences.

We spent a week in Sofia, during which I delivered a speech about the computers in an overflowing hall with the remaining public listening over loud speakers outside in the cold. The next week they took us around the country and we visited my father's native village. I was embarrassed and kissed by more than 200 people, which proved to be my relatives. I met a cousin of my father, who was several years younger than me, but still yet was remembering his departure. But as I know that my father did not like to write letters. I was doubtful when they show me a letter, written by my father – in Bulgarian – in 1954. But the envelope was very clearly addressed by my mother. In a nearly small town I met my father's sister, who was born, after he has left Bulgaria.

The last week we were again in Sofia. I did not feel very well from so many celebrations in my honour, but at the end of my visit, we felt we did not like to go. On the day before our departure, I had a telephone call from the Secretary of the Academy, asking me if I could postpone my departure with one day. It seems, some academicians had suggested to the Sobranje for a reward, and they have just received the approval to present me officially with the orden of Cyril and Methodius I-st. For my "great merits and scientific contribution". I suppose, that decision has been influenced by the fact, that my grandfather has participated in the uprising against the Turkish. To Sts. Cyril and Methodius is attributed their contribution for creating the cyrilic alphabet in 850 A.D. Although, that they have invested the cyrilic alphabet with religious purposes, the Bulgarians have called their highest reward, given to scientists, on their name. Even Communist Bulgaria is proud of the work of these saints. The award was delivered to me the next day in the presence of the Ambassador of the USA and his advisors. There was at the same time some international incident, which caused tension betwwen Bulgarians and American officials, but my reward changed this attitude.

While the Chairman of the Academy Angel Balevski has completed his official speech, I was listening to my translator. I suddenly realized, that it is necessary to reply and it should be done immediately. Then I remember that in fact, I know something about the Sts. Cyril and Methodius. I told at the Academy about my great interest towards the writing. I pointed out that Bulgaria is one of the few nations, which owns a system of written signs; the Cyril's alphabet stands equally, on a level with the other alphabets of the world. My own studying, I underlined, show, the necessity of efforts towards invention of a new alphabet, which to serve for the goodness and future of mankind.

A letter from John Atanasoff to Prof. Sendov

1970,02 September,

Dear Prof. Sendov,

I received your kind letter this morning. Sitting at my bureau. I was evaluating the large number bits, needed, in order to reply properly to your letter. I am sure, that this letter is not enough, but I hope, that will give you an idea about some moments from the history of the computing machines. Our earliest works in the State University of Iowa (by that time – a college) are not well known. But, during the last three years different investigations found what fundamental and principle important meaning they had. These investigations have been done as a consequence of a million dollars patent claim, instituted in the Federal Court of the USA. My testimony in the Federal Court of Minneapolis took 9 days and comprise of 1250 written pages. And of course, all the lot of evidences covers not everything in the question you have raised in your letter.

Somebody has told me, that my family name is as popular in Bulgaria, as Smith in England. In any case, my father was a Bulgarian born on 06.01.1876 (according the Gregorian calendar). When he was three months old a Turkish bullet killed his father, leaving also a scar on his head. After the uprising the young widow had married again and the family's difficulties compeled my father, then 13 years old, to depart to the USA with his uncle to trade with rose oil. At the age of 15 he was left all alone there and by some miraculous chance learned English and obtained a good education. That was his occupation until 1901, when he graduated from the university of Colgate.

My mother (she is now 89) is a typical American with a mixture of Irish, English and French blood, and so the Bulgarian language was never spoken in our home. Bulgarians have seldom visited us and with none have we been closely related. Later, when I was graduating from the university, I got acquainted with one Bulgarian, Boris Iliev. It was in 1926 and 1927. He was studying Agricultural machine constructions and occupied some position in your Agriculture faculty. I still remember, by some chance one address in Sofia, which he gave me, Chatalja str. 21. Could you check if he is still alive?

For your general information about my life, I enclose a copy of the information contained in the edition " American scientists ". At present, I am retired in favorable condition and good health, at age 67. During the last five years I had no close relations with any organization, but from time to time I consult in my specialty. During the last three years I devoted my attention mostly to the court trials, I mentioned above. Sometimes, I join different programs for research and development, which are of interest to me, and in this way I lead a vigorous and happy life. I own a small farm and one of my favorite occupations is to grow vegetables. Some of my friends, that know all these things, assure me, that a similar, uncommon (for America) occupation is typical for the Bulgarians.

I started to work on my M.Sc. degree in the State University of Iowa at the end of 1925 and received the title Master of Science in the summer of 1926. I continued my work in the State University of Iowa, but during the spring of 1929 I moved to work at the University of Wisconsin, where I obtained Ph.D. in theoretical physics in the summer of 1930. At the end of the same year I returned back to the State University of Iowa, where I devoted my time to active lecturing and research work. About 1935 I was lecturing post-graduate students and guided the scientific work of Ph.D. applicants. I worked together with my students in different fields as quantum mechanics, elasticity and physics of crystals. For almost all problems we encountered solution of linear formal differential equations. Usually, it was impossible to solve the systems directly, so we had to resort to the methods of approximation from the type of Rely-Ritz and Trefz. At the same time the students with a better theoretical background began developing new methods of a more general character. In all cases we reached large systems of linear algebraic equations. My whole program was burdened with the solving of such systems.

This problem became to some extent my idea-fix. First of all I tried analog models for solution. Very soon I was convinced, they lacked punctuality. Then I used some table devices from the type Holerit and started thinking about using a mechanically connected calculating systems. In all the cases the computing ability and speed proved to be unsatisfactory and finally I was encouraged to approach the construction of new calculating elements. It was in the spring of 1937.

In one very cold night in the late Autumn of 1937 I went back to my study in the University, to work on that problem. I tried to predispose on the problem, thinking over every detail, but nothing came up. Disappointed I went out to my car, and drove more than 300 km with speed well above 100 km/h, went out in the cold night and entered a bar or tavern. In a few minutes I left my mind very calm and clear and as if I saw in front of me, without any reference books and notes, all my knowledge and experience. When I started driving home early in the morning, to an extent I had reached a fundamentally new approach to the computation process.

I will skip the details. At first I worked alone, but towards the autumn of 1939 I found some means and hired Clifford Berry. Late autumn of the same year, the first our prototype computer, performing the operations adding and subtracting was brought into the light. In chronological order we demonstrated :

1. The first implementation of binary number system in DECM

2. The first regenerating memory

3. The first logic schemes, very similar to the schemes, used today

4. In fact, the first implementation of consecutive calculating

5. The first automatic DECM and other less important details of the contemporary computing machines

Here I will try to stop and put an end to my letter. I would like to devote some time for more detailed cooperative work. Would it be possible for you to come to USA? On the other hand I had been thinking for years to visit Bulgaria, and see my father's native place (Boyadjik, Yambol district) and to feel the nature of people, I originate from. But, yet, I have no particular plans about this visit. I could supply you with much more details, but it will impose the complication of taking copies. Please, write to me, if you have any question.

Sincerely Yours,
JOHN ATANASOFF

LIVING WITH A MAN WHO IS CONSTANTLY INFATUATED WITH STRANGE IDEAS IS QUITE EXCITING

ALICE ATANASOFF'S STORY

John and I married late. We have lived together for 35 years now. He has three wonderful children and we have ten grandchildren from our son and two daughters.

When we met, he did not talk about his great invention. He worked on other inventions and was totally engulfed by that. He was sorry that he could not continue working on the computer and avoided mentioning the topic. The lawyers came one day and asked him to tell them about his work. At first, he refused but later he agreed to show them some of his old archives. There, they found all they needed for the turning of the lawsuit, which was an important precedent in commercial law. I was helping to collect all details left in the archives.

There was a funny moment. At that time, he did not get any financial aid for the invention of the computer. The lawyers were surprised to find that he wrote on both sides of the sheet to save paper... Paper cost a penny then; later it became 10 cents. Telephone conversations were very expensive and people preferred to write letters or to send post cards. So he had kept many letters, which served as evidence before the court.

After the trial my husband was very upset and depressed because nobody recognized his work. The trial was a turning point for him because only then did he realize that his old idea about a new calculating machine was behind all modern computers. Even now, when he has a computer of his own, he studies it closely and identifies his original ideas... Often, he would call me to explain, "I have invented this." And his confidence grows. Some time ago, there was a congress of young teachers of Mathematics from different universities. About a thousand people attended. My husband was invited too. He was very pleased because the young people did not know anything about the lawsuit. The only thing they knew was that there before them stood the man who had invented the first computer. It was wonderful!

At the beginning, we were surprised by the fact that, after the trial, there was no reaction in the national press. The papers were busy with the Watergate case. One of the most popular newspapers in the State of Iowa published a brilliant article about the trial. Later one of the most popular CBS commentators prepared a whole program for the evening news but the political events – the invasion in Grenada and the Beirut massacres – did not allow its broadcast.

When I was young, I taught at a primary school. Later, I became a drafts person and, when my husband founded his own company, I began working there. I did anything that was necessary; I was a drafts person, an accountant and a secretary. We worked long hours together. We went on working together even after our marriage. We have bought a farm and bulls. The work on such a farm is heavy but we both like the open space. We both like gardening. We grow many vegetables. I freeze or can them and so we always have homegrown vegetables.

Once, we were traveling in the country. A beautiful garden, in which an elderly man and woman were working, attracted our eyes. We stopped and asked them why they kept working and caring for such a large garden – they were quite old. The woman answered, "That's because my husband is Bulgarian." Before preparing for our visit to Bulgaria, my husband ploughed the land with a tractor, tilted the soil and we planted the garden. When we go back, everything should have sprouted... We grow eggplants and okra, which thrives in the southern parts of the United States. It is a popular plant in Bulgaria. Also, we cultivate tomatoes and peppers. We have stopped bottling wine lately – we cannot drink it... But we were famous among our friends for our wine. Our guests would always bring bottles so that we could pour of our homemade wine. And from the apples we made apple wine.

Living with a man who is constantly infatuated with strange ideas is quite exciting. It is never boring. Sometimes I tell him that other people go and buy what they need but he wants to invent his own machine, to build some device. Of course, that takes much more time but in the end we both are happy because we have exactly what we need. To find what exactly you need also takes a lot of time. All sorts of original ideas occur to him in our everyday life. Everybody wants to make something better and to make it cheaper and more functional.

We both like reading together a lot. John buys many scientific journals, which are difficult for me but he patiently explains to me the interesting papers published in them. I keep learning new things. He is very careful to everybody in the family.

John has a clear memory and remembers many details of the past. For example the hospital room, in which he stayed more than 40 years ago, or the exact place or page where he read something many years ago. He remembers clearly our first date. It is so nice to be remembered when you were young and attractive...

His mother lived with us during her last years. She died at the age of 101. His father died in 1956 (note by D.Sh. – at the age of 80; John Atanasoff died aged almost 92; they all were marked by longevity). He was a handsome man with a great vitality. After his death, the mother lived for some time with each of her eight children. She was a very active woman; she would stay with one of her children for two months and then move to another one. She moved constantly. During the last years her strength drained out and she stayed with us. She was a wonderful person. I had never imagined that one could be charming even at an old age but she made me believe that. She was a very independent woman but she would allow us to service her. I think that I would not be able to agree to that. I suppose my pride would prevent that. I would not feel good if someone else would wash my hands. But she accepted our help gladly.

My husband was very kind and careful with her. Despite his work, he kept a small alarm clock, which rang every hour. He took her up from the chair and walked her round the room every hour. Then she would sit down again but these walks kept her physically active until the very end. When she could not see and read, she made enormous calculations to keep her brain active – she was a very good mathematician. Also, she solved crossword puzzles to keep her mind. She liked writing letters and, after losing her sight, we would read to her. She had written her memoirs and she wanted us to read them to her. Once we had a meeting of the whole Atanasoff family – all children, grandchildren and great grandchildren. The meeting was in Florida. Many Bulgarians were present. I remember two or three of them, with whom we have been together. Otherwise there would have been more opportunities to speak in Bulgarian. The expression, mother tongue, is not without a reason – every man learns his mother's language first.

ANTENI NEWSPAPER, 1985, № 23–26

THE SECOND AND LAST VISIT

THE LONG LIFE OF A GREAT MAN: JOHN ATANASOFF
/4 October 1903 – 16 June 1995/

Dimitar Shishkov

In May 1985 he visited Bulgaria for the second and last time as an honored guest of the International Conference: “Children in the Information Era” held in the city of Varna, Bulgaria.

Post scriptum made by John Atanasoff:

“At that conference representatives from 48 countries had arrived, to discuss important problems, and I hope, that in the forthcoming week I should carry on conversations with a lot of them. The subjects of the discussion are really the most important in the modern world and are stressing the significance of the computational machines, although it is impossible to include all these problems…

Surely a lot of people, who had read my works concerning the computational machines are surprised that I am here.

My family name is an answer of the secret.

When I was young, after becoming an Associate Professor in Physics and Mathematics, I was lecturing graduate students. I remember that in my lectures on Electrical Engineering I had not included lectures on electronics. I knew I should do something about it that’s why I found the best book on the matter. It turned out it was written by a South-African Professor called Makomo – If you look for it in the library, may be you will find it, though it is now very old. Having carefully examined this book, I carried out a number of experiments in the field of Electronics.

From my Bulgarian father I have learned to do everything with my own hands. Even when I was engaged in Higher Scientific Physics, I did not abandon experiments. That is how I taught my students. Some of them took in my style.”

JOHN ATANASOFF

EXCEPTIONAL SCIENTIFIC ENLIGHTENMENT

On May 17, 1985 the vice-premier of the Council of Ministers and chairman of the Committee for Culture George Yordanov bestowed on Prof. John Atanasoff an award "People's Republic of Bulgaria, I[st] class". The citizen of USA with Bulgarian lineage John Atanasoff is the first developer of the Digital Electronic Calculation Machine. George Yordanov delivered a speech as follows:

I am delighted to perform the task of the State Council of People's Republic of Bulgaria to award you, Prof. John Atanasoff with the highly appreciated medal – People's Republic of Bulgaria, I[st] class.

On this occasion I am delighted to express our respect and sincere honor to you. We are pleased to congratulate you again in Bulgaria, the native country of your father. The land that lives in our hearts, inspiring a deep and permanent sense of humanism and patriotism.

I would like again to stress: Prof. John Atanasoff was awarded with the highly prised Bulgarian medal. We would like with pleasure to note that the first man, who achieved the audacious research idea in using electronics for the purposes of calculations, the man, who transfered that idea in a creative and perspective work with world significance, has a Bulgarian lineage (origin).

In our electronic century your research is a symbol of progress. Today the computers have transformed into a miraculous power, that occup all fields of life. And we are happy that the basis of this significant creative work was built by the name and talent of our fellow-countryman, Prof. John Atanasoff.

We would like to believe that somewhere in the deep descents of your magnificent creative work, a result of an exceptional scientific enlightenment, underlines the investigative impulse of the talent of the Bulgarian people.

In your presence, my dear Prof. Atanasoff, we congratulate the scientist, whose contribution to the human intellect and spirit to be provided with powerful means of progress. The future development of the world is an inseparable of the wide application of the computer approach. That goal is important for the science, economics, culture and education in socialist Bulgaria.

Let us remind the words of the president of People's Republic of Bulgaria, Todor Zhivkov in his salutatory address to the participants in the International conference and exhibition under the title "The Children in the information era", held recently in our country: "Within its possibilities People's Republic of Bulgaria establishes a great activities in the field of electronics and informatics. We carry out a national program for education and engagement of the youth in the electronic – computational machinery, for realizing a large-scale issue of the second computation competence.

Expressing our admiration for your character and our respect for your scientific work, with all my heart and spirit we wish to implement it for the purposes of people and the progress in a peaceful world.

I Congratulate you from my heart with this honorable award! I would like you to accept it as a expression in courtesy and recognition towards you for your significant contribution of the world creative work.

Be in high spirit and healthy, dear Prof. John Atanasoff! Let your Bulgarian origin support you, let us give you new power to the meaning of your contribution in the scientific world.

I wish you new life and family joys, happy and fruitful creative longevity. Once more: congratulations for long life!"

The ceremony was attended by the president of the Bulgarian Academy of Sciences, acad. Angel Balevski, the President of Sofia University, distinguished representatives of Bulgarian science. The ceremony was also attended by the US Ambassador to Bulgaria, Melvin Levitsky.

Narodna Kultura, 1985, No. 21

AN HOUR SPENT WITH PROF. JOHN ATANASOFF: THE COMPUTER CANNOT REPLACE MAN

A big bouquet of roses and somewhat more than the usual excitement at the airport. And then there was a flurry of curiosity because the passenger, was the inventor of the first computer. Prof. John Atanasoff, we knew him by name, and that he was of Bulgarian origin. And later, as he joked, the inventiveness and buoyancy are undoubtedly inspired by the Bulgarian half of his blood.

[...] Only a half of a century has passed since the first computer had been invented by prof. John Atanasoff and his assistant Clifford Berry, at the dawn of the computer revolution. But as the engineers confirmed that "in the world of computers, time runs faster than the chronological time". We have witnessed several fundamental changes in the machines. And it seems that by now we have become used to this dynamic change – new electronic generations emerge before our very eyes.

"The Children of The Information Era: The Forthcoming Problems of Today", the subject of the International Conference held in the city of Varna, attempts to answer the questions of the future, developing a program for further computer training. Can we predict the future innovations of the contemporary children, whose free time is engaged with computers? The interest toward the great scientist is only natural. We understand his emotion, when Prof. Atanasoff began to talk adressing the overcrowded conference room.

The same day, in the calm hotel room, decorated with still fresh bouquet of roses, we spoke with Prof. Atanasoff.

"Early in my life my mother had taught me not only to read and write, but to hear and interpret each speech. Not to learn the letters but to know the phonetics of the words. I hear them, I hear the voices and the hearts of the people, who pronounce them. In ones life, man has few real teachers, those who serve as role models. To a great extent, I owe my successes, my diligence, to the fact that I have been persistent in setting and achieving the goals. But we learn most from books".

Recently the professor had counted approximately how many words he knew. About eighty thousand! Talking about this, he is categorically sure – the computer could never replace "reading and writing", first of all we are obliged to educate our children.

In calculation as well as in communication "the intelligent machine" can help. It can offer faster and international connection between people. During 1940 that idea obsessed Prof. Atanasoff and it consumed his free time. After 1961 his focus centers around the development of a universal dual code, namely a machine that would encode sounds: "I do that rather discreetly – he noted – because I would like to create an alphabet, applicable to all languages". He has not published his latest work.

"It is possible and I must carry that work to its end! I want each letter or each symbol to carry more meanings, to support with full power the alphabet".

His own creation serves his needs. Using it Prof. Atanasoff is writing his memoirs and his books. A year ago, a foreign newspaper announced that "the farther of the computer" is learning the language Basic.

– Yes, I am – he afirmed – new and new machines appear and I have to improve my knowledge.

– Are there limits to the computer, Prof. Atanasoff, beyond which man cannot subjugate the electronic devices?

– No, the computer has no soul. It is a facility, a device, an instrument.

It would be dangerous and an error, should the computers "grasp" human thought. We should not let our children forget how to study because of the computers.

Rabotnichesko delo, 1985, No 130

Unforgettable meetings with fellow Bulgarian compatriots

John V. Atanasoff tombstone in Mt. Airy, Maryland near the Atanasoff home

High relief of the great inventor, placed on the facade of the building of Science and Technology in Yambol, Bulgaria

THE FIRST AMERICAN ENCYCLOPEDIA OF COMPUTER SCIENCE

1st ed., Antony Ralston (ed.), Van Nostrand Reinhold Co., 1976, 1523 p.

ATANASOFF, JOHN VINCENT

John Atanasoff (b. Hamilton, N.Y., Oct. 4, 1903) received his B.S. at Florida State in 1925 and his M.S. at Iowa State in 1926.

Impeded by the cumbersome solution of large systems of equations and other complex calculations while working on his Ph.D. (Wisconsin, 1930, in math-physics), Atanasoff dismantled the desk calculators in an attempt to adapt them and increase their computational capabilities. After receiving his doctorate, he returned to Iowa State in 1930, where he remained until 1945 as a professor in mathematics and (later) in physics. During his tenure there, he revamped an IBM punch card machine in another attempt to speed the tedious calculations for his graduate students.

Rejecting the analog devices because they were too slow and not adequately accurate, he concentrated on the digital approach. With the help of a graduate student, the late Clifford Berry, Atanasoff had built a prototype of the computer by December 1939. A working model of the Atanasoff – Berry computer was completed in 1942. It was a serial, binary, electro-mechanical machine, and employed various new techniques that Atanasoff invented, including the novel uses of logic circuitry and a regenerative memory.

Atanasoff did not completely understand the extent of the contribution he had made to the advancement of technology and did not anticipate the wide use of computers. IBM and Remington Rand rejected Atanasoff's overtures, and Iowa State – not fully realizing the potential importance of his computer – failed to obtain patent rights. Discouraged by his own attempts to obtain a patent, Atanasoff gave up. He spent the rest of his professional career in various governmental and industrial jobs, including the presidency of two companies he founded. Ordnance Engineering Corporation and Cybernetics, Inc. For his work with the Navy Ordnance Laboratory during World War II, received the U.S. Naval Distinguished Award in 1945.

Only very recently did Atanasoff receive the recognition as one of the fathers of the digital computer. In a patent infringement law suit filed in 1973 by Sperry Rand against Honeywell, Atanasoff and others testified concerning the development of the first electronic computer, the ENIAC, by John Mauchly and J. Prosper Eckert of the Moore School of Electrical Engineering at the University of Pennsylvania between 1942 and 1946. The decision on the case, by Federal District Judge, Earl R. Larson, concluded that Eckert and Mauchly had derived some of their ideas from Atanasoff, partly as a result of a visit Mauchly made to Atanasoff at Iowa State in 1941.

New York, 1976 C. Mollenhoff

THE EARTHLY EPILOGUE BUT A PLACE IN ETERNITY

JOHN ATANASOFF WAS BURIED WITH BULGARIAN MUSIC

FREDERICK, USA. I am proud that I have Bulgarian origin and my great grandfather was Bulgarian, said Fred Eastler, great grandson of John (Ivan) Atanasoff.

Fred's grandfather – John Vincent Atanasoff, the inventor of the first electronic digital computer, was buried yesterday in Frederick, Maryland, 80 km away from Washington D. C.

"We attend the man in the path of immortality, who belongs to America and Bulgaria as well as to the whole mankind" said in her parting words, the Ambassador of Bulgaria in USA, Snezhana Botusharova, who was invited to participate at the funeral ceremony by the family of John Atanasoff. Condolence letters were read, sent by then President of Bulgaria Zhelyu Zhelev and by the President of the Bulgarian academy of Sciences Blagovest Sendov.

Ambassador Snezhana Botusharova expressed the high respect of Bulgarians toward the contribution and the personality of John Atanasoff and remembered the distinguished prizes, that Bulgaria presented to the great scientist.

The order Cyril and Methodius, Ist class, among the awards, were placed on a special spot at the home of John Atanasoff.

The funeral ceremony was attended by the John Atanasoff family – his wife, brother, both of his daughters and his son, grand children and great grand children, eminent professors and scientists from the Universities in Iowa and Wisconsin.

Bulgaria was present in the parting words of all. "I tried to study Bulgarian when I was a little girl, and now I remember many words" – said his daughter Joan.

"Sofia is a very beautiful city" – said Alice, John Atanasoff's wife, who has been twice to Bulgaria.

"He lived 91 years – almost a century, and with him has gone on an entire era" – said his son, who is also called John Atanasoff. "It is a very important era, that opened the doors to new computer technologies" – added the professor in informatics Arthur Oldihont at the State University in Iowa. There John Atanasoff was a professor for 10 years and it was there he created the first prototype of the electronic computer.

The urn with John Atanasoff's ashes were accompanied by ecclesiastic songs sung by Philipopolis group, which were presented to the Atanasoff's family from the Bulgarian Embassy.

Demokratzia, 1995, No. 141

A TELEGRAM BY PRESIDENT ZHELYU ZHELEV ADDRESSED TO THE FAMILY OF THE DEAD SCIENTIST, JUNE 16, 1995

"On behalf of the People's Republic of Bulgaria and myself I express the deepest condolences over the death of Prof. John Atanasoff. Throughout the world, as well as in Bulgaria, his works and scientific achievements are known and are used with high respect. Bulgaria, the native place of his parents, conferred Prof. Atanasoff with the most prestigious government prizes and he received a honourable place at the Bulgarian Academy of Sciences. By creating the first prototype of the electronic computer, Prof. John Atanasoff drew up mankind to its future."

* * *

MRS. ALICE ATANASOFF –
PLEASE, CONVEY TO
MR. JOHN V. ATANASOFF II
BOULDER COLORADO 80304
USA

Dear Mr. Atanasoff,

Please, accept our deepest regards as being the son of John Atanasoff.

We are The Bulgarian Computer Society "John Atanasoff". We are as well TANGRA TanNakRa All Bulgarian Foundation. We work together with leading scientists from BULGARIAN ACADEMY OF SCIENCES and SOFIA STATE UNIVERSITY to promote knowledge on ancient Bulgarian civilization. This is reflected in a number of editions, published by the foundation.

In contemporary aspect we find the universal achievements of your father, the great John Atanasoff – the Father of the Computer as a brilliant expression and emanation of Bulgarian creative spirit.

We intend to organize the construction of a John Atanasoff Memorial in Sofia[...] We have paid the Iowa University for the film "...from one John Atanasoff" in order to propagate it in Bulgaria. We want to translate and edit books about your father. Every piece of written or visual information will be useful [...]

In all this we would be glad to have your moral support.

Best regards,

PETKO KOLEV – CHAIRMAN OF TANGRA FOUNDATION
DIMITAR M. DIMITROV – CO-CHAIRMAN OF TANGRA FOUNDATION

SOFIA
January, 2000

* * *

1 FEBRUARY 2000
MR. PETKO KOLEV AND MR. DIMITER M. DIMITROV
TANGRA FOUNDATION

Gentlemen:

Mrs. Alice Atanasoff forwarded your letter to me. You have our support in your plans to construct a John Atanasoff memorial in Sofia. I would appreciate your sending us information as to your plans and progress.

Two books written about John V. Atanasoff, I, my father, are:

Atanasoff: Forgotten Father of the Computer by Clark R. Mollenhoff, Iowa State University Press, Ames, Iowa, 1988

The First Electronic Computer: The Atanasoff Story by Alice R. Burks and Arthur W. Burks, The University of Michigan Press, Ann Arbor, Michigan, 1988

We look forward to hearing of your progress.

Yours truly,

John V. Atanasoff, II

* * *

During October 2000, an Initiative committee for the creation of a monument to the inventor of the computer was established in Sofia.

* * *

WED, 4 OCT 2000
TO:
TANGRA FOUNDATION
THE INITIATIVE COMMITTEE

I am very pleased to hear that Bulgaria is honoring my father by planning to build a monument and publish a book. As you know we are of Bulgarian ancestory and we have close ties and wonderful feelings about Bulgaria. We would be very pleased to provide information, pictures or assistance on your project.

I am planning to visit Bulgaria in the Spring of 2001 and I would be pleased to meet with you and discuss this project. If I can be of immediate assistance please don't hesitate to call me.

Again I would like to give you my very best wishes and thanks.

Sincerely yours,

John V. Atanasoff II

Boulder, Colorado 80304

* * *

During December 2000 Bulgaria honorred John Vincent Atanasoff posthumusly with the orden "Stara Planina" Ist class.

BIBLIOGRAPHY

SCIENTIFIC PUBLICATIONS OF JOHN ATANASOFF

(WITHOUT HIS PUBLICATIONS ON MILITARY PATENTS)

1. *Atanasoff. J. V.*, Dielectric Constant of Helium. Physical Review, 36(1930)7, 1232–1242.

2. *Atanasoff, J. V., A. E. Brandt*, Application of Punched Card Equipment to the Analysis of Complex Spectra. Journal of the Optical Society of America, 26(1936)2, 83–88.

3. *Atanasoff, J. V., H. L. Wilcke*, Measurement of Viscosity of Eggs by Use of a Torsion Pendulum. Journal of Agricultural Research, 54(1937)9.

4. *Thorne, C. J., J. V. Atanasoff*, A Functional Method for the Solution of Thin Plate Problems Applied to A Square, Clamped Plate with A Central Point Load. Iowa State College Journal of Science, 14(1940)4, 333–343.

5. *Atanasoff, J. V., P. J. Hart*, Dynamical Determination of the Elastic Constants and Their Temperature Coefficients for Quartz. The Physical Review, 69(1941)1, 85–96.

6. *Atanasoff, J. V., E. W. Hammer*. A Determination of the c44 Elastic Constant for Beta-Quartz. The Physical Review, 59(1941), 97–99.

7. *Kammer, E. W., J. V. Atanasoff*, A Determination of the Elastic Constants of the Beta-Quartz. The Physical Review, 62(1942)7, 8. 395–400.

8. *Atanasoff, J. V., G. Murphy*. A Mechanical Device for the Solution of Equations Involving the Laplacian Operator. Iowa Engineering Experimental Station Bulletin, 166(November 1949).

9. *Atanasoff J. V., B. L. Snavely*. Upper-Atmosphere Temperatures from Helgoland, Big Bang. Journal of Meteorology, October 1949.

10. *Atanasoff. J. V., B. L. Snavely*, J. Brown. Modern Breadboard Chasis. Electronics, 22(1949)7.

11. *Atanasoff, J. V.* Computing Machine for The Solution of Large Systems of Linear Algebraic Equations, 1940. Originally unpublished Memorandum. In: The Origins of Digital Computers, Selected Papers, Br. Randell, B. (ed.), Chap. 7.2. Berlin, Springer Verlag. 1973, 305–325; 2d ed. 1982.

12. *Atanasoff, J. V.* A Proposal for the Adaptation of the Binary Alphabet to Modern Persian. To Minister of Education, Government of Iran. Cybernetics Inc., Frederick, Maryland, 1976.

SELECTED PUBLICATIONS ABOUT JOHN ATANASOFF

1. *Апокин, И. А., Ю. А. Белый, Л. Е. Майстров*. Вычислительная машина Дж. В. Атанасова. Историко-математические исследования, вып. XXIII. М., Наука, 1978, 168–180.

2. *Апокин, И. А., Л. Е. Майстров. Развитие вычислительних машин. М., Наука, 1974.*

3. **Атанасов, Дж. Началото. С., Народна младеж, 1985, 40 с. Съкратен бълг. превод.**

4. ***Атанасова, Алис. Разказва Алис Атанасова. Антени, бр. 23, 5.06.1985, бр. 25, 19.06.1985 (в бр. 25 – 2 пъти в Неизвестния процес).***

5. *Бончев, Н.* Бащата на компютъра. *Наука и техника за младежта*, 33(1981)9, 26–30. Препечатана в: Компютърът за вас, 1. С., Народна младеж, 1984.

Азбука за всички езици. Мечтата на проф. Джон Атанасов.

За буквите. Кирилометодиевски вестник, бр. 6, май–юни 1982, с. 12. Препечатана в книгата: Компютърът за вас, 2. С., Народна младеж, 1985, 37–38.

6. **Бончев, Н. Джон Атанасов. Изобретателят на компютъра.** С., Университетско изд. Св. Кл. Охридски, 1990, 164 с.

7. Как Джон Атанасоф стана българин. Computer World/България, бр. 1, 18.01.2001.

8. *Миланов, А.* Бояджикският бунт. Варна, Изд. Георги Бакалов, 1977.

9. *Сендов, Б.* Изчислителна математика – стара и нова. С., Наука и изкуство, 1972.

10. *Фолта, Я., Я.* Нови. История на естествените науки в дати. С., Народна младеж, 1984, с. 188, 189, 191,192.

11. **Atanasoff, John V. Advent of Electronic Digital Computing. Annals of the History of Computing, 6(1984)3, 229–282**
(за противоположната гледна точка вж. [7, 26, 32, 33]).

12. *Berry, C. E.* Design of Electrical Data Recording and Reading Mechanism. Unpublished M. S. Thesis, Library, Iowa State College, 1941.

13. *Berry, C. E.* Journal of Applied Physics (1946)4.

14. *Burks, A. W., A. R. Burks.* The ENIAC: First General-Purpose Electronic Computer. Commentaries by J. V. Atanasoff, J. G. Brainerd, J. Presper Eckert, Kathleen R. Mauchly, Br. Randell, and Konrad Zuse, together with the authors responses. Annals of the History of Computing. 3(1981)4, 310–389.

15. *Burks, A. W., A. R. Burks.* Recent history of computers. New York, 1987.

16. *Burks. A. R., A. W. Burks.* The First Electronic Computer. The Atanasoff Story. Ann Arbore University of Michigan Press, 1988.

17. *Eckert, J. P.* A Survey of Digital Computer Memory Systems. *Proceedings of the Institute of Radio Engineers,* 41(1953), 1393–1406.

18. ENIAC Trial Records. Pretrial depositions, affidavits, complaints, transcripts. exhibits, briefs and decision. Honeywell, Inc. vs. Sperry Rand Corp. et al. № 4–67 Civ. 138, U. S. District Court, District of Minnesota, Fourth Division, 1 June 1971 to 13 Mar. 1972, and pretrial depositions taken from 26 May 1967 to the trial date of 1 June 1971. Decided 19 October 1973. General Services Administration, Federal Records Center, Chicago.

19. *Goldstein, H. H.* The Computer from Pascal to von Neumann. Princeton, NJ, Princeton University Press, 1972.

20. Honeywell, Inc. Computerized Trial Arguments and Brief, filed 30 September 1972, 509 pp.

21. **Larson, Earl R., U. S. District Judge, 19 October 1973, Findings of Fact, Conclusion of Law and Order of Judgement, U. S. District Court, District of Minnesota, Fourth Division. Honeywell, Inc. vs. Sperry Rand Corp., et al. Defendants, Civil Action File No 4–67, Civ. 138. U. S. Patent Quarterly, 180(1974), 673–773.**

22. *Mackintosh, A. R.* The First Electronic Computer. *Physics Today*, 40 (March 1987)3, 25–32. *Макинтош, А. Р. Първият електронен компютър. ФМС (1987)2, 116–127.*

23. *Mackintosh, A. R.* Dr. Atanasoff's Computer. Scientific American, 259(1988)2, p. 72.

24. *Mauchly, J. W.* The Use of Hight Speed Vacuum Tube Devices for Calculating, 1942. Originally unpublished Memorandum.

25. *Mauchly, J. W.* The ENIAC. В [29].

26. *Mauchly, K. R.* John Mauchly's Early Years. Annals of the History of Computing, 6(1984)2, 116–138.

27. *Metropolis, N., J. Howlett, and C. Rota* (eds.). A History of Computing in the Twentieth Century. NY, Academic Press, 1980.

28. **Mollenhoff, C. R. Atanasoff: Forgotten Father of Computer. Iowa State University Press, Ames, 1988, 275 pp.**

29. *Randell, B.* (ed.). The Origins of Digital Computers: Selected Papers. NY, Springer Verlag, 1973, 2d ed., Berlin, 1982.

30. *Richards, R. K.* Electronic Digital Systems. NY, John Wiley, 1966.

31. *Richards, R. K.* Electronic Digital Computers and Cirquits. NY, John Wiley, 1967.

32. *Stern, N.* From ENIAC to UNIV. New York, 1981.

33. *Stern, N. Abacus,* 1(1983), 7–15.

34. *Stewart, R. M.* The End of the ABC. *Annals of the History of Computing,* 6(1984)3, p. 317.

35. *Taylor, J. M.* A College Algebra, Boston, Allyn and Bacon, 1895.

36. The first electronic computer. Physics Today, March 1987, 25–32.

JOHN VINCENT ATANASOFF

PERSONAL

BORN	4 October, 1903, Hamilton, New York
FATHER	John Atanasoff, born 1876, Bulgaria, emigrated to USA 1889, married 1900; B.Ph. Colgate University 1900; electrical engineer; died 1956
MOTHER	Iva Lucena Purdy, born 1881; school teacher (mathematics); died 1983.
SIBLINGS	Nine, of whom seven survive: Ethelyn, Margaret, Theodore, Avis, Raymond, Melva, Irving.
FAMILY	Married Alice Crosby, 1949; three children: Elsie, Joanne, John Vincent II; ten grandchildren
ADDRESS	P.O. Box 503, Frederick, Maryland 21701.

EDUCATION

HIGH SCHOOL	Mulberry, Florida 1920
BSEE	University of Florida, Gainesville 1925 MS, Mathematics PhD, Theoretical Physics University of Wisconsin, Madison 1930 Thesis title: "The Dielectric Constant of Helium" Research adviser: Professor John H. Van Vleck Committee (Van Vleck was in Europe): Professors Wentzel, Weaver, March, Mendenhall and Ingersoll.

PROFESSIONAL

OCCUPATION	Mathematical Physicist, Inventor, Businessman
POSITION	Phosphate prospector 1920–21 Gainesville H.S., Teacher, Head of Science Dept. 1925–26 Iowa State College, Mathematics, Graduate Assistant and Instructor, 1926–29

University of Wisconsin, Mathematics, Instructor 1929–30
Iowa State College, Mathematics and Physics
Assistant Professor 1930–36
Assistant Professor 1936–42
Professor in Absenia 1942–45
US Naval Ordnance Lab., Washington, D.C.
Chief, Acoustics Section 1942–45
Chief, Acoustics Division 1945–48
US Army Field Forces, Ft. Monroe,
VA, Chief Scientist 1949
Naval Ordinance Lab., Director, Fuse Program 1949–52
The Ordnance Eng. Corp., Frederick,
MD (sold to Aerojet Gen. Corp. 1957)
Founder, President, Director 1952–57
Aerojet General Corp., Frederick, MD
Manager, Athlantic Div 1957–59, Vice Pres. 1959–61
Cybernetics, Inc., Frederick, MD, President 1961–80

CONSULTANT

Steward-Warner Corp. 1961–63
Control Data Corp. 1967–71
Honeywell 1967–71

PATENTS 32

MAJOR INVENTION

Electronic Digital Computer 1936–42

MEMBERSHIPS

Phi Beta Kappa
Phi Kappa Phi
Sigma Tau
Pi Mu Epsilon
Tau Beta Pi
Sigma Xi
Cosmos Club
American Assoc. for the Advancement of Science
Foreign Member, Bulgarian Academy of Science
Honorary member, Computer Medicine Society

HONORS

U.S. Navy Distinguished Service Award
(Navy's highest honor awarded to civilians) 1945
Citation, Seismological Society of America 1947
Citation, Admiral, Bureau of Ordnance 1947
Cosmos club membership 1957
Order of Cyril and Methodius,
First Class, Bulgarian Academy
of Science, (Bulgaria's highest honor awarded to a scientist) 1970
Iowa Inventors Hall of Fame

Plaque, Iowa State Univ. Physics Building 1974
Honorary Membership, Society for Computer Medicine 1974
Doctor of Science, University of Florida 1974
Doctor of Science, Moravian College 1981
Distinguished Achievement Citation,
Iowa State Univ. Alumni Assoc. 1983
Doctor of Science, Western Maryland College

May-June 1985 –John Atanasoff's second visit to Bulgaria. Awarded with People's Republic of Bulgaria Medal, Ist class

1985 – Then Vice-President George W. Bush honoured John Atanasoff with the Holley medal – the hignest prize of the US Society of Engineers.

1986 – Coors American Ingenuity Award, founded by Adolph Coors Company, Colorado State. For the first time it is given to John Atanasoff.

1986 – Atanasoff scholarship for excellent students in computer science, founded by Adolph Coors Company.

1987 – D.Sc. at the State University in Wisconsin.

1988 – "Atanasoff" is the asteroid (one of the little planets near Mars), discovered and researched by Bulgarians at the National Astronomic Observatory in Rozhen. That logo is registered by the Special Commission for naming the new discovered astronomic bodies at the International Astronomic Union and the International Planet Center in Cambridge (Great Britain) suggested by DSc Vladimir Shkodrov, MSc Violetta Ivanova and Angelina Georgieva (Bulgaria).

1989 – Information Resource Management Hall of Fame, Washington, DC

1990 – National Medal of Science and Technology for 1990, presented by President George Bush in the White House. This is the most important prize received by Atanasoff.

1995 – John Atanasoff died at 91, spending a long and exceptionally fruitful life.

Prof. Dimitar Shishkov – editor

Shishkov, Dimitar Petrov (1939), graduated from the Faculty of Physics and Mathematics of the State University of Sofia, Bachelor and Master of Mathematics (1961–1962), one of the 15 founders of computer technology and computer informatics (CSc) in Bulgaria (1 June 1961), PhD in Math & CSc (1976, BAS), DSc in Technical Sciences (CSc, 1996, TU-Sofia), Professor of the Faculty of Economics of SU (2000), expert of Soros's Open Society Foundation (1993–1995), scientific advisor to the American company Great Bear Technology Ltd. in Sofia (1994–1997), scientific consultant to the company Information Services PLC (since 1998). Over 40 years teaching in Higher Education. Author of 5 books, 78 scientific publications and over 30 popular scientific papers.

Dr. Plamen Pavlov – author of the introductory part

Dr. Plamen Pavlov, (born 12 July 1958) – Historian, whose focus area is Byzantium and the Balkan States of the Middle Ages (14th–15thcentury). Lecturer University of Veliko Turnovo, Plovdiv, Shumen and Varna. Chairman of the Agency for Bulgarians Abroad, attached to the Council of Ministers.

Amongst his better known publications and monographs as author and co-authorship are: "Lectures on Bulgarian History", v. I–II, S., 1991; "Bulgaria, Byzantium and the Cummans" (the 1070s and the beginning of the 14th century), dissertation, 1991; "A Short History of the Bulgarians" (1993), S., 1999; "Prince Presian II", S., 1993; "Who's Who in the Bulgarian Middle Ages", S., 1994, 1995, 1997; "Chronological History of the World" v. VI (Byzantium and the Byzantine World), S., 1994; "History of Bulgaria" v. I–II (1995; 1998); "Bulgaria and the Ottoman Expansion, End of the 13th Century – Middle of the 15th century", S., 1995; "Avocation: Lives of Three Saints"; S., 1999; "The Fall of the First Bulgarian Empire", S., 1999.

TABLE OF CONTENTS

TABLE OF CONTENTS

ТАНГРА ТанНакРа ОБЩОБЪЛГАРСКА ФОНДАЦИЯ
и ЦЕНТЪР ЗА ИЗСЛЕДВАНИЯ НА БЪЛГАРИТЕ

имат за цел да издирват, публикуват и разпространяват научни знания, хипотези, митове и легенди, свързани с историята на българската народност. Книгите от поредица „Българска вечност“ търсят отговор на въпросите за произхода и богатото културно наследство на Българите в областта на философското осмисляне на света, държавното управление, социалното устройство, военното изкуство, писмеността, езиковата култура, строителството, астрономията и религията, за тяхното влияние и принос в световната култура. Нашият стремеж е да дадем човешко и историческо самочувствие на децата на българския род, разпръснати като пясък по света от превратностите на историята. Българите могат да имат много по-значимо присъствие в съвременния интегриращ се свят.

ДОСЕГА В ПОРЕДИЦАТА:

1. БЪЛГАРСКИТЕ ОГНИЩА НА ЦИВИЛИЗАЦИЯ НА КАРТАТА НА ЕВРАЗИЯ – ст.н.с. д-р Петър Добрев
2. ДВЕ ИЗРЕЧЕНИЯ НА ИСУС ХРИСТОС – Й. Вълчев, съвместно издание с Универитетско издателство „Св. Климент Охридски“
3. СЛАВЯНИ ЛИ СА БЪЛГАРИТЕ – доц. д-р П. Цветков
4. АЛМА – ЛЮБОВТА НА КАН ТЕЛЕРИГ – Елена Димитрова
5. ИСТОРИЯ НА БЪЛГАРИТЕ: ПОТРЕБНОСТ ОТ НОВ ПОДХОД. ПРЕОЦЕНКИ (Първа част) – ст.н.с. Петър Добрев; гл. ас. д-р Цветана Тафраджийска; гл. ас. д-р Цветелин Степанов; доц. д-р Пламен С. Цветков; ст.н.с. д-р Валерия Фол; ст.н.с. д-р Божидар Димитров.
6. ИСТОРИЯ НА БЪЛГАРИТЕ: ПОТРЕБНОСТ ОТ НОВ ПОДХОД. ПРЕОЦЕНКИ (Втора част) – проф. д-р Георги Бакалов; доц. д.и.н. Петър Ангелов; гл. ас. д-р Цветелин Степанов; н.с. Свилен Станимиров; доц. д-р Пламен Митев; проф. д-р Марко Семов; Атанас Семов; доц. Рая Заимова и др.
7. ИСТОРИЯ НА БЪЛГАРИТЕ: ПОТРЕБНОСТ ОТ НОВ ПОДХОД. ПРЕОЦЕНКИ (Трета част) – проф. дин Александър Фол, доц. д-р Атанас Стаматов, проф. д-р Снежка Панова, проф. Емил Боев, ст.н.с. д-р Валерия Фол, Георги Владимиров, ст.н.с. дин Николай Овчаров
8. ГЛАДСТОН И БЪЛГАРИТЕ. ПОЛИТИКА НА ПРАВЕДНА СТРАСТ – Проф. д-р Андрей Пантев и доц. д-р Румен Генов
9. ЦАР СИМЕОН ВЕЛИКИ – Николай Станишев
10. ЗА КИРИЛ И МЕТОДИЙ – д-р Михаил Маргаритов и Ангелика Маргаритоф-Хофер Едле фон Сулмтал
11. ЗАГАДКИТЕ ОКОЛО ЕТНИЧЕСКИЯ ПРОИЗХОД НА СОЛУНСКИТЕ БРАТЯ СВЕТЦИТЕ КИРИЛ И МЕТОДИЙ – дин Гатя Симеонова
12. ДОБРОДЕТЕЛИТЕ НА БЪЛГАРИНА – проф. дфн Марко Семов
13. БЪЛГАРИ И ЕВРЕИ – част 1 и част 2, авторски колектив
14. ОБУЧЕНИЕТО ПО ИСТОРИЯ В НОВИТЕ УСЛОВИЯ – Сборник
15. БОЙНИТЕ ИЗКУСТВА И ВОЕННО ДЕЛО НА ДРЕВНИТЕ БЪЛГАРИ – д-р Дориян Александров
16. КАЛЕНДАР И ХРОНОЛОГИЯ – Йордан Вълчев
17. БЪЛГАРИТЕ/THE BULGARIANS - авторски колектив
18. ДРЕВНАТА БЪЛГАРСКА ЦИВИЛИЗАЦИЯ – д-р Марин Димитров
19. ПОБЕДИТЕ НА ЦАР КАЛОЯН – доц. дин Н. Овчаров
20. БЪЛГАРСКИЯТ НАРОДЕН КАЛЕНДАР – ОСНОВИ И СЪЩНОСТ – Георги Велев

21. БЪЛГАРИ И АРМЕНЦИ ЗАЕДНО ПРЕЗ ВЕКОВЕТЕ – Сборник, авторски колектив
22. ПЪТЕВОДИТЕЛ БЪЛГАРИЯ. – съвместно издание с „Александър тур“, на български и на английски език
23. СРЕДНОВЕКОВНИТЕ БЪЛГАРИ – НОВИ ФАКТИ, ИНТЕРПРЕТАЦИИ И ХИПОТЕЗИ – гл.ас. д-р Цв. Степанов
24. АРАБСКИ ИЗВОРИ ЗА БЪЛГАРИТЕ – Райна Заимова
25. ОБЛЕКЛОТО И ОРЪЖИЕТО НА СТАРАТА БЪЛГАРСКА ВОЙСКА – проф. Геза Фехер /Унгария/
26. ЗВЕЗДНИ МИГОВЕ В БЪЛГАРСКОТО МИНАЛО. ПРИНОСЪТ НА БЪЛГАРИТЕ В СВЕТОВНАТА ЦИВИЛИЗАЦИЯ ПРЕЗ АНТИЧНОСТТА И СРЕДНОВЕКОВИЕТО – Борис Чолпанов, съвместно издание с Академично издателство „Проф. Марин Дринов“
27. БЪЛГАРИТЕ-АТЛАС/ THE BUL GARIANS-ATLAS – авторски колектив
28. ДРЕВНИТЕ БЪЛГАРИ (ИСТОРИЧЕСКА БИБЛИОГРАФИЯ) – Петър Чолов
29. ДЖОН АТАНАСОВ – съставител проф. дтн Димитър Шишков, на български и на английски език
30. КИПРИАН-БЪЛГАРИНА – МИТРОПОЛИТ МОСКОВСКИ И НА ЦЯЛА РУСИЯ – Петър Куцаров, Бистра Николова, на български и на руски език
31. ПОУКИ ЗА ДЪРЖАВНИЦИТЕ – проф. дин Георги Марков
32. МЕЖДУНАРОДНА КОНФЕРЕНЦИЯ „100 ГОДИНИ ОТ РОЖДЕНИЕТО НА ЧЛ. КОР. ПРОФ. БЕШЕВЛИЕВ“

СПИСАНИЕ „БЪЛГАРСКИ ВЕКОВЕ“ – Бр. 1, 1999 г.

СПИСАНИЕ „БЪЛГАРСКИ ВЕКОВЕ“ – Бр. 2, 2000 г.

СПИСАНИЕ „БЪЛГАРСКИ ВЕКОВЕ“ – Бр. 3, 2001 г.

БИБЛИОТЕКА ЗА МЛАДИТЕ ЧИТАТЕЛИ „БЪЛГАРИТЕ ПРЕЗ ВЕКОВЕТЕ“ ДОСЕГА В ПОРЕДИЦАТА:

1. ИСТОРИЯТА КАТО ПРИКАЗКА. Част 1 ЗЕМЯТА НА БЪЛГАРИТЕ – Ангел Каралийчев
2. ИСТОРИЯТА КАТО ПРИКАЗКА. Част 2 КРИЛАТИЯТ ЮНАК – Ангел Каралийчев
3. ПО ПЪТЯ НА НЕБЕСНАТА СЪРНА. КНИГА ЗА НАЙ-СТАРИТЕ БЪЛГАРСКИ ЦАРСТВА. Част 1 БЪЛГАРСКАТА ТРОЯ – ст.н.с. д-р Петър Добрев
4. ПО ПЪТЯ НА НЕБЕСНАТА СЪРНА. КНИГА ЗА НАЙ-СТАРИТЕ БЪЛГАРСКИ ЦАРСТВА. Част 2 БЪЛГАРСКИЯТ ЩИТ НАД ЕВРОПА – ст.н.с. д-р П. Добрев

ОЧАКВАЙТЕ

- АЛЕКСАНДЪР МАКЕДОНСКИ И БЪЛГАРИТЕ – ст.н.с. д-р Божидар Димитров
- ИЗМЕРЕНИЯ НА БЪЛГАРСКАТА МЕДИЦИНА – Сборник, под общата редакция на проф. дмн М. Апостолов
- TEMPORA INCOGNITA НА РАННАТА БЪЛГАРСКА ИСТОРИЯ – доц. дфн Атанас Стаматов (второ преработено и допълнено издание)
- АРХИТЕКТУРА И СТРОИТЕЛСТВО НА ДРЕВНИТЕ БЪЛГАРИ – Сборник, авторски колектив
- Пътеводител „БЪЛГАРИЯ“ – руски и немски език.
- СПИСАНИЕ „БЪЛГАРСКИ ВЕКОВЕ“ – бр. 4/2001 г.